Organizational
Research Methods

Organizational Research Methods

A Guide for Students and Researchers

Paul Brewerton
and
Lynne Millward

SAGE Publications
London • Thousand Oaks • New Delhi

© Paul Brewerton and Lynne Millward 2001
First published 2001

Apart from any fair dealing for the purposes of research or private study, or criticism or review, as permitted under the Copyright, Designs and Patents Act, 1988, this publication may be reproduced, stored or transmitted in any form, or by any means, only with the prior permission in writing of the publishers, or in the case of reprographic reproduction, in accordance with the terms of licences issued by the Copyright Licensing Agency. Inquiries concerning reproduction ouside those terms should be sent to the publishers.

 SAGE Publications Ltd
6 Bonhill Street
London EC2A 4PU

SAGE Publications Inc
2455 Teller Road
Thousand Oaks, California 91320

SAGE Publications India Pvt Ltd
32, M-Block Market
Greater Kailash - I
New Delhi 110 048

British Library Cataloguing in Publication data

A catalogue record for this book is
available from the British Library

ISBN 0 7619 7100 9
ISBN 0 7619 7101 7 (pbk)

Library of Congress catalog card number is available

Typeset by Organisational Solutions, Brighton, East Sussex
Printed in Great Britain by Cromwell Press Ltd, Trowbridge, Wiltshire

To all you sources of inspiration out there for getting me here
(you know who you are).
And especially to Ana, who never ceases to amaze me.

For Rick, for life.

Paul Brewerton BA MA MSc PhD C.Psychol (Occ)
Managing Director, Organisational Solutions

Paul heads the occupational psychology consultancy Organisational Solutions, which specialises in added-value employee surveys, individual selection/development, employee motivation, organisation development and the construction and validation of psychometric instruments. Paul's academic studies have included psychology to doctoral level and social research to Masters level. He lectures regularly at the University of Surrey and continues to publish papers in psychology and management journals, as well as contributing to texts on the practical application of occupational psychology to business. Paul's current research interests include the impact of organisational culture on performance at work, the contemporary employment relationship (in terms of the employee-employer 'psychological contract'), and staff motivation.

Dr Lynne Millward BA PhD C.Psychol (Occ) AFBPS
Senior Lecturer, University of Surrey

A leading-edge researcher into organisational and leadership psychology, Lynne heads the MSc Occupational & Organisational Psychology postgraduate degree at the University of Surrey. Previously a consultant in private industry, she now consults both through the University and privately to government and commercial organisations, as well as publishing in numerous academic journals, and writing major texts in the field. Lynne's current research interests include exploration of the psychological contract concept within the workplace, the impact of the psychological contract on employee behaviour and performance, identification of optimal leadership styles for work teams in stressful environments, team development through promotion of 'shared mental models', issues of identity in the workplace and the role of group processes in organisational effectiveness.

Contents

List of Figures   xi
List of Tables   xii
List of Boxes   xiii
List of Case Studies   xiv

Preface   xv

1   Introduction
1.1   Research in organizations: debunking the myths   1
1.2   Objectives of the book   2
1.3   The role of the researcher   3
1.4   References and further reading   6

2   Applying Social Science to the Real World
2.1   Introducing the scientist–practitioner model   7
2.2   Tackling the question from a scientific perspective   8
2.3   The practitioner approach   9
2.4   Scientist–practitioners: applying science in a practical environment   10
2.5   Can science be qualitative?   11
2.6   The 'action research' model   13
2.7   References and further reading   14

3   Starting off the Research Process
3.1   Some common fears and worries about research   16
3.2   Establishing a research framework and getting yourself a supervisor   19
3.3   Project planning   22
3.4   One step on … the project proposal   27
3.5   The internet as a research resource   30
3.6   The literature review   36
3.7   Operationalizing the research question(s)   40

4   Obtaining and Using Access to an Organization
4.1   Introduction   44
4.2   Obtaining access from 'scratch'   44
4.3   Getting 'buy in' across the organization   47
4.4   'Managing' the organization throughout the research process   48

5　Project Design

5.1	Introduction	52
5.2	The case-study or 'now' design	53
5.3	The correlational design	57
5.4	The experimental design	58
5.5	Selecting a research design	60
5.6	Ethical considerations in organizational research	61
5.7	References and further reading	65

6　Methods of Data Collection

6.1	The research process continues	67
6.2	Criteria for selecting a method	68
6.3	Interviews	69
6.4	Techniques for use in interview contexts	75
6.5	The focus group method	80
6.6	Psychometric research	87
6.7	Observation	96
6.8	Survey and questionnaire design	99
6.9	Diary methods	109

7　Sampling Considerations

7.1	Introduction and definitions	114
7.2	Probability sampling	115
7.3	Non-probability sampling	117
7.4	Limitations of sampling approach on analysis	118
7.5	Conclusion	120
7.6	References and further reading	120

8　Assessing Performance in Organizations

8.1	Performance, effectiveness and productivity	122
8.2	The criterion issue	123
8.3	Individual performance	125
8.4	Group performance	129
8.5	Organizational performance	135
8.6	Conclusion	140
8.7	References and further reading	140

9　Data Analysis

9.1	Introduction	143
9.2	Statistical data analysis: finding a test	144
9.3	Statistical data analysis: the tests	147
9.4	Content analysis	151
9.5	Multi-dimensional scalogram analysis	155
9.6	Meta-analysis	161
9.7	Structural equation modelling	165

10   Reporting Research Findings
10.1 Introduction   171
10.2 Reporting to an academic audience   171
10.3 Writing up for academic publication   174
10.4 The client report   177
10.5 References and further reading   180
10.6 Presenting research findings   181

11   Concluding Words   191

Glossary   *192*

Index   *201*

List of Figures

1.1	The research process: a working model	3
3.1	Starting the research process	19
3.2	Suggested project plan	23
3.3	The project plan as a Gantt chart	26
6.1	The research process continues	68
6.2	An example of a Q-sort template	79
6.3	Example of a 7-point response scale anchored with 'Strongly disagree' and 'Strongly agree'	102
6.4	Example of a semantic differential attitudinal scale	103
6.5	Kunin's (1955) 'faces' rating scale	103
9.1	MSA plot for advertising agents	159
9.2	MSA plot for police officers	159
9.3	Proposed measurement/structural model for predicting construction workers' intention to leave	167

List of Tables

6.1 The use of psychometric instruments within organizational research 88

6.2 Makin et al.'s (1996) estimates of relative utility of various criterion-related validity co-efficients 92

7.1 Participants required per condition according to effect size and statistical test in order for adequate statistical power to be achieved 119

8.1 Typical performance/outcome criteria at various levels of analysis 123

8.2 Example of a graphical rating scale for evaluating training effectiveness 127

9.1 Bivariate data analysis: applications, restrictions and interpretation 148

9.2 Multivariate data analysis: applications, restrictions and interpretation 149

9.3 Alternative goodness of fit statistics and their acceptable value range 168

10.1 Analysing your presentation performance 188

List of Boxes

3.1	Help frame and focus the supervisory process	22
3.2	Writing as an integral part of the research process	27
3.3	Tailoring the project proposal to an organizational audience	29
3.4	The literature search	37
3.5	References	38
6.1	How *not* to conduct the research interview	72

List of Case Studies

1   When a lack of confidence can severely let you down   16
2   Research proposal to a software development company   46
3   Use of repertory grid technique with a nursing sample   75
4   Team identities (Jacobs, 1988)   77
5   Exploring organizational culture with focus groups   82
6   Developing a measure of organizational culture   93
7   Communicograms: applying diary methods   111
8   Sampling problems with an organizational survey   114
9   Exploring the psychological contract using MSA   157
10 An example of an executive summary presented to a call-centre   178
    company

Preface

As both academic researchers and organisational consultants (see our website www.organisational-solutions.co.uk for more about our research interests), we had long been aware of the need for a practical 'how to' guide for those planning research into the activities of organisational life. Feedback from students and discussions with colleagues, however, led us to realise that there was a need for more than simply a 'cookbook' of organisational research methods. So, we set out to identify the core areas of concern to organisational researchers: the obstacles to best practice research (selecting an appropriate research question, securing organisational access, selection of statistical tests for analysis, for example); the research methods available (qualitative and quantitative, to gather and to analyse data); and a framework to structure the research process (what to do and when). The focus of our book, then, began to broaden from a straightforward introduction to applied research methods. Instead, we felt that what was needed was a more wide-ranging consideration of those issues specific to the design, implementation and delivery of sound organisational research.

It has been our intention throughout this book to integrate techniques and approaches traditionally associated with *academic* research with those of *applied* organisational study. The Q-sort method for eliciting employee perceptions (based on Kelly's Personal Construct Theory), for example, sits alongside classical project management techniques (identifying timescales, project milestones and presenting these in Gantt format). By bridging the gap between these two areas of practice, we have tried to demonstrate the potential synergy that lies in integrating and applying both schools of thought.

We were also keen to provide practical advice to researchers and we have drawn on case studies and real-world examples in an attempt to achieve this. We have tried to keep in mind the need for researchers to apply these techniques in a very real environment and so have presented an introduction to each topic that focuses primarily on *application*, with theory a secondary consideration. Conscious that this would necessarily limit our coverage of each area, we have also provided numerous suggestions for further reading for more in-depth treatments.

We did not want to be prescriptive in our suggestions, and felt that by presenting as comprehensive a picture as possible, we could provide organisational researchers with a sufficiently broad platform on which to base their research decisions. So we have tried to present our discussion of each area in as impartial a way as possible. While, as researchers, we may draw more frequently on some methods than others, we wanted to ensure that any prospective researcher is given the full picture before embarking on their project.

Based on our own (both personal and partly vicarious) research experiences, we were conscious of the particular areas that repeatedly present problems to students and practitioners of organisational research. We have firstly attempted to bring structure to the process of identifying a sound research question to ensure that the goals of the research are specific, measurable, achievable, realistic and time-bounded (SMART). We have devoted an entire chapter to the often sticky problem of securing organisational access and subsequent management of the client relationship throughout the course of a research project. A major portion of the book focuses on the various methods of data collection available to organisational researchers and we have paid special attention to the selection of appropriate statistical tests when analysing quantitative data. We introduce the classical methods of data generation and analysis, such as interviews, focus groups and questionnaires. We were also keen to outline some emerging techniques and have included introductions to structural equation modelling, multidimensional scalogram analysis and psychometric measurement. Finally, we wanted to provide readers with some guidance on the 'writing up' process and on the presentation of research findings both to academic audiences (project supervisors, internal/external examiners and academic editorial committees) and to organisational sponsors (project stakeholders at various levels within host organisations).

Ultimately, what has motivated us to develop this book is an underlying belief in the value of organisational research. It is only by studying behaviour, motives, attitudes, values and beliefs in organisational settings that we can really come close to fully understanding people at work. The potential of this knowledge should not be underestimated. On the one hand, it can lead us towards more efficient and effective individual employees, teams, departments and organisations. On the other hand, our findings have the potential to enhance and enrich the working lives of people at work. It is at the confluence of these goals that we believe the most stimulating and exciting contemporary research to be taking place. We hope that this book can assist both new and established researchers in achieving their aims and look forward to hearing readers' thoughts on how we might bring further clarity and direction to the conduct of best practice organisational research.

Paul Brewerton: *Managing Director, Organisational Solutions*
Lynne Millward: *Senior Lecturer, University of Surrey*

February 2001

1 Introduction

1.1 Research in organizations: debunking the myths

In our experience, the majority of students entering into the applied sciences in a professional capacity are put off by the prospect of 'research'. Many potentially highly research-competent students perceive the research side of their degree to be something just to get through, a self-contained task to be completed and then forgotten about. Most are not short of ideas for neat and manageable research projects but these are too often sacrificed to pressures of time, an inability to get access to an appropriate sample (in part often due to a lack of advance and/or contingency planning) and/or a lack of confidence in actually getting a project off the ground. This is not due to incompetence. On the contrary, most trainee practitioners in the social sciences are well qualified in their discipline, often with broad experience of the real world and usually deeply enthusiastic about their subject. They are at the same time keen to liaise with 'real-world' clients and tackle live organizational issues.

Herein lies the problem. Many students in the applied sciences tend to distance themselves from what they construe to be more basic and distal approaches to their discipline. This is true too of qualified practitioners in many fields of the social sciences (Anderson, 1998). These students and practitioners perceive research as something done only by those more academically inclined, largely operating at a distance from the real world. To us, as both academics and practitioners in our field, this separation of the applied social science professions from their research bases represents a missed opportunity. The assumption that 'only academics do research' affords an image of research as largely consisting of experiments run in laboratories by scientists out of touch with reality, thereby perpetuating the myth that research is irrelevant to the real world, and thus a distraction from what one would really like to do. We feel that it is this set of assumptions and images which is also partly responsible for students' lack of confidence and belief in their ability to 'do' research.

In this book, we challenge the myths about research, its white-coat image and supposed irrelevance to the practice of the social sciences. We demonstrate how research is an integral part of professional activity and that acknowledging this is fundamental to issues of accountability. We argue that research is an essential part of what social science is all about and, as such, is something that all social science students must become competent in, and must maintain competence in, as responsible practitioners in their respective fields.

To assist in facilitating such competence, this book takes the reader through the research process from beginning to end. We operate within a framework of applied science and to this end we address issues arising from the pursuit of research 'in the field', including obtaining organizational samples, the political context of the research, research design, data collection and analysis and report writing (in both client-friendly and academic versions).

1.2 Objectives of the book

It is intended that this text should help the reader to:

- Plan and make informed and systematic research decisions;
- Gain access to organizational settings;
- Understand the ethical implications of applied organizational research;
- Select appropriate methods for collection and analysis of organizational data;
- Implement, report and present the findings of meaningful applied research with a view to achieving the highest of academic and professional standards.

To achieve this, the book will provide the organizational researcher with a comprehensive understanding of the research process, presented according to the framework described in Figure 1.1. This framework model will be revisited throughout the text.

As you will see, while there is a linear, directional nature to the model (i.e. there are a number of stages which need to be completed *en route* to 'reporting and presentation of findings'), it also has a cyclical, iterative flavour (i.e. at several stages it may be necessary to review progress and return to earlier tasks, particularly during the preliminary planning and reviewing phases). We feel this is a fair representation of the research process: review and revision should be seen as necessary and crucial parts of the process. Research *is* iterative and it is critical that organizational researchers accept this prior to embarking on a research project.

Throughout this book, we will emphasize the importance of several key activities: advance planning, strict time management and writing as integral parts of the research process. Advance planning ensures that the project is properly scoped and mapped out from beginning to end in terms of key steps and milestones. Strict management of time is essential to progress in line with this plan and will help promote a sense of calm as regards achieving project goals. Writing is an activity that can begin immediately and will help shape the research. It will also provide a focus for discussion during supervision and the basis for regular feedback, both of which are crucial to constructive progress.

The book provides clear pointers for how to reconcile ideals with reality and for maintaining project momentum. It provides overviews of a wide variety of different research strategies, methods of data collection and analysis well beyond those ordinarily discussed in mainstream textbooks. It also helps with the report-writing task, indicating ways in which the project material can be most effectively organized for academic and also feedback purposes.

Figure 1.1   The research process: a working model

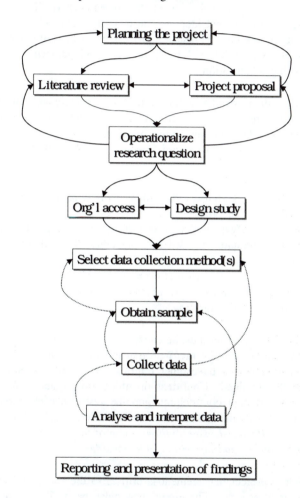

Finally, the book offers a clear, manageable procedure for preparing a presentation to an organizational or academic audience.

1.3 The role of the researcher

The research process requires the researcher to adopt a variety of roles and to uphold a number of professional objectives. The researcher will be called upon to be objective, scientific, to think creatively and to conduct his/her research ethically. S/he will also be required to act as manager, data gatherer and 'synthesizer', as well as data analyst and presenter. The following explanation of the various roles of the researcher in the research process indicates relevant chapters which discuss each issue in more depth.

- **Objective** – in practical settings, the researcher is likely to enter the organization as an outsider, or third party, and will need to retain objectivity throughout the research process, regardless of external pressures and the method(s) selected for generating and gathering data from the participating organization.

- **Scientific** – the researcher will need to think critically and objectively at all times, examining the research question posed in detail and leaving 'no stone unturned' in seeking answers to that question.
  See Chapter 2 – Applying Social Science to the Real World – for more on the science of research.

- **Creative** – any research effort is likely to require the researcher to think 'outside the box' in order to generate a testable research hypothesis, for example, to identify a suitable project design or method for data collection, and to accommodate the differing agendas of academic and applied research.
  Chapter 5 – Project Design and Chapter 6 – Methods of Data Collection, discuss in depth the various approaches which can be taken when addressing a research question.

- **Ethical** – the researcher must be conscious of and respect any ethical issues raised. Research projects involving participants of any kind are likely to raise expectations, or have other implications for the organization or the participants involved. Confidential information gained from whatever source must remain confidential, and the researcher must retain a high degree of integrity in conducting research within a 'live' setting;
  Chapter 5 – Project Design outlines some of the key ethical issues which the prospective researcher will need to consider.

- **Manager** – project management is critical to the successful execution of the research process. The researcher must be well organized, setting realistic deadlines and milestones, meeting representatives from the participating organization on a regular basis and communicating progress. In an academic environment where there are numerous pressures on the student to spread his/her time across multiple projects, management of this kind is invaluable to ensure that the project remains on track.
  Chapter 3 – Starting off the Research Process – outlines the basic tenets of project management and provides some guidelines for using project management principles when developing a research proposal and plan.

- **Salesperson** – it may be that organizational access can only be secured by 'selling' an idea to a potential participating organization. This requires an articulate statement of the aims of the research and its practical significance, particularly in terms of tangible benefits for the organization. At the same time, the researcher needs to be sure not to overstate these benefits in order that the organization retains realistic expectations of what is being offered.

  Chapter 4 – Obtaining and Using Access to an Organization – explains how to 'sell' your research into an interested organization and how to manage the relationship with that organization throughout the research process.

- **Data gatherer and 'synthesizer'** – the researcher will be called upon to gather and interpret large amounts of information during the early stages of the research process (particularly during the literature review). It is crucial that the researcher is able to analyse and synthesize this information rapidly and critically, identifying key issues and how they might impact on the research question.

  Chapter 3 – Starting off the Research Process – discusses in detail the literature review and its role in the research process. Chapter 6 – Methods of Data Collection – provides details of the many and varied methods available to the organizational researcher.

- **Data analyst** – analysis of data gathered is an integral part of the research process and the researcher will need competence in qualitative and quantitative analytic methods. It is likely that this will involve at least some bivariate or multivariate statistical analysis.

  Chapter 9 – Data Analysis – provides some pointers as to which statistical tests (or other forms of data analysis) should be used when analysing and interpreting project findings.

- **Presenter** – the researcher will need to be able to present and communicate research findings in a digestible and appropriate way, depending on the audience (i.e. academic or organizational). This will require honed interpersonal skills for one-to-one or group presentations to participating organizations, in addition to scientific writing skills for the preparation of the project report or dissertation.

  Chapter 10 – Reporting Research Findings – gives some detailed guidance on how to construct research reports and presentations tailored to a particular target audience.

1.4 References and further reading

Anderson, N. (1998). The practitioner–researcher divide in work and organizational psychology. *The Occupational Psychologist, 34*, 7–16.

Hackman, J.R. (1985). Doing research that makes a difference. In E.E. Lawler III, A.M. Mohrman Jr., S.A. Mohrman, G.E., Ledford Jr. and T.G. Cummings (Eds.), *Doing Research that is Useful for Theory and Practice*. San Francisco, CA: Jossey-Bass.

2 Applying Social Science to the Real World

2.1 Introducing the scientist–practitioner model

The 'scientist–practitioner' model highlights the role of research in the practice of applied science on at least three different levels:

1. *Research as a formal activity* pursued in the form of a specific project with a clear beginning and a clear end (e.g. research into the antecedents of turnover decisions in nursing staff);

2. *Research-based practice* – i.e. drawing on the knowledge base of the discipline in an informed and critical way (e.g. uncovering motivations to leave their employing organisation in order to improve retention of nursing staff and overall performance of NHS Trusts);

3. Application of knowledge, experience and skill using the *research process,* i.e. systematic practice based on inquiry, a process of hypothesis formulation and testing, and model development (e.g. building a model of nursing turnover synthesizing theory and practical findings, obtained through application of appropriate data collection and analysis methods).

All of these uses of the term 'research' are built into the term 'scientist' as a preface to the term 'practitioner', and as such are highly pertinent to the practice of the social sciences. Unfortunately, the terms *science* and also *research* are imbued with a white-coat laboratory-based image of a quest for knowledge for its own sake rather than for its applicability and relevance to the real world, and largely addressed to basic and often highly trivial questions. However, this need not be the case. Research can be pursued on a highly applied yet nonetheless highly *scientific* basis, in either a laboratory or a field context.

For example, the question of 'what constitutes team effectiveness?' has fundamental relevance to how we approach the task of team development in real organizational settings. This example will form the focus of the following sections.

2.2 Tackling the question from a scientific perspective

There are many ways in which such questions can be addressed, drawing on both theoretical and applied forms of literature. In pursuit of research in the form of a neat and manageable project, we might draw on several different types of literature to form hypotheses about what might differentiate an effective team from an ineffective team: the theoretical and applied literature on group processes; the theoretical and applied literature on teams and team processes; and the team-building literature. The literature may also straddle several different disciplines in this instance, including psychology, sociology and management science. A systematic review of this diverse literature may enable us to identify some key themes. For example, it might strike us from our reading that there is no one definitive set of factors that differentiates the effective from the ineffective team since the issue of *effectiveness* can only be judged relative to the situation. Each situation or type of team setting will, on the surface, throw up a different set of 'effectiveness' factors. We may thus conclude that team effectiveness is situation-specific, and that the only thing definitive of the effective team is 'flexibility' to adapt to a situation and its requirements. Is it valid then to talk about 'the effective team?' At one level it is not, for the reasons we have described: factors which make for an effective team in one situation (e.g. cohesiveness, which may be functional in instances where the team must operate in a highly co-ordinated manner) may not be so pertinent to another (cohesiveness is less critical when a very important decision needs to be made). But, at another level, we can talk about the 'effective' team.

If we reframe the question into one of 'what makes team effectiveness possible?' or 'what are the causes of team effectiveness?' then some tentative suggestions can be reached. If an effective team is a flexible team, what makes it possible for a team to be 'flexible'? A shared understanding of the team and its capabilities, an ability to size up a situation and its requirements, an ability to draw on experience of 'success' and 'failure' in similar situations in working out the most appropriate way of responding? Such 'hypotheses' thus lead us away from focusing on 'team processes' into focusing on 'team cognition'. The closest we get to this when digging around in the literature is the notion of 'team identity' and the notion of 'team mental model'. We thus begin to hone down our notion of the effective team. The effective team, we may argue, is one that has a strong sense of its own identity 'as a team' and which has a clear insight into its capabilities, the situations it is likely to encounter and how best to handle these situations *as a team*.

Such hypotheses can be tested, and are indeed most appropriately tackled, using both basic and applied methods. In a basic sense, various teams could be constructed for laboratory purposes and assigned a particular task with clear, measurable performance outcomes against which to judge 'effectiveness' or otherwise. Team members would ideally be randomly assigned such that it becomes reasonable to assume comparability across laboratory teams. The task should be sufficiently challenging so as to test the competence of the team and to allow variability in team competence to be detected. It should not, however, require too much prior experience or previously acquired expertise, thus ruling out the potential for bias in favour of experience to creep into the equation. Various measures of 'team cognition' would thus enable us to test the hypothesis that 'team identity' and 'team insight' account for significant variation in team performance. It is not possible to ensure such control in the field, which would require access to a huge number of comparable teams (in terms of team composition, history, size and focus) operating within a similar industry, with similar goals and against similar criteria of success.

This does not rule out the feasibility of fieldwork; it will simply need to be tackled on a different basis. A survey, for example, can be distributed to different teams across different industries with a view to unravelling the concept of 'team cognition' and evolving appropriate measurement indicators. Critical incident interviews might help us to fathom out how team members *think* in various challenging team situations and in particular how they deal with emergency situations which put team resources and competence to the test. On-site observation of team meetings and other team scenarios would enable us to capture 'team talk' and action *in situ*, thereby affording a rich picture of how teams operate in practice. Each of these approaches to the question of team effectiveness throws some light on the issue, contributing in an important way to the piecing together of a much larger puzzle. No single approach or method is valid in and of itself, but is dependent on the purpose to which it is directed and on what kind of evidence is sought. Laboratory research may help sharpen up the hypotheses ready for testing in the field. In turn, fieldwork may generate new questions and possibilities most appropriately tested in the laboratory setting.

2.3 The practitioner approach

This picture of the research process as a formal activity demonstrates the kind of analysis involved in the process of forming viable hypotheses and the decisions involved in how to test them. The practitioner, however, may come at the same question from a completely different (but equally valid) angle. S/he may draw more fundamentally on his/her own experience and observations derived from working with teams and from team development activity. S/he may form hypotheses about what constitutes an effective team derived from a working model or 'theory-in-use' (Argyris, 1960) developed over time and with experience. S/he may also consult the literature to ensure the viability of these hypotheses, and may also harness the expertise of others working in the same field via published case studies, anecdotal records and extensive networking. Such hypotheses can be considered to be grounded in reality, and may be similar to those formulated in more conventional academic terms. The practitioner may then evolve a team development programme informed by these hypotheses, the implementation of which provides a 'test' of their power to guide the engineering of real improvements in team performance. Some practitioners may operate with definite theories about, say, *effective teamwork* which inform their work (e.g. transactional analysis, goal-setting theory); others may operate in a more integrative fashion, drawing on a range of different theories deemed appropriate to the circumstances at hand (e.g. goal-setting theory, role theory, theories of interpersonal and intra-group dynamics). Yet others will prefer not to use theory at all, operating eclectically with a range of techniques to draw upon, and within a general problem-solving framework. Whatever the style or theoretical preferences of the practitioner, each in the course of his/her work will operate with implicit models and some form of hypothesis about the power of one kind of intervention relative to another. The scientist–practitioner can thus draw on 'science' in the form of a knowledge base and/or operate in a systematic manner to determine the most appropriate action to take given the circumstances at hand.

The practitioner and/or researcher who is driven by pragmatics, fads and fashions is not the scientist–practitioner, nor is s/he someone who can be considered to be truly professional. By definition, a professional is someone who is informed and who can apply his/her knowledge to practical situations in an intelligent and skilled manner. Consumer-led practice – i.e. giving clients what they ask for, without critical reflection and analysis of its appropriateness or relevance – is *not* professional practice. Unfortunately, it is all too common for the practitioner to operate in this way, in part because it would not be in his/her interests to question the validity or value of the solution being requested and in part because of time and resource constraints. The scientist–practitioner, however, is fully accountable for his or her actions (their success or otherwise) and to this extent is distinguishable from the cowboy and the jack-of-all-trades. The scientist–practitioner is to all intents and purposes, the *scientist in practice*.

2.4 Scientist–practitioners: applying science in a practical environment

The concept of the scientist–practitioner is fundamental to the application of all science, and is in essence part of what it means to be professional. Nurses, for example, are prime exemplars of the scientist–practitioner breed. Their work is based on the 'science of care' and is practised in a systematic, scientific way (i.e. through adequate research of a client's clinical and care needs and the formulation of a care plan) using the nursing process. Various theories or models of care are also available for nurses to draw upon in formulating the care plan. In addition, nurses are encouraged to pursue research in a formal sense, as part of developing the knowledge base of the discipline. Some have criticized the professionalization of nursing and the scientific thrust of the discipline, arguing that caring is an art and *not* a science. Science, the argument goes, is a cold and highly ritualized activity not appropriate for the pursuit of care. Care is something highly individualized and personal, underpinned by intuition and warmth. Yet the practice of science does not preclude this. By definition, the application of science might be said to constitute an art insofar as the 'universalistic' (i.e. the accepted methods and approaches underpinning medical science) must in each instance be translated into something 'particularistic' (to cater for the individual needs of each patient). In this sense, the art is in the practice of science and does not necessarily require detachment or distance of the kind imagined of the white-coated laboratory scientist. The art of science then is in its application. The use of intuition and experience makes the 'art' possible, and is thus not precluded from the scientist–practitioner scenario.

2.5 Can science be qualitative?

2.5.1 Positivism or qualitative investigation?

The white-coat image of science originates from its positivistic roots. Positivism signals an approach to research in search of objective truth which in turn is assumed to be made up of general principles and laws. Positivist science is experimental and quantitative. That is, it prescribes a method of investigation which presupposes complete control over particular 'variables' and their 'effects' on, or 'interactions' with, other variables as a means of identifying quantifiable cause-effect relationships. Positivistic science originates from the natural sciences and has been imported wholesale into the social sciences as the best practice model to which we should all aspire in the pursuit of valid and reliable knowledge. Those who operate in this paradigm derive knowledge by forming and testing hypotheses. Theory evolves accordingly in a *hypothetico-deductive* fashion (that is, *deducing fact* by testing generated *hypotheses*).

Within the social sciences, however, some have challenged this paradigm of science as inappropriate to the investigation of psychological and social phenomena. Such a challenge has spawned the evolution of various non-positivist paradigms of research, including the phenomenological and interpretative sciences. Common to these approaches is the assumption that reality is constructed and cannot be fathomed out or explained with direct reference to universal laws. The interest of researchers operating in this tradition is in *meanings* and *interpretations*. Knowledge is gleaned using qualitative techniques and theory thus evolves in a 'grounded' (i.e. largely *inductive* rather than *deductive*) way.

Qualitative research paradigms are becoming increasingly fashionable in the social sciences as a valid alternative to positivism and in part as an ideological criticism of positivistic science (Hayes, 1997). Qualitative science is now a recognized means of generating knowledge in the social sciences. On a more pragmatic (or less theoretical) note, researchers are now harnessing a whole range of qualitative techniques as part of their methodological repertoire, either as stand-alone tools or to complement the use of quantitative methods (Cassell and Symon, 1994). In practice, qualitative methods can be used to generate quantitative data (e.g. interviews can be content analysed for different themes and these themes can then be frequency analysed) and vice versa (e.g. a survey incorporating a series of open comment boxes).

2.5.2 How different are qualitative and quantitative approaches?

The difference between qualitative and quantitative approaches to research is well illustrated both currently and historically in the organizational culture literature. Quantitative approaches to studying culture emphasize its quantifiable nature and are concerned with identifying its predictive power (e.g. the relationship between organizational culture and performance), categorizing organizations into cultural 'types' (e.g. 'power', 'role' and 'macho' cultures) or otherwise measuring distinct elements or dimensions of culture in as objective a way as possible.

Qualitative approaches to culture, by contrast, seek to characterize its rich, emergent, constructed and multi-dimensional nature using ethnographic approaches, often requiring 'psychological immersion' in an organization (e.g. participant observation, depth interviewing).

These two different approaches to exploring organizational culture are most often pursued separately and in terms of a completely different (yet equally valid) language. Martin and Frost (1996) in their critique 'Organizational culture war games: a struggle for intellectual dominance', analogize the inherently confrontational field of published culture research to a series of wargames between researchers adopting alternative theoretical and pragmatic viewpoints. Rousseau (1990), however, explains how the two approaches can be used in tandem to provide a comprehensive overview of organizational culture from as many perspectives as possible.

Generally speaking, qualitative methods are distinguishable from quantitative methods insofar as they:

> focus on interpretation rather than quantification; an emphasis on subjectivity rather than objectivity; flexibility in the process of conducting research; an orientation towards process rather than outcome; a concern with context – regarding behaviour and situation as inextricably linked in forming experience; and finally, an explicit recognition of the impact of research process on the research situation. (Cassell and Symon, 1994: 7)

Here is not the place to enter into a debate about the appropriateness of either a quantitative or qualitative approach (refer to Cassell and Symon, 1994 for more on this). Suffice to say that organizational research is a fundamentally practical endeavour and that to this end researchers are best advised to draw on whichever technique is most appropriate to the questions posed by the situation at hand. This does not mean to suggest that the research process need be entirely consumer-driven or characterized by technical eclecticism without regard for theoretical concerns or coherence. The point is that debates about what constitutes 'valuable' knowledge are limited in their utility, since this depends largely on what the question is and how best it can be answered or addressed.

The scientist–practitioner who 'grounds' his or her theories or models of organizational life in interpretative or experiential data is operating fundamentally within the qualitative paradigm. This does not invalidate the process or render it less 'scientific'. Equally the researcher in a more formal sense need not necessarily operate within the quantitative paradigm. He or she can potentially draw on a whole range of different techniques, both qualitative and quantitative, in addressing the issues of interest.

2.6 The 'action research' model

The action research model is becoming increasingly popular in the applied social sciences (Whyte, 1991). Cohen and Manion (1989: 223) describe action research as:

> essentially an on-the-spot procedure designed to deal with a concrete problem located in an immediate situation. This means that a step-by-step process is constantly monitored (ideally, that is) over varying periods of time and by a variety of mechanisms (questionnaires, diaries, interviews, and case studies, for example) so that ensuing feedback may be translated into modifications, adjustments, directional changes, redefinitions, as necessary, so as to bring about lasting benefit to the ongoing process itself.

Rapoport (1972: 23) states that action research differs from other social science approaches in the 'immediacy of the researcher's involvement in the action process.'

Cummings and Worley (1993) suggest that action research involves 'a cyclical process of diagnosis–change–research–diagnosis–change–research. The results of diagnosis produce ideas for changes; the changes are introduced into the same system, and their effects noted through further research and diagnosis.'

In effect, this means that the research task is never-ending: the process is an ongoing one of iterative and incremental review and improvement of practice. It is essentially a problem-solving process, appropriate to any situation where specific knowledge is required to address a specific problem or when a new approach is to be introduced into an old system. The research process within the action research model is systematically pursued just as for any piece of research. Its aim, however, is not to generate knowledge for its own sake but for the improvement of the research participants' situation over the long term.

These definitions also point to the close involvement of the researcher with study participants within the action research framework. Whilst retaining a scientific objectivity in his/her aims and methods, the action researcher is keen to develop a partnership with participants, exploring together the various issues surrounding the research question in an effort to develop mutually beneficial research aims and objectives and to ensure that the research programme has a lasting beneficial effect for all involved. Uzzell (1995) points out that the action research framework has been employed in many different areas of social investigation, including public policy, police management, industrial organization and management, community development and education research.

Zuber-Skerritt (1992) differentiates action research approaches from traditional social science and natural science approaches to research in the following ways:

- Action research is intended to make a *practical* difference to participants (note the intentional avoidance of the term 'subject'), with advancement of the theoretical field or discipline a second goal;
- Action research is participative and collaborative, empowering and involving participants in the research process and demystifying the 'researcher' as a white-coated academic, instead fostering a partnership approach to achieve the research goals;
- Action research regards as valid the views of each participant, with participants asked to reflect continuously on their situation in order to explore as many avenues for action as possible.

The practical, problem-solving nature of the action research approach does not devalue the role of theory in the process. There must be some means of organizing or interpreting the 'evidence', in the form of either an analytical or a conceptual framework. The framework may be one that has been derived deductively (i.e. using logical thought) or inductively (i.e. from empirical work). In addition, the action researcher must remain keenly aware throughout the research process of his/her role as researcher and the responsibilities which this brings with it. Rigorous and objective investigation of the area is central to any research project and this continues to apply within the action research framework. While the action researcher encourages participation and involvement and is likely to form part of the change process (thereby engaging psychologically and emotionally with participants), sound methodological and theoretical principles should remain core to the researcher's approach since it is through this that s/he can add the greatest value to any change initiative.

The above discussion should illustrate the important role played by both theory and practice in applied organizational research. The scientist–practitioner, then, is able to draw on the advantages of objective, critical, scientific thinking, while retaining a practical focus to a research project. Recent growth in (and growing acceptance of) areas such as action and qualitative research suggest that the scientist–practitioner model is enjoying healthy and sustained uptake within academic and organizational settings alike.

2.7 References and further reading

General

Argyris, C. (1960). *Understanding Organizational Behavior*. Homewood, IL: Dorsey.

Qualitative vs quantitative research

Cassell, C., and Symon, G. (1994). *Qualitative Methods in Organizational Research: A Practical Guide.* London, UK: Sage Publications.

Hayes, N. (Ed.) (1997). *Doing Qualitative Analysis in Psychology.* Hove, UK: Psychology Press.

Lee, T.W. (1999). *Using Qualitative Methods in Organizational Research.* Thousand Oaks, CA: Sage Publications.

Martin, J. and Frost, P. (1996). Organizational culture war games: a struggle for intellectual dominance. In S.R. Clegg, C. Hardy and W.R. Nord (Eds.), *Handbook of Organization Studies.* London, UK: Sage Publications.

Rousseau, D.M. (1990). Assessing organizational culture: the case for multiple methods. In B. Schneider (Ed.), *Organizational Climate and Culture.* San Francisco, CA: Jossey-Bass.

Action research

Cohen, L. and Manion, L. (1989). *Research Methods in Education* (Third Edition). London, UK: Routledge.

Cummings, G. and Worley, C.G. (1993). *Organization Development and Change* (Fifth Edition). Minneapolis/St. Paul, MS: West Publishing Company.

Rapoport, R.N. (1972). Three dilemmas in action research. In P.A. Clark (Ed.), *Action Research in Organizational Change.* London, UK: Harper and Row.

Uzzell, D. (1995). Ethnographic and action research. In G.M. Breakwell, S. Hammond and C. Fife-Schaw (Eds.), *Research Methods in Psychology.* London, UK: Sage Publications.

Whyte, W. (1991). *Participatory Action Research.* London, UK: Sage Publications.

Zuber-Skerritt, O. (1992). *Action Research in Higher Education.* London, UK: Kogan Page.

3   Starting off the Research Process

3.1 Some common fears and worries about research

A number of concerns tend to crop up consistently when faced with a research remit, most of which derive from a lack of confidence with respect to the prospective researcher's ability to 'do research' and all that this signifies. Worries commonly pertain to:

- Formulating a research objective and/or set of hypotheses;
- Gathering relevant research material;
- Making decisions about what to do and how;
- Obtaining and/or constructing means for assessing and measuring a given phenomenon;
- Getting it 'right' and making the 'right' decisions;
- Getting access to an appropriate and adequate sample;
- Data analysis, especially that involving the use of statistics;
- Getting a significant result;
- Getting it all done in time;
- The protocol for writing up.

In this chapter, we attempt to allay these fears by encouraging you to engage in advance planning, and to be thoroughly prepared and organized. Treat the research project as an exercise to be *carefully and systematically managed.*

> This requires planning, control and continuous monitoring and evaluation.

It may be in your nature to leave everything to the last minute, and/or it may be through avoidance of anxiety about the project that it ends up being left till it is almost too late. However, you cannot afford to do this, as the following case scenario illustrates. Please note that the following Case Study is based on a real example although names and other personal details have been changed.

Case Study 1: When a lack of confidence can severely let you down

Esther is a highly competent mature student who lacks confidence in herself and her ability to pursue research. She waited for nearly two whole academic semesters before she made any contact with lecturing staff for potential supervision. By then, the majority of students had lodged themselves with supervisors and had got projects underway, in some cases with data collected and ready to be analysed. Esther presented a few rather ambitious and vague ideas to several people who told her to go away and rethink them into something more specific and manageable within the time-frame (by now with only 4 months to go before the deadline). Esther withdrew even more than before and refrained from contact with any of the lecturing staff until it was noticed by course administrators that she had not got herself signed up with a supervisor.

One of her friends on the course expressed concern that Esther was not going to get anything done in time and that she was getting more and more anxious and depressed. Urgent steps were taken by lecturing staff to seek contact with Esther, who still had not firmed up any of her ideas and was in quite a panic-stricken state about it all. After some considerable discussion, one of the lecturing staff decided to get the ball rolling by providing Esther with a specific research question which she could address using a survey method within the time scale, given a bit of firm management between then and the project deadline. Esther appeared satisfied with this as a starting point and was given the tasks of (a) obtaining access to a sample and (b) constructing a measure. She was encouraged to contact her supervisor within the next couple of weeks to indicate her progress on these two tasks and for help with survey construction. Esther did not contact her supervisor. Through the student grapevine it was learned that Esther was still unsure about what she was doing and was hence feeling rather embarrassed and 'incompetent'. Her reaction to this was retreat and avoidance of contact.

As time was now getting very tight, Esther was strongly advised to make contact with her supervisor. She did and the survey was constructed there and then. With only six weeks to go before deadline, there was no time to pilot the survey: it was imperative that she distributed the survey immediately. The only way she could do this was via friends and relatives. She succeeded in obtaining a reasonable sample size on this very opportune basis but then appeared to retreat once again from seeing her supervisor for help with the data coding and analysis phase. With only a week to go, she finally appeared. She was guided step by step through the data analysis process and was advised on how to interpret the findings and write them up. Two weeks after the deadline she finally came up with her first draft which needed substantial reshaping because of the hurried way in which it had been written up. Three weeks after the deadline she submitted her final dissertation.

The project received a very low mark (although it did just scrape a pass) for the following reasons:

- The student had made very little personal contribution to the project and had had to be 'hand-held' throughout; she had not made any of the decisions involved and needed to be told what to do and how;
- The project was designed and implemented in a hurried and rather messy fashion;
- The sample was inappropriate to the project objectives;
- The write-up reflected little real grasp of the project objectives, of how the study addressed the objectives, or the implications of the findings.

The submitted project clearly did not do Esther justice. She was a competent student who, through lack of confidence, failed to get herself organized in time to do anything worthwhile. She had no ownership of the project and this was reflected in its write-up. The project was a last-minute scraping together of something manageable, requiring a lot of time and energy from the supervisor to very little avail.

The above student was more than capable of pursuing high-quality publishable research. Students of lesser or equivalent intellectual capability with advance planning, foresight and much commitment throughout can be cited whose research projects obtain marks of distinction. It is not enough to be *able* on an intellectual level, one must be *organized* in advance and throughout. No amount of advice or support can substitute for advance planning and tenacious pursuit of a project from this point on. The experience, as many of our students will tell you, is challenging and at times quite painful but overall extremely fulfilling and fun. These students:

- Commit themselves to a topic area early on in the year and get themselves signed up with a supervisor immediately;
- With the help of their supervisor, map out the project from beginning to end across the year in terms of key phases and milestones;
- Once the project is designed, take immediate steps to seek access to organizations for the pursuit of the research well in advance of the data gathering stage which afford the possibility of research collaboration and partnership;
- Adhere as closely as they can to the project timetable;
- Demonstrate enthusiasm, energy and commitment throughout, despite set-backs and difficulties.

The sections below are intended to dispel further the common fears and concerns about research, and introduce the following key themes and topics, explaining the role of each activity in the early stages of the research process:

- **Section 3.2: Establishing a research framework and getting yourself a supervisor** – communicating your research idea;

- **Section 3.3: Project planning** – the value of applying project management principles to the research process;

- **Section 3.4: One step on … the project proposal** – formalizing your ideas and interests;

- **Section 3.5: The internet as a research resource** – using the internet and WWW to (amongst other things) generate research ideas;

- **Section 3.6: The literature review** – a means of organizing and tracking your thinking;

- **Section 3.7: Operationalizing the research question(s)** – making the question measurable;

- **Chapter 4: Obtaining and using access to an organization** – tips and pitfalls;

- **Chapter 5: Project design** – the approach most appropriate to answering the research question.

Figure 3.1 provides on overview of the research process at its early stages. As the diagram suggests, the process of planning and starting out on a research project is an iterative and cyclical one and the researcher may need to revisit earlier stages as necessary. However, the overarching aim of this part of the research process should be to identify and define the **specific research question** or questions which will be addressed by the project. The operationalization of this question will then lead into the development of the project's design and will arm the researcher with enough information to seek out and secure organizational access.

Figure 3.1   Starting the research process

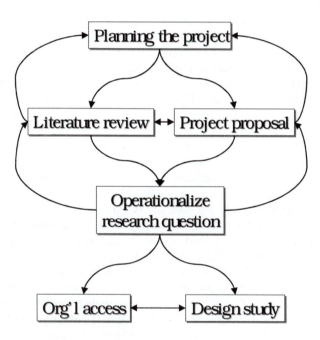

3.2 Establishing a research framework and getting yourself a supervisor

Like any project, the research project must be carefully managed from the start. This will require that you map out the project in terms of its key phases and milestones well in advance of its commencement and that you adhere as closely as you can to this plan. This should not be taken to mean that the process is a mechanical one that flows from one stage to the next in a linear and progressive fashion. There will be setbacks and difficulties to overcome, and the process will in practice be much more iterative and fluid than perhaps portrayed here. The point is that careful 'project management' using the framework provided below will:

- render the project less global, abstract and fuzzy by casting it into a **manageable, tangible and more evidently achievable form;**

- which will, in turn, promote a feeling of **confidence and self-efficacy;**

- which will, in turn, **motivate, inspire and thus facilitate successful project completion.**

Deciding on a topic is perhaps one of the hardest decisions to make for the research student because it implies a commitment from which there is no turning back. This is not necessarily the case, as your project supervisor is unlikely to be this draconian! Nonetheless, a commitment to a topic will provide some relief from the inevitable sense of anxiety about 'getting started' and will also afford a framework which will help to focus your reading. Some supervisors do require that you have a tangible project in mind, although most will be happy to discuss potential projects or research questions. Find out about the research interests of various potential supervisors and if possible read something of what they have published to get a 'feel' for these interests at a more concrete level. Make appointments to see those supervisors whose interests are broadly aligned with your own or whose interests you might wish to pursue.

If you have no particular interests (even at a broad level), take time out to scan through some of the recently published journals in the organizational domain to see if anything strikes you as worthwhile pursuing. Talk to other students and think about the kind of thing you hope or anticipate doing after the course. It may be that you could pursue a topic or interest that will provide you with an edge in your application for jobs or in progressing in your existing job. For those of you already in a job, think about the kind of research opportunities that your place of work might afford you. Look at previous dissertations/projects completed by ex-students to see if there are any research avenues worth pursuing or building on. Consulting previous dissertation material (particularly project work that has attained a high mark) will also enable you to work out what exactly is required in terms of research scope and standard.

Once you have made contact with a supervisor, s/he may throw some ideas into the pot of possible research avenues or projects, and will also advise on the feasibility of implementing the ideas you have already within the time scale available. There is no substitute for time spent at this stage, thinking about what to do and making a commitment to invest in it. The topic must interest and inspire you since it is something you will have to live with for a substantial proportion of your time. Some supervisors may have projects available for you to sign up to. Make sure you understand exactly what the research question is and do some background work on it before you commit yourself to it.

Once you have decided on a topic, sign yourself up with a supervisor with whom you can now start to do some planning. Different supervisors have different styles of working. Some supervisors will be reluctant to commit to a project until a clear proposal has been written and agreed. Others will help you with the process of shaping your proposal. Either way, a proposal of some kind is the next step of the project process and should be seen as the primary vehicle for project planning and discussion. Without a plan of sorts, the supervisory process has little to build on and will be largely aimless and unhelpful. Make sure you are comfortable with your supervisor and his or her style. Seek to develop a 'contract' with the supervisor regarding his or her role in the project process. This will enable a clarification of expectations, roles and responsibilities. If you feel that your supervisor is not being constructive or that you are being repeatedly 'fobbed off' in your attempts to get the project off the ground, make sure that:

- You have a research proposal which has, as its focus, a worthwhile and answerable question. This research question should be realistic in what it will require of you and others in the time you have available to answer it. Section 3.4 will give you an insight into developing a research proposal;
- You have communicated this to your supervisor in an enthusiastic way, and have demonstrated your interest in, and ownership of, the research question (perhaps by discussing reading you have done in the area) and the research process (perhaps by securing one or more organizational samples).

The vast majority of supervisors, regardless of their personal approach to the supervisory relationship, should respond to this sort of approach. You may need to put your ideas across forcefully and on more than one occasion really 'catch the attention' of the supervisor. If your supervisor does not respond constructively at this stage, it may be worth approaching an alternative supervisor. Of course, all the work you have put in up to this point will have been very much worthwhile since you will more than likely have a robust research proposal with which to impress the new supervisor.

Remember, it is *your* project, for which *you are responsible*. The supervisor is merely an advisor and facilitator and is not responsible for making decisions or managing the project on your behalf. There is a fine line between 'assessment' and 'apprenticeship' during the project process. The project is an assessed piece of work and in most cases the *process of pursuing a project,* as well as the report produced at the end, is taken into consideration in the assessment. On the other hand, your supervisor will also be there to guide you in the process and to provide constructive feedback, advice and mentoring throughout.

See Box 3.1 for some advice on framing and focusing the process of supervision (i.e. *managing* your supervisor during the course of the project).

Box 3.1: Help frame and focus the supervisory process

Where possible, always provide the supervisor with something to read before you meet him or her, perhaps with some key issues or questions you wish to discuss. This will focus the supervision and also help the supervisor orient to the project in advance, particularly if s/he has multiple projects to supervise as well as his/her own personal research projects. It is common for supervisors to have up to 20 projects to supervise, plus fingers in almost as many others. Help the supervisor to keep track of what you are doing, your thought processes and to orient to your project just prior to a meeting. Otherwise you may risk him/her not remembering what you have been doing since the last meeting (or at least the finer details), and spending most of the supervision seeking an update on your progress before they are able to be of any constructive help or support. Why not provide your supervisor with a written update on one page of A4 plus any other material you wish to obtain feedback on? The supervisory process will then have a firm basis on which to progress. Even if the supervisor has not had a chance to read the progress report in advance, s/he can quickly skim over it and be firmly reminded of your project there and then without wasting too much meeting time. Remember, your supervisor is only human and may need help to intellectually 'switch into' your project.

The issue of supervisors keeping track or being 'on the ball' with respect to student project work is perhaps less salient in instances where you have been in regular contact with him/her, where you are pursuing research highly pertinent to his/her own interests and/or where s/he has only a small number of projects to supervise. It is increasingly likely nowadays, however, that the supervisor is supervising multiple projects at undergraduate, masters and doctoral level and needs you to take responsibility for keeping him or her regularly informed and focused.

If you find that the supervisory process is not of any value or at least not in a constructive sense, then talk to your course director or course representative. Bear in mind that this is more likely to be due to misunderstanding about the role of the supervisor and of what each can expect from the other than any malevolence on the part of the supervisor.

3.3 Project planning

The first step is to agree a project plan with your supervisor. Map out the project into divisible stages (planning and preparation, project design, project implementation, data analysis and interpretation, report), sub-stages (e.g. data input and coding, data analysis, data interpretation) and also measurable milestones (e.g. literature review, formulate a research question, produce/agree a proposal, obtain access to organization(s), construct/obtain measures, etc.). Identify time-scales with your supervisor for the achievement of each milestone and completion of each project phase. Build in contingency time (e.g. difficulties in obtaining access or obtaining measures, holidays and sickness), taking into account your own circumstances in combination with those of your supervisor. The plan will 'get you started' and will indicate the various things to aim for, watch out for/think about, and achieve along the way.

Many students may start off in this way but then get side-tracked by coursework demands and deadlines. To this extent, the research side of things becomes subordinate to the coursework timetable and more often than not forgotten about until assignments have been submitted. This is unfortunate, since in many departments, the research component is weighted much more heavily than the coursework component. This suggests that what students should be doing is planning their coursework timetable around their research timetable rather than vice versa. In practice, this means that, once the plan is mapped out and agreed, the student is best advised to commit one day a week (or 6–8 hours equivalent) to the research project regardless of coursework requirements. This can be spread out into an hour a day, across two or three days per week or contained within one day. What matters is that time is being spent keeping the project alive.

One of the main reasons why the project must be kept alive is because the **process of obtaining organizational access to appropriate and adequate samples can take a long time to get organized** (even when the researcher has available contacts). Organizational access is an issue to be dealt with very early on, even months in advance of project implementation. Where possible, the research should be done in collaboration or partnership with an organization or set of organizations for it to achieve the best results. The issue of securing and using access to an organization is dealt with in more detail in Chapter 4.

A project plan may look something like that shown in Figure 3.2. Note that write-up activities appear in italics.

Figure 3.2   Suggested project plan

Phase	*Activity/task*	*Completion date*
Phase 1	**Planning and preparation**	**Sept–end Jan**
	Literature review	By mid Dec
	Formulation of research objective/question/ hypotheses	First week of Dec
	Completion of research proposal	Mid Jan
	Decision on design, method/measures, appropriate sample/organizations	Mid Jan
	Writing to organizations to seek access	Mid Jan
	Identifying project deliverables, resource requirements	End Jan
	Write up first draft of introduction	*End Jan*
	continues	

Phase	Activity/task	Completion date
Phase 2	**Project implementation**	**End of Jan to May/June**
	Ongoing inquiry through reading, writing and discussion	Ongoing
	Second draft of introduction	*End Feb*
	Obtain/design measures and/or means of data collection	End Mar
	Meet with organizational contacts and elicit involvement and ownership	Mar/Apr
	Seek feedback on proposed methods/measures from organizational contact	Apr
	Seek ethical approval, if necessary, following organizational procedures	Apr
	Decide and agree project logistics with organization including sampling considerations, issues of confidentiality, collation procedures, etc.	Apr–May
	Run project	May
	Write up first draft of research procedures/methods	*End May*
Phase 3	**Data handling/analysis and interpretation**	**End June**
	Data coding and input (quantitative)	First week June
	Data coding/content analysis (qualitative)	First week June
	Data Analysis (e.g. statistical, thematic)	Mid June
	Data Interpretation/Model Development	End June
	Write up first draft of results	*Mid–end June*
	Polish introduction in the light of results/recent papers	*Ongoing to end June*
Phase 4	**Report writing**	**End July**
	Sharpen up first drafts of method and results	*$1^{st}/2^{nd}$ week July*
	First draft of discussion	*Mid July*
	Final overall draft report	*Last week July*
	References, appendices, figures/tables, contents	*End July*
	Submit dissertation	*End July*

Phase	Activity/task	Completion date
Phase 5	**Organizational report/feedback**	**Mid/End Aug**
	Draft out report for organization	By end Aug
	Present results	End Aug
	Seek feedback	Early Sept
Phase 6	**Publication**	**Sept–Oct**
	In collaboration with supervisor work out a publication plan	Sept–Oct

The plan outlined in Figure 3.2 takes into consideration 'contingency' time, particularly at the implementation stage which is very much at the whim of the organization in which you are seeking to obtain samples. It also takes into consideration that all project planning and design is undertaken with the guidance and support of the supervisor, and all written material (literature reviews, notes/commentaries, proposals, drafts of various sections of the report, etc.) is reviewed by the supervisor who will provide detailed feedback and advice along the way. You might also want to seek peer feedback on what you are doing over lunch or coffee. Discussions taking place outside of the project are just as important as the discussion taking place within it, and also prevent feelings of isolation as you become increasingly involved in the project process. Some students may prefer to operate with a more visual 'plan', but a plan nonetheless such as provided by a Gantt chart (see Figure 3.3 for an example). Note the following key:

Key:

═══	Phase duration
───	Task duration
▲	Project milestone

Figure 3.3 The project plan as a Gantt chart

	Sept	Oct	Nov	Dec	Jan	Feb	Mar	Apr	May	June	July	Aug	Sep	Oct
Phase 1: Planning and preparation														
Literature review														
Formulation of research objective														
Approach organizations to seek access														
Completion of research proposal														
Write up first draft of introduction														
Phase 2: Project implementation														
Ongoing inquiry														
Obtain measures/other means of data collection														
Meet organizational contacts														
Seek feedback on proposed methods														
Seek ethical approval if necessary														
Agree project logistics with organization														
Run project														
Write up first draft of method														
Phase 3: Data handling/analysis and interpretation														
Data coding														
Data analysis														
Data interpretation														
Write up first draft of results														
Polish introduction														
Phase 4: Report writing														
Sharpen up method and results sections														
Write up first draft of discussion														
Final overall draft														
Submit dissertation														
Phase 5: Organizational report/feedback														
Submit organizational report/feedback														
Phase 6: Publication plan														

Those of you with ready organizational contact or access can bypass the stage at which 'access' is sought. However, whether you are *in situ* (i.e. already working for the organization) or are an affiliate of some kind (i.e. an advisor, ex-employee, consultant), ready access can bring with it other problems (e.g. being driven down an avenue of research which is primarily in the organization's interests but with little academic content; project logistics being dictated by the organization and its time scale). These problems are addressed in Chapter 4. Let your supervisor know what the project constraints are in the 'ready access' scenario so that s/he can help you work out a way of reconciling your interests and the academic requirements with organizational interests and timetables.

3.4 One step on ... the project proposal

When asked to formulate a project proposal many students panic. This need not be the case. The purpose of the proposal is:

- to get you writing;
- to help you clarify and unpack your research question into testable hypotheses and/or its operational implications;
- to scope out the research project into manageable tasks;
- to help you check out the feasibility and manageability of the research question in terms of design, sample, implementation and analytical/ interpretative requirements;
- to prompt you to map out the time scale of the project from beginning to end.
- to help you with the process of operationalizing and sharpening up the project idea;
- to focus and guide you.

See Box 3.2 for an explanation of how writing is a critical and integral part of the research process, right from the outset of the research project.

Box 3.2: *Writing as an integral part of the research process*

It is commonly assumed that writing is relevant only to the 'writing up' stage of a research project. On the contrary, writing is part-and-parcel of the *process* of research. To write is to think on paper. In so doing, ideas can be formed and shaped, and issues can be better grasped. In the early stages of a project the important thing is to start writing, and start immediately. Not only write notes on the papers you have read but write up a commentary or review of these papers. This will help you to *engage* in the issues addressed and will help you to organize your thoughts. Simply copying out chunks of text is a waste of time and of little ultimate value or use. Similarly, simply highlighting or underlining blocks of a text will not actively engage you nor does it constitute a true process of inquiry. Many students worry that they must provide their supervisor with highly polished pieces of writing. This is rarely what they expect. Polished writing often requires several drafts, taking into consideration detailed feedback in the process of drafting and redrafting.

At the outset of a project, however, writing is more appropriately construed as an activity of thought, reflection and synthesis rather than as a *product* of some kind. The supervisor may require that you conduct a literature review in advance of writing a proposal. The purpose of this is not so much that you produce an excellent piece of work but that it provides you with a forum in which to 'think'. By providing your supervisor with your thoughts and commentaries on paper throughout the literature review stage, he or she has a basis on which to focus the supervision and to get a feel for where you are at. It is a basis for contact, and a focus for discussion.

Writing can also help you keep track of your thinking over time. Many students get to the 'report writing' stage as if it were an activity tacked on to the project at its very end, without being able to remember how they got started or what their question is, or even what they have read. These students effectively have to start from scratch, retrospectively trying to bring order to the process and trying desperately to remember why they chose one method rather than another and so on. Writing up along the way, no matter how seemingly incoherent, creates a diary of your thought processes and will enable you to trace back a line of thinking to a particular idea and its source.

Writing up along the way means that the 'report writing' stage is relatively straightforward, since most of the work has already been done. It instead becomes a process of synthesis, integration or summarizing of what has been written before.

Writing can aid the task of obtaining organizational access and eliciting organizational commitment to a piece of research. By providing organizational contacts with a clear set of aims and objectives, they can help with the process of project design and implementation or provide you with feedback and contributions to what you have already *tentatively* planned. Obtaining commitment to access is essential for worthwhile projects to get off the ground and will yield high return. Writing in this sense is a means of keeping people informed and for engaging in constructive dialogue. It can also help bring clarity to the project at the operational level and encourage you to write clearly and concisely for a non-psychological audience.

Writing builds confidence and maintains focus. It helps sharpen one's thinking and to see patterns more clearly. It promotes understanding and reflection, raises issues and questions and provides structure to the research process and its supervision.

Some people prefer to write notes on separate sheets of paper, in a project notebook, on a set of cards, or in a designated computer directory. Whatever the chosen method, all writing pursued as part of the research process needs to be kept in one place where it is easily retrievable.

The proposal requires that you make the following decisions:

- What is my primary research objective?
- What exactly are the hypotheses or questions to be addressed?
- How were these hypotheses/questions derived?
- What are the theoretical issues raised? What theoretical frameworks have been developed/utilized already?
- What is the most appropriate design in this instance? Why?

- What kind of sample do I need? Where from? How many participants?
- What methods of data gathering will I use? Why? How will they enable me to address the questions I have asked or test the hypotheses I have formed?
- How will I handle the data?
- What is my time scale?
- What resources will I need?
- Is the project manageable within the time scale? Does my proposed method really address the question? Will I be able to get access to an appropriate sample in time? What steps will I need to take to obtain organizational access?
- What can be delivered, i.e. what kind of evidence will my research yield and how will this be of practical use to an organization? The *practical* relevance of the research is a critical consideration, one that needs to be thought out in advance and used as a marketing device in securing organizational access.

A proposal is one of the first steps in the process of pursuing research and is a particularly important form of planning document enabling you to establish goals and milestones as detailed in the Gantt chart shown in Figure 3.3. It will also help you to frame the final report.

It might also be necessary for you to rewrite the proposal in more accessible plain English terms for the purpose of securing organizational access. Essentially, the proposal document will provide the vehicle for marketing the research and securing commitment and involvement from suitable organizational participants. The proposal document must emphasize the added value of the research in terms that collaborating organizations can understand and relate to. You will need to answer the questions likely to be posed by the organization: 'What's in it for us?' 'Is it worth the hassle?' 'What are the practical benefits to be gained?' 'What are the resource requirements?' 'To what extent will the project interrupt normal organizational operations?'

When tabling a project proposal with a potential participating organization, it is worth noting the points laid out in Box 3.3, below.

Box 3.3: Tailoring the project proposal to an organizational audience

Your research proposal, as prepared for consumption by your project supervisor and containing, as it will, extensive details of the theoretical reasons for your project, technical aspects of previous research efforts, etc., is unlikely to be an ideal 'selling' device when attempting to secure organizational access. The following tips should provide some ideas as to how to tailor your research proposal to impress an organizational audience:

- **Keep the proposal short and punchy** (the shorter the better) – take an 'executive summary' type approach providing top line information wherever possible;

- **Avoid jargon and technical terminology** – write in comprehensible 'English' terms, avoiding theoretical discussion and focusing on the practical elements of your proposal;

- **Explain what tangible benefits your project can provide** to the organization. If you are collecting performance or attitudinal data, this could be very useful to the company. If you will be able to provide comparative data from other organizations, this is also worth mentioning. It may be worth 'selling' your project as an opportunity for the organization to participate in academic research, thereby communicating their links with the wider community;

- As part of this, **explain exactly what you will deliver** as your part of the 'deal' – this may include progress and final reports on findings, a copy of the dissertation itself, presentations to the Board, to key staff, etc.;

- **Describe exactly what resources you will need from the organization** – the time it will take staff to complete questionnaires or interviews, for example; photocopying, materials costs, etc.;

- **Outline likely time scales, project milestones and deadlines** – this will both aid the organization's understanding of the research process and will also serve to communicate your competence as a research 'project manager'.

For more on this, see Case Study 2 in Chapter 4, which gives a 'real world' example of a research proposal tailored to an organizational audience.

3.5 The internet as a research resource

Over the past several years, the internet has become increasingly widely recognized as a resource for researchers in all areas of academic study. This section provides some background to the use of internet resources during all stages of the research process (but particularly during the initial exploration and data-gathering phases, i.e. planning the project, undertaking the literature review and developing the project proposal). We start by providing some broad definitions of internet-relevant terms, moving on to discuss the use of search engines, critically evaluating internet resources and citing electronic information obtained via the internet.

There are some critical issues surrounding the use of the internet as a research resource. These include the following:

- The internet can be a very valuable source for generating ideas and for initial data gathering;

- The value of an internet research session should be assessed by setting the *quality* of information obtained against the *time* taken to obtain that information;
- Because the internet is a 'public domain' resource, it is often difficult to assess the credibility of a particular source of information. Section 3.5.3 provides you with some guidance on this topic;
- Before you start out on an internet research session, you will need to identify: the general research topic/area you are interested in; the key concepts and ideas which underpin this area; words and phrases which **uniquely** describe your topic; and a number of search engines with which you feel confident and which you can operate competently.

3.5.1 Definitions

Alongside the internet's rapid growth has been a similar expansion in the use of new technical terminology and jargon. The following definitions should clarify some of the topics covered in this section.

Internet – the internet is a global collection of inter-connected computers and computer 'networks' (a collection of individual computers linked to each other), using a common set of standards and protocols (known as 'TCP/IP') which establishes a framework for the way in which information is accessed and exchanged. No one owns or controls the internet since it comprises independently operated but co-operative computer networks, working together to supply and exchange information.

Internet service provider (ISP) – a company providing a 'gateway' or link into the internet.

Internet 'browser' – the software used to 'browse', navigate or explore (i.e. interface with) the internet (most typically Microsoft Internet Explorer or Netscape Navigator).

WWW – the World Wide Web (WWW) is currently the most popular method for accessing and communicating information to internet users. The WWW is a 'document retrieval' system which uses 'hypertext' links (i.e. a way of linking documents together) to set it apart from other means of locating and retrieving information on the internet. The World Wide Web uses a number of unique concepts (and associated language), which include the following:

- **Hypertext and hypermedia** – in a hypertext system, key concepts and images in a document are linked to other documents (and images). The user can connect to new documents by following **highlighted** or <u>underlined</u> links;

- **Hypertext transfer protocol (HTTP)** – the means by which computers running web software communicate with each other and retrieve and exchange required information;
- **Uniform resource locator (URL)** – this is a standardized electronic addressing and resource-finding system which allows users of the web to locate specific internet resources. Each site, page or document has a unique URL or address. URLs generally begin with protocols such as HTTP (see above), which computers use to recognize and communicate with each other;
- **Domain** – each URL will contain information about its content at various levels, and this is described as its 'domain name'. At the highest level, a URL will describe something about its origin as, for example, a commercial organization (using domain 'extensions' such as '.com' in the US and '.co.uk' in the UK), an academic institution (denoted by different extensions in different countries, e.g. '.edu' in Australia, '.ac' in the UK), a non-commercial organization (fairly universally denoted as '.org'), or a government institution (again fairly commonly denoted as '.gov'). At lower levels of description, a domain name provides a more detailed description of the URL's content, and often the country of origin of the URL or site (see the examples given below);
- **Hypertext markup language (HTML)** – web documents are created using this specific language, which specifies the format of the document including text styles, positioning of graphics, paragraphs and the location of hyperlinks. Most web or document pages available on the WWW will use '.html' as a suffix;

So, for example, the URL 'http://www.surrey.ac.uk' contains the following information:

- The URL is using HTTP protocol to communicate with other computers and users ('http');
- The URL is located on the World Wide Web ('www');
- The URL is associated with an academic institution ('ac');
- This institution is based in the UK ('uk');
- The site designer has chosen the word 'surrey' to describe the institution.

If we arrived at the URL 'http://www.surrey.ac.uk/research.html', we would have reached a specific web document ('.html'), entitled 'research' by the web designer.

The URL 'http://www.organisational-solutions.co.uk/home.html' is likely to describe the 'home page' (first page – 'home.html') of a commercial site operating in the UK ('.co.uk'), via the World Wide Web ('www'), whose designer chose to name the site's domain as 'organisational-solutions'.

Search engines – these are specific programs designed for the search and retrieval of documents from the internet. They allow the user to specify 'terms' which the engine will then search for across particular parts of the WWW and internet. Section 3.5.2, immediately below, describes some of the most popular search engines and the methods they use to search the internet.

3.5.2 Search engines

Search engines allow the user to specify topics of interest by entering search 'terms' which the engine then uses to explore its database of information. There are a number of different search engines available, each of which can be used to search the internet for research information. The most popular search engines include: AltaVista, Yahoo, Excite, Lycos, Infoseek and Webcrawler. Each of these search engines is different, employing alternative methods for organizing and searching for information on behalf of the user. No search engine indexes the entire World Wide Web, which means that the researcher will probably need to try alternative engines in order to cover an area of interest comprehensively. Search engines use different 'robots' or 'spiders' (programs which scour the internet for new information on an ongoing basis) with different levels of complexity and coverage. It is important to bear in mind that each search engine has its own 'rules' for specifying search terms and syntax – exploring the help pages provided by a search engine's designer can be very helpful in improving the utility of internet searches.

A general introduction to searching with search engines (i.e. the use of search terms) appears below:

'Simple' word or phrase searching – entering a single word or phrase into a search engine will usually result in the engine using its 'default' program to search for relevant information. Some default programs are better than others at returning accurate results. More specific information can be obtained by punctuating a word or phrase with 'operators' such as plus and minus symbols, and *Boolean operators*, explained in more detail below.

Using plus and minus – most search engines allow the user to search for documents which contain more than one word. For example, if we were searching for information on organizational culture and climate, we could enter the following: '+organizational +culture +climate'. The engine would then search for documents containing all three target words. If we were interested in the same topic, but wanted to find documents without any reference to 'typologies' of culture (see Chapter 8 for more on this), we could enter the following phrase: '+organizational +culture +climate –typology'. This would instruct the search engine to omit any relevant documents which contained the word 'typology'.

Phrase searching – specific phrases, such as *performance related pay* for example, can be entered into most search engines using double quotation marks, i.e. "performance related pay".

Upper/lower case words – different engines have different rules for searching with upper and lower case letters (you will need to check the engine's help pages for more on this). Some recognize upper case letters, while others do not.

Wildcards/truncation – the asterisk symbol can be used to 'wildcard' a word after entering a certain number of letters (usually at least three letters are required before the asterisk symbol becomes active). If we were interested in information relating to assessment, assessors or assessing, we could enter the phrase 'assess*'. Some engines use a different symbol from the asterisk to denote a wildcard search and this information will appear on their help pages.

Boolean operators – So-called 'Boolean' operators include the following words: AND, OR, NOT, NEAR and ADJ. Different search engines require the user to include these in either quotation marks, or capitals. In general, AND finds pages that include two terms. OR finds pages that include either term or both terms. NOT finds pages that include the first term but not the second, e.g. 'team NOT building'. NEAR finds pages in which both terms appear within a certain number of words of each other in either direction. ADJ finds pages in which two terms appear next to each other in a specified order.

Once you have found a site or sites containing information of potential use, it may be worth identifying whether these sites contain any further links to other sites. This can be an excellent way of widening your search, allowing you to 'surf' between information-providing sites. However, it is easy to become side-tracked when adopting this approach and 'bookmarking' useful sites is good practice, i.e. saving the URL information of relevant sites using your browser software. It is often the case that internet searches will return information which is out of date, or to which hyperlinks are no longer functional. This is to be expected and should not detract from the overall goal of the internet session – to gather information on a particular topic.

3.5.3 Evaluating research resources

Finding relevant information using the internet is only the first step in the research process. More than is the case with conventional research resources (obtained via journals, books, periodicals, etc.), the internet researcher needs to fully evaluate any information obtained, judging it for likely reliability, accuracy and utility. Much of the information available on the internet (particularly the WWW) has not been subjected to the rigorous editing and verification of facts normally given to traditional print and commercial electronic databases. When a researcher uses an academically recognized library, they know that the information contained within the library has been evaluated by a librarian and other academics and has been deemed to be reliable and informative. When a database is interrogated for articles, only journals that are considered professional or scholarly are usually indexed. None of these filters are used on the World Wide Web.

The following checklist should help to guide you through the evaluation process – if you are unable to obtain adequate evidence on the information sources you have found, it may well be worth omitting them from your review.

- **Site** – the site on which the information appears may give clues to its reliability. A site maintained by an academic or government institution is probably more credible than one published by a private user. See Section 3.5.1, above, for more information on identifying the purpose and nature of the site (by referring to the top-level domain name, e.g. 'edu', 'ac', 'gov', etc.).

- **Author(s)** – the status of the author is of critical importance in ascertaining the reliability and accuracy of internet-posted information. It should be safe to assume that material written by a known expert in the field will be reliable (in the same way that information posted by a recognized institution or organization can be assumed to be reliable). However, see the paragraph on 'purpose' below for more on this. For lesser known, or unknown, authors you may well have to undertake some further cross-checking with other information sources to establish their credibility (e.g. by checking their track record of published material, their affiliations to credible organizations, etc.).

- **Age of material** – identifying the age of material can be problematic with the internet. Many pages are published and then left unattended for months or even years, without being revisited or updated. It is therefore important to establish when a particular article was written. Some search engines provide this information when reporting results of a web search (by stating, for example, when a page was 'last updated'). If in doubt, write to the author or maintainer of a site to obtain this information. This criterion is of most importance when obtaining information with a specified 'shelf-life', e.g. *current* statistical data.

- **Purpose** – as a researcher, you need to think critically about the underlying motivation for the author in publishing the information/document which appears on a given site. Some sites may appear academically authoritative but have an alternative agenda. Many 'special interest groups' exist, for example, which post what may be useful information, but perhaps with something of a bias in terms of selection and presentation of information to the reader. It is important to determine whether the author of an internet document is stating an argument for personal gain, offering an opinion (a commentary written by an authority in the field remains an opinion unless substantiated by evidence), presenting factual reports (about recent research findings, for example), or relating a personal observation. You will often need to take an executive decision as to whether the reasons underpinning the author's publication of a document may have led to bias in the way the in which information is presented to you.

- **Sources/references** – it may also be important to determine from where an internet author has gathered his/her evidence. Sources and references may be included in the document itself, which will allow you to cross-check and validate some of the arguments stated. You need to identify whether the information presented derives from original research, observations or interviews or secondary sources such as books and documents, keeping in mind throughout the possible reasons why the author has published the information in a publicly accessible forum such as the internet.

3.5.4 Citing internet resources

There is a specific protocol for citing all electronic information, whether obtained via e-mail, CD ROM, or internet. The following protocols and examples are drawn from the APA (American Psychological Society's) style of citation and include protocols for individual works and journal articles available via the internet:

Individual works (protocol and example)

Author/editor. (Year). *Title* (edition). [Type of medium]. Producer (optional). Available Protocol (if applicable): Site/Path/File [Access date].
Rigdon, E. (1998). What is structural equation modeling? [Online]. Available: http://www.gsu.edu/~mkteer/sem.html [2000, February 22].

Journal articles (protocol and example)

Author. (Year). Title. *Journal Title* [Type of medium], *volume* (issue), paging or indicator of length. Available Protocol (if applicable): Site/Path/File [Access date].
Taggar, S., Saha, S. and Hackett, R. (1999). Leadership emergence in autonomous work teams: antecedents and outcomes. *Personnel Psychology* [Online], *52*, 4, abstract only. Available: http://www.wcnet.org/~ppsych/vol-52/524/taggar.htm [2000, February 22].

3.6 The literature review

The literature review is essential as a means of 'thought organization' and a record of evidence/material gathered. Although it might seem that the literature review is a task with a clear beginning and a definite end, it is more ongoing and open than this. As new evidence and material comes to light throughout the project, the review can be appended and reshaped as necessary. At the first stage, however, one must get started, and this can be hard. Where do I start? How will I know what is relevant? How will I know when I have read enough? How does it need to be structured?

Generally speaking, the review will need to begin broadly, narrowing down as your focus of interest becomes clearer. Given a tight time scale, it is unlikely that you can or should endeavour to read everything. A first trawl through an academic journal database (see Box 3.4) may reveal hundreds, even thousands, of papers of some relevance to your area of interest, although this will depend on the scope of the topic you have selected. Some topics will be relatively seldom addressed because they are 'new' (e.g. emotional intelligence), whilst others will have almost a century of literature behind them (e.g. employee motivation). Yet other topics may not have been examined in the context of organizations, in which case you will need to take some pretty strict decisions about relevance.

Box 3.4: The literature search

The literature search can be time-consuming and unwieldy unless approached systematically. There are many ways of obtaining literature. CD Rom databases like PsycLit and Psyc Info (psychological), SocioFile (sociological), and ABInform (management) are usually available for consultation in higher education libraries, as are many relevant books, dissertations and journals from which relevant citations and bibliography lists can be gleaned. The internet (see Section 3.5 above) may also provide some useful leads, containing as it does many complete research papers (often including reference lists), and links to other relevant sites.

Consultation of all these sources will often yield an overwhelming number of potential sources of information and evidence. One way of keeping the information pool manageable is to locate the most recent journal articles on the topic which will usually provide neat concise summaries of the 'state of the art' on a topic or issue, or which will throw up important avenues of research yet to be addressed. Recent articles can be identified from CD Rom databases and/or by scanning the recent journal sections of your library for relevant papers. Pertinent papers may not always be available in your library either because they are obscure or the journal is not often consulted by members of staff in your department. To obtain these papers, you can usually complete an 'inter-library loan' request form which the library will process for you and then you should receive the paper(s) of interest within a couple of weeks. There are usually limits on the number of loan requests you can make, so it may be worthwhile making inquires at other libraries about whether they house the journal(s) you need, and visiting them as necessary.

Once you have obtained these articles, you can then track down the 'classic', much-cited papers or books for your own use. It is important to go back to the original source (rather than to rely on secondary sources) because (a) you might find that somewhere along the line a point made by an original author got distorted or lost along the way, (b) you need a firm basis for forming your own interpretation of what was said and (c) because the author may have said/found other interesting things which were never taken up by researchers or systematically pursued. Go back to the original whenever you can.

Keep track of the references you wish to follow up and log them once you have managed to get hold of them. If you take photocopies, take heed of copyright regulations. Also, be careful not to be lulled into a false sense of security through having obtained a whole pile of photocopied articles: you must also read and digest them. Unfortunately, the information will not enter your brain by a process of osmosis!

To really get to grips with the literature you need to start writing immediately even if only in note form. Avoid leaving it for too long before you 'act' on the information gleaned - i.e. start reviewing, ordering and synthesizing the material early on. Identify gaps and inconsistencies, key themes and issues, theoretical approaches and their strengths and weaknesses.

Many researchers are faced with the question 'Have I read enough?' at some point during the review process. If you feel able to generate and discuss in depth your chosen research question, drawing and building on the principal work undertaken in the field to date, then the answer is probably 'Yes'. Don't make the mistake of searching for the 'Holy Grail' of research papers – the one that you *must have* before you are sure that your research project is heading in the right direction. It is very unlikely that this paper is even out there – all researchers take their own stance and approach to their own research question. For you to truly *own* your research, you may well have to take a leap of faith, which may mean stepping beyond the known (i.e. the published) into the unknown (i.e. new and unpublished research).

Once you have gathered some material and have started to identify patterns, themes and issues, theoretical approaches and such like, you can start to categorize and order. This will only be possible once you have started writing (see Box 3.2). Once you have started forming a 'story' or picture of the literature you can afford to be more selective about what you read. Your supervisor can advise on whether you have missed out on a key paper or book. There may be time for you to contact researchers who have published relevant material recently to see if they have anything currently in press or preparation, and which may be otherwise unavailable. Most researchers will be delighted and flattered by your interest in their work. Throughout your early explorations of the literature be sure to keep records (and, where possible, copies) of all that you have read (see Box 3.5).

Box 3.5: References

Take steps to keep records of all references you consult. It is common for students to forget what they have read or the source of what they have read, or forget to note down citation details. Most departments have their own house style for writing bibliographies or reference lists, which you need to ascertain in advance, to avoid wasting time retrieving material you have already read. There are several ways in which you can record references:

- On index cards;
- In a computer file;
- In a bibliography package;
- In a designated notebook.

If you are likely to be pursuing research on a more long-term basis, then it may be worth investing in a bibliography software package. Such packages can be used to download reference material from databases and will scan a document with a view to inserting all necessary references (so long as the bibliography record is kept up to date). These packages can save a lot of time, since preparing reference lists by hand can be an endless and laborious process requiring painstaking attention to detail.

If you do end up compiling the reference list by hand, the process can be aided by ensuring that you do keep records of everything you have read, that you have correctly recorded the author's initials, spelled names correctly, identified the volume number, page numbers, date and place of publication. Most of the time-consuming nature of reference compilation is attributable to lost references and having to retrace one's steps to locate them. Whatever means of recording references you choose, keep it consistent (avoid recording references across several sources, e.g. written on scraps of paper, cards, several notebooks and in various different unidentifiable files on the computer!)

During the process of reviewing the literature, make regular contact with your supervisor to discuss what you have read and how you have made sense of it all, and seek feedback to help you shape your ideas and thoughts.

The ultimate purpose of the literature review is to help you to formulate a clear research objective or question, and also as the basis for hypothesis derivation (where appropriate). In our experience, students sometimes find it hard to formulate questions at the outset of the research process other than in generic all-encompassing forms, e.g. 'I want to look at leadership and gender', 'I am interested in the psychological contract among nurses', 'I want to do something on the impact of organizational change'. Such 'objectives' are of little practical use to the research planning and design process. A research objective needs to be phrased in such a way as to afford a clear set of testable hypotheses and/or a direct means of investigation.

The literature review may generate many questions and issues. Only one question is required, however, and a commitment should be made to this *and only this* question. Too many students are inclined to take a 'scattergun' approach to the research process either because they want to examine everything they can in connection with a topic or due to reluctance to narrow down the focus too soon for fear of missing out on something important. Those who take this line tend to find it difficult to identify what it is they have found and its relevance, and have a terrible task writing it all up because there is no coherent 'story' to tell. The more focused the research from the start, the neater and more focused the whole process from beginning to end and the more concise the report. This does not, of course, preclude the researcher from including things in a study that are only of 'tangential' interest (particularly if they have open access to an organization and a whole host of research opportunities to pursue or the organization wishes to examine a number of extra issues). However, it does mean that there is even more reason to keep track of the primary research objective.

Examples of manageable research objectives or questions include:

The aim of the research is:

- to predict turnover among a sample of the nursing population by examining their motivations for staying with or leaving their employing organization;

- to identify the role of management style in determining team effectiveness;

- to examine the impact of teleworking arrangements on family relationships;

- to examine the construct validity of the notion of 'growth need' within the job characteristics model;

- to construct a valid and reliable measure of organizational honesty;

- to develop an objective means for measuring personality;

- to examine the role of attribution bias in the selection process;

- to identify the role of culture in helping group members cope with an identity as 'airforce wife' and the possibility of 'losing' their husbands to the job;

- to examine the coping strategies of dual career families in juggling responsibilities of home and work.

These kinds of broad objectives then enable more refined and specific questions to be asked and, if need be, hypotheses to be formed. You will have by now formed a rationale for asking a particular question and have identified an appropriate theoretical (or epistemiological) framework in which to address it. The latter will incline you to adopt a quantitative and/or qualitative line of inquiry on the issue.

You may benefit from feedback on the review from your supervisor (in some instances the review stage is a formal requirement, in others it simply provides the basis for the proposal). Some supervisors will request that you provide them with a review so that they can get a feel for the literature on the topic (particularly if it is outside their main area of interest) and/or as an aide to focusing the research and to taking decisions about ways in which to answer the research question.

3.7 Operationalizing the research question(s)

Once you have derived your questions or hypotheses, they will need to be operationalized. Operationalizing the questions requires that they are translated into a testable and/or measurable form. It is conventional within the social sciences to state questions in the form of hypotheses which are statements of prediction about what result will be obtained given the conditions under which the hypothesis is tested. The more precisely formulated the hypothesis, the easier it is to envisage how it should be tested (i.e. what methods and measures to use, and under what circumstances). Example hypotheses include:

- A significant amount of variance in staff turnover will be explained by staffs' stated level of commitment to the employing organization;

- The more 'transformational' the leadership style, the stronger the group bond within a given team;

- Gender of group members will interact with leadership style in determining the character of the group dynamic and performance on a standardized task;

- Women in dual-career families will self-report experiencing significantly more stress than women in families where only the male member is pursuing a career.

Hypothesis statements will also 'frame' the research by suggesting or implicating a particular research design as appropriate. In the case of 'turnover' the hypothesis presupposes a correlational design with quantitative data, perhaps obtained by survey. The investigation of leadership by gender interaction on the group dynamic and with reference to a standardized task implicates a more controlled experimental or quasi-experimental design, as appropriate.

It is often hard for students to form questions and then to state them in the form of testable hypotheses. Many are inclined to express their interests in rather vague terms, often with a method in mind even before the question is properly formulated in their mind. This is to put the cart before the horse. Strictly speaking, the method should be suggested by the question rather than the other way round. This is not to say that in practice the feasiblity of one's research question will not need to be adjusted or reformulated in the light of practical research possibilities and constraints. The important point is that the method selected should be appropriate to the question being asked.

The difficulty of formulating questions and/or hypotheses may stem from a reluctance to commit to something in advance. To form precise predictions requires confidence in one's thinking and one's ability to obtain valuable data that will produce 'significant' results. It is this desire to obtain a 'significant result' (or the fear of *not* producing a significant result) that can engender reluctance to commit to one prediction or another. Thus students may prefer and feel more comfortable with a scattergun approach that will yield potentially all sorts of possibilities for writing up. Yet this can generate its own problems, not least due to the complexities of finding a *story* to tell. The data may be so rich and complex that it is difficult to identify the really worthwhile findings. It can then be difficult to find a focus, which in turn may mean that the student feels inclined to write everything up. Projects of this kind are usually messy and incoherent, and whilst they often reflect considerable effort of time, energy and enthusiasm, do not do the student justice.

Formulating questions is also something we tend to forget how to do and may be even inhibited from doing because of educational practices that emphasize passivity and conformity among the student population. All 3 and 4 year olds ask the most amazing questions, more often than not underpinned by curiosity and the need to make sense of the world. To a certain extent, many of us manage to unlearn this very natural, human skill because of the negative reactions we have had to face whenever we have asked questions in the past. The educational system encourages an examination driven mode of learning that requires the rapid assimilation of knowledge which can then be cognitively regurgitated during an examination. Thoughtful and critical inquiry is something that is relatively little encouraged (and to some extent may even be actively discouraged) for a whole variety of reasons: individual inquiry can disrupt the flow of learning in a group, and can involve too much 'individual' time and attention. Inquiry also invites challenge and many teachers operating in the pedagogical mode will prefer to adopt the 'expert' role in relation to the 'learner'. Indeed, there are a whole host of reasons why we stop asking questions. Research requires that we relearn this skill; that when we read, we actively engage in the material by asking questions of the text and raising queries and challenges. Many students do not feel confident enough in their ability to do this, feeling that they do not know enough to warrant the taking of a critical and reflective stance. But how much knowledge does one need in order to decide that now is the time to start questioning and reflecting?

Act like a 3 or 4 year old: ask questions incessantly!

There may be instances where hypothesis testing may well be inappropriate. This will usually arise when the literature is thin or atheoretical with respect to a particular research issue or problem (e.g. bullying at work is a relatively ill-investigated phenomenon which is also fairly ill-circumscribed as a problem in the workplace). This may require that a more 'inductive' stance is taken on the issue, requiring some degree of exploration with a view perhaps to problem identification and circumscription, or to an in-depth investigation of meanings and experiences using qualitative techniques. Such investigations are conducted in what is known as an *a posteriori* vein, although in practice, the researcher may nonetheless deploy existing concepts or frameworks (either implicitly or explicitly) in deciding what to ask participants and how to go about gathering the data.

Exploratory work can be used as the basis for hypothesis derivation, for trialing a particular method of data collection or as the basis for developing a quantitative measure. Whatever the use of exploratory work, it should be driven by aims of some kind in order to lend it direction and focus.

There are instances when students may be reluctant to form hypotheses on *epistemiological* grounds. Rather, they may prefer to identify a field issue or problem to investigate that requires that a more 'qualitative' approach is taken.

This may come about as a result of a literature search which suggests one particular approach rather than another or because the student feels that the existing paradigm has not yielded data of much significance or use. One of our students, for example, came to the conclusion that corporate identity could not be investigated adequately using conventional measurement techniques and that instead she would apply 'narrative analysis'. She reasoned that corporate identity was about the use of language and about the process of communication (of the organization to the outside world and of the organization to itself and its own members). Narrative analysis would enable her to investigate the kinds of 'stories' the organization tells about and to itself. This signified an epistemiological leap in thinking which in turn yielded different kinds of questions and ways of investigating the concept of corporate identity. The 'paradigm-busting' nature of this realization felt exciting but was also quite daunting for someone largely unacquainted with this way of thinking and firmly socialized in the positivist tradition. Other more 'inductive' ways of investigating organizational phenomena may include a 'grounded' approach to concept development, whereby the concepts that are evolved from the data are nonetheless still firmly grounded in the data. This is an approach to data collection and analysis described briefly in Chapter 5 on project design.

4   Obtaining and Using Access to an Organization

4.1 Introduction

Once you have decided on your research idea, have devoted time and effort to exploring literature in the area, have developed a detailed proposal, and have been able to operationalize your research question, the issues of organizational access and project design need to be addressed in more detail.

It is often the case that students are so worried about securing access to a sample that they do so before they know what it is exactly that they want to do. This is an understandable sentiment given the demands for 'real' research required by many of today's social science study courses. However, unless you are really clear about what to do and how, the task of securing access, even with ready contacts, can be even more problematic in the long run. The more vague the project outline, the more opportunity an organization has to 'take the lead' in scoping and organizing the project, which could mean that practical considerations may start to overshadow academic ones. If you are someone who does have organizational access, either because you work for an organization or because you have good contacts, this is not to say that you should not use this situation to your advantage. Instead, the issue is one of how to combine practical need with academic standards and requirements. This is why you need to have an accurate and comprehensive picture of exactly what you need from an organization before you approach them.

For some student researchers, then, securing access is not particularly problematic since they have links and contacts they can draw on to obtain organizational samples. For others, recruiting a willing organization represents a significant challenge and one which will require a good deal of effort and time to achieve. This section introduces some of the issues associated with gaining access to organizations, securing 'buy in' from everyone involved in the research project, and 'managing' the organization and your contacts as the project progresses.

4.2 Obtaining access from 'scratch'

If, like the majority of student researchers, you need to secure access from scratch (i.e. you do not have a suitable organization/contact lined up to assist you in the project), you will need to be very clear about what it is you wish to do and how, as this will form the basis on which to contact potential organizational participants:

- Potential participating organizations can be obtained from various company directories, including the business telephone directory, and/or from databases held by business centres or libraries;

- Ring up companies to find out the names of board members (managing directors, HR directors, etc.), asking some preliminary questions about the nature of the business and its size. You can then make some preliminary decisions about whether to pursue any given organization;

- Draft an organizational research proposal with a covering letter, which briefly outlines the proposed research, its aims, methods and resource requirements, and in particular the benefits to the organization of participation. Indicate the time scale of the project as a primary research constraint so that organizations are aware of exactly what the commitment will involve. See Box 3.3 in Section 3.4, above, for more on tailoring an existing research proposal to an organizational audience, as well as the Case Study below for a 'real world' example of an organizational research proposal.

> **Tip 1**: Take steps to secure access as early as you can, but only when you are clear on what you want to do and how, or if you are confident you can pursue something meaningful and academically sound on a collaborative basis.

Always let your supervisor help you with putting together a proposal and a covering letter. Not only will this provide you with important and useful feedback, but the involvement of the supervisor in securing access can add legitimacy and credibility to the research exercise.

> **Tip 2**: The way you present the proposal is critical: it should look like a professionally prepared document with clarity, focus and the ability to engage the reader's interest. If you present it as an academic document without attention to presentational style and flow, accessibility and so on, it will not inspire interest or enthusiasm and may not even get past the CEO's secretary! Use plain English, short punchy sentences, headings and sub-headings, and above all keep it brief. Take time to prepare the document and to get it 'looking right'. Senior people are busy people, inundated with letters, reports and other documents to read. Why should they take the time to read yours? Make them **want** to read your document: make it worth reading and responding to.

The research proposal outlined in Case Study 2, below, is taken from a 'real-life' example where the researcher required access to several hundred participants in order to validate a personality-based selection instrument. It should provide some indication of the style and level of detail required of an organizational research proposal. Please note that names and specific project details have been changed in the interests of confidentiality.

Case Study 2: Research proposal to a software development company

PROPOSAL TO ABC SOFTWARE – PERSONALITY RESEARCH

1. Introduction

In late 1998, the University of Southern England's School of Social Sciences embarked on a research project into the nature of personality at work. Initial research, conducted by MSc students from the university, succeeded in identifying critical elements of personality. A tentative model was developed and, in parallel, a measure of personality was constructed using state-of-the-art psychometric techniques.

This questionnaire measure now requires extensive validation in order for its psychometric properties to be confirmed. This will provide information on the 'reliability' and 'utility' of the instrument in an organizational setting.

It is understood that ABC Software have expressed an interest in participating in this validation research and this document aims to outline the proposed project process, and identify project deliverables which may be of direct value to ABC management.

2. Project process

There are several available methods for collecting data from organizations via questionnaires, including pencil-and-paper, corporate intranets and the internet. Whichever approach is used, the guarantees of *anonymity* and *confidentiality* are paramount. Respondents must be assured that their responses will remain confidential at all stages of data collection. This is critical both from an ethical and practical viewpoint in that doubts about confidentiality are likely to compromise accuracy of responses.

Once the survey is distributed, it is recommended that 1–2 weeks' completion time is provided, during which period reminder e-mails/memos be distributed to employees to maximize response rates. On return of surveys, data analysis and interpretation is likely to take around 4 weeks, after which time a full report will be made available to ABC management on the outcomes of the survey (see Section 3 below for more on this). Total project time, from distribution of surveys to submission of final report, is thus estimated at 6 weeks.

3. Value to ABC

The principal advantage to ABC of participating in this project is in obtaining valuable information relating to employees' attitudes and intentions. It is intended that biographical data be collected via the survey, which will allow data to be analysed by staff group. The data of particular interest to ABC are likely to be as follows:

- Stated intentions to stay with, or leave, ABC;
- Self-report absenteeism rates over the past 12-month period;
- Organizational citizenship behaviours and organizational commitment.

4. Cost to ABC Software

The cost to ABC Software of participation in the research project will be the time taken by each respondent in completing the questionnaire. In total, this is estimated at 15–20 minutes x the number of respondents actually completing the questionnaire. To offset this cost, it is possible to request that employees complete the questionnaire outside of office hours.

Once proposals and letters have been sent, it will probably be worth following up some or all by telephone. At this stage, some organizations will turn you down due to political sensitivities but will express an interest nonetheless. Others will express a firm interest in pursuing the research. Yet others will not reply at all. Take all replies seriously, and respond accordingly. Whilst it might at first feel like there is 'too much to handle' (particularly if several companies get back to you), you may end up either having to be selective in who becomes involved or in selecting the organizations in which the research will take the least time to pursue. Be careful not to make false promises for the sake of keeping contacts 'on the boil'. If they are interested, keep them interested but ensure that you can manage the load it will entail. Otherwise, be honest about the scope of the project and its time constraints, and the academic requirements which underpin it.

There are times when a company will let you down at the last minute. Whilst this is everyone's dread, such instances are unavoidable. Build contingency time into the project to allow for delays brought about by organizational procedures or events. If possible, have two or three companies to draw upon for a sample so that if one company withdraws altogether then you have the others to fall back on without total detriment to the project (although remain mindful of these organizations' expectations and be as honest as you can about their likely involvement).

4.3 Getting 'buy in' across the organization

Securing access of any kind, whether you have contacts or not, can take a lot of time and energy: more than is usually anticipated. The research may need to be sanctioned by an ethical committee which requires forms to be completed, and decisions to be made by committees that perhaps meet only two or three times a year. The research may obtain the 'go ahead' from the top, but if agreement is not obtained lower down the hierarchy, senior people have the power to seriously restrict the research.

For instance, in the NHS, senior nursing and medical executives may agree to a particular piece of research being undertaken involving nursing and medical staff in a particular NHS Trust. If agreement (and in some cases 'involvement') is not sought from those who manage particular units, wards/clinics or departments within the Trust, then the research effort may be thwarted there and then. To this extent, whilst you may get permission to distribute 5,000 questionnaires to employees within the Trust, only a very small percentage (e.g. 5–10%) of them may actually get completed and returned unless lower level managers are notified (and are encouraged to get involved). The larger the organization, the more complex the issue of research communication and involvement and the longer it can take to secure a satisfactory response rate.

Even if you do obtain access and permission to pursue your research from the most senior to the most junior members of the management hierarchy in an organization, this does not guarantee involvement from their staff.

Questionnaires, for example, get left in in-trays, stuffed in bags/lockers, or even dumped in bins, unless there is some incentive to complete them. If a directive from above is issued via a covering letter attached to each questionnaire, an imperative to respond can be created. However, the anonymity of the process may mean that people will not always take the completion of questionnaires as seriously as they might, using them as forums in which to offload personal gripes, leaving whole sections incomplete or simply refusing to complete them altogether. Even the most user-friendly and brief questionnaire on which a memo from the Board is attached may not be completed properly (or at all) if an atmosphere of cynicism or mistrust prevails within the organization.

Tip 3: Involve people as far down the management hierarchy as you can in seeking permission to pursue the research and/or research involvement.

To a certain extent, 'political' problems such as these can be pre-empted with good planning and a thorough anticipation of all potential problems and reactions associated with the proposed research.

Tip 4: Anticipate people's reactions to your research and take steps actively to pre-empt these reactions or to manage them systematically. Think about how *they* will view and react to the research, given the type and nature of the company, and current organizational issues facing them.

It is good practice to forewarn all potential project participants of the scope, duration and purpose of the research. By communicating with organizational members (via company newsletters, the corporate intranet, company memos, a direct presentation/briefing to staff, etc.) the project's aims, what is needed from them, what they will get in return, likely time scales, etc., they are far more likely to respond positively when asked to complete surveys, or participate in interviews, role-plays, etc. Of course, emphasizing confidentiality and anonymity (where appropriate) can be a very powerful way of increasing accuracy and volume of responses, particularly in organizations where a climate of distrust or suspicion prevails.

It may be possible to involve key staff in the development of the project plan and even in the construction of measurement instruments which will be used during the project (as long as this does not compromise the overall academic aims of the research). This is likely to increase participants' sense of involvement and commitment to the project. Maximizing 'buy-in' of as many organizational members as possible is likely to make for a successful project and one that the organization too feels it has benefited from.

4.4 'Managing' the organization throughout the research process

Any participating company will expect you to behave professionally throughout the course of the project, to treat the organization, its staff and any information obtained from it with the appropriate respect and in confidence. The organization will also expect you to *manage* the research process from the outset, since you are effectively its project manager.

So, meet up with organizational representatives face to face and, where possible, seek their involvement in the research. 'Involvement' can range from ideas about what questions to ask in a survey, about the wording of particular questions, the logistics of the research, through to data analysis and interpretation. The company representative you end up meeting may not have time to get involved, and may pass you on to someone who does, having given you the go-ahead. To some degree, you will need to go with the flow in this instance, although you will need to put limits on the extent to which you can change the research (or incorporate particular methods/questions) to suit the company's practical interests and needs. At the same time, accommodate the request for 'extra' questions on a particular issue or topic wherever you can, even if not of any academic interest.

Tip 5: Meet or talk regularly with company representatives assigned to the project, to maintain commitment and interest, and to ensure that the project timetable does not 'drift' as they are inclined to do. Seek decisions on practicalities and secure commitment to dates and times for, e.g., questionnaire distribution, interviews, etc. Keep the project salient in the mind of company representatives and keep it in 'on the boil' throughout the project's course.

You will need to gain the confidence and respect of all organizational representatives involved in the project. If you are able to gain 'buy in' from a senior or respected figure in the organization at an early stage, this can be invaluable in the process of 'selling' and 'championing' the project across the organization. Take time to identify the needs and expectations of your project 'champion': perhaps s/he has an underlying personal/academic interest in the research you are undertaking; perhaps the information you obtain will be of direct and practical use to him/her. If you are able to identify such a person at an early stage of the project, this is likely to work in your favour in the following ways:

- The champion can act (on a day-to-day basis) as your representative when presenting the project idea to other organizational members;
- They will be able to identify the 'movers and shakers' within the company, i.e. the people who can help and hinder the project process;
- They will be able to give you an insight into the 'culture' of the organization, i.e. the way things are done within the company. This can be invaluable if you are to conduct the project sensitively and with the minimum of disruption to normal organizational operations.

> **Tip 6**: When dealing with organizational members (particularly senior decision-makers) combine assertiveness with sensitivity and respect for the participating organization and its ways. Take care not to take over, step on people's toes or bulldoze your way in, but, at the same time, engineer momentum and movement with respect to the project and its deadlines.

Assure the client that any findings deriving from your research will remain confidential and *stick to this promise*. Confidentiality of research findings forms one of the cornerstones of professional practice in any area of social science and should be upheld at all times. Do not reveal the identity of the client company to anyone outside the research project unless you request and receive the explicit permission of that company. Breaking this assurance of confidentiality, especially in the area of occupational psychology, where individuals and organizations are required to divulge personally and politically sensitive information, can be extremely damaging to you and the company and may even have legal implications.

> **Tip 7**: Keep your findings confidential. They are *not* public information.

Respect the 'psychological contract' that exists between you and the organization, particularly with the contacts you have made. It is likely that your contact will have had to 'champion' the idea for your research to his/her seniors and peers, possibly even going out on a limb on your behalf, and will have become increasingly invested in the outcomes of the research. If you fail to follow time scales or are unable to deliver what you have promised, this psychological contract will be placed under severe strain – your contact may become disenchanted with the research and may even be placed in a compromising position with his/her peers or seniors. Alternatively, fulfilment of, or even exceeding the expectations of, this psychological contract can reap enormous benefits.

So, make sure that you *manage* the psychological contract between yourself and the client organization: make clear what you expect from the organization, and what they should expect from you at the end of the project as early as possible. This will avoid compromising expectations and putting the relationship with the client under undue strain.

> **Tip 8**: Respect and manage the psychological contract you have developed with the client organization – for accommodating your research project, your contact will expect certain deliverables in return. Make these expectations explicit – the client contact may not state his/her expectations in this way and may use this lack of initial clarity later to demand extra work from you as a 'freebie'.

So, by following a project through and reporting/presenting back to a 'client' in as professional a way as possible, you will have:

- Succeeded in fulfilling the applied requirements of your project and boosted your chances of securing a high mark for the research report;
- Broken down any preconceptions the client organization may have had about the casual, unprofessional way that 'academics' or 'students' do things;
- Raised your own profile within the client company – it is often the case that students are offered further projects, or even full-time positions, within a company in which they have carried out research;
- Gained valuable (further) experience of consultancy work, including: client liaison, project scoping, project management, data analysis, interpretation, reporting/presenting and developing recommendations.

5   Project Design

5.1 Introduction

Based on the operationalization of your research question, and, to some extent, the constraints placed on you by time (and by your study organization), you will now be in a position to decide on a suitable project design. The design of a project pertains to the particular way in which hypotheses or questions are tested or investigated:

- At its broadest level, the researcher must decide whether the investigation is going to be largely quantitative or qualitative (or both) – i.e. what type of evidence is required.

- At the next level of consideration, the actual design of the study must be decided upon. The study may be case-study based (i.e. dealing in-depth with a single organizational sample or issue), correlational (exploring relationships between factors within an organizational setting) or experimental (examining differences between groups, perhaps over time or across situations).

- At the lowest level, a decision is made about how 'evidence' is to be collected (e.g. interviews, focus groups, survey, experiment, field observation). If a quantitative approach is adopted will the data need to be in 'correlational' and/or 'experimental' form? If a qualitative approach is selected, what will be the most expedite method or methods which can be drawn upon to collect data?

Formally defined, the *design* of a study pertains to the strategy or schedule used to collect evidence, to analyse the findings and from which to draw conclusions. *Measurement,* on the other hand, refers to the systematization of information using a standardized unit of recording.

As outlined above, there are three broad classes of design:

- case-study;
- correlational;
- experimental.

All classes of design presuppose that something has occurred or is occurring which needs to be examined. This occurrence can be referred to as an event or series of events, in relation to the activity, practice or procedure under scrutiny. The event(s) may be an everyday occurrence or something which is staged specifically for research purposes. The latter usually involves an intervention of some kind (e.g. a new organizational practice is introduced). The evaluation of an intervention follows the same logic as the 'drug trial': something new is tried out and its outcomes are then compared in some way to the previous way of doing things to identify whether any change has occurred. Designs vary in the degree of control one is able to exert over the target event (i.e. the character of the event and the logistics of its implementation). Some designs assume little or no control of the target event by the researcher, whilst others require strict control over what happens, with whom, exactly how and when.

The following sections explore in more depth the three basic approaches to research design.

5.2 The case-study or 'now' design

5.2.1 Introduction

This is the simplest of all designs. It involves the description of an ongoing event (e.g. organizational change) in relation to a particular outcome of interest (e.g. strategies of coping) over a fixed time in the 'here-and-now'. Advantages of this design are:

- It enables a more in-depth examination of a particular situation than other designs;
- The information it yields can be rich and enlightening and may provide new leads or raise questions that otherwise might never have been asked;
- The people involved usually comprise a fairly well-circumscribed and captive group, making it possible for the researcher to describe events in detail.

Problems with this design arise largely from difficulties with interpretation. There is no guaranteed method for determining the impact of an event that has not been systematically controlled, or where there is an absence of baseline information against which impacts can be compared. One way of overcoming the difficulties of interpretation is to compare the outcomes against some absolute standard of success (i.e. something agreed in advance as the criterion against which the event can be compared). For example, the change has/has not yielded the desired consequences identified on an *a priori* basis as 'desirable'.

Other problems with this form of design include:

- Getting caught up in minutiae, making it difficult to 'see the wood for the trees';

- Getting so involved that impartiality is lost;
- The information yielded can be difficult and time-consuming to analyse;
- The 'now' design produces evidence that cannot be generalized beyond local circumstances;
- Project participants may feel under intense scrutiny if they know they are being 'researched'.

Hilliard (1993) suggests a number of different forms of case-study research, including narrative case-study research, single-case experiments, single-case quantitative analysis and combined quantitative/qualitative studies. Each of these design types is introduced below.

5.2.2 Narrative case studies

Narrative case studies employ qualitative techniques to elicit and analyse descriptive accounts. These narratives are concerned with making sense of the 'stories' people tell about aspects of their experience. There are a number of different ways of gathering stories (e.g. stimulated recall of critical events, interviews, diaries or journals, open-ended questionnaires, observation of meetings).

The main issue in this kind of research is one of authenticity and completeness of the information derived, which will depend largely on the amount of trust the 'informant' has in the researcher. Analysis of data obtained relies on the ability of the researcher to understand the *meaning* of what is said to him/her. In a review of the biographical writings of Van Gogh, Runyan (1981) found 13 competing but plausible psychological explanations for why Van Gogh cut off his ear. Studies of historical figures show how one can 'construct' a reading or version of a life. It is not, as supposed by positivist philosophers, that the accumulation of data leads inevitably to a convergence on an 'agreed truth'. The situation is more one of interpretation being open to reinterpretation and so on.

To overcome problems of interpretation, Bromley (1986) has suggested that case-study research should apply a quasi-judicial approach, involving the seeking out of alternative views of the data or appointing an 'adversary' to the research team. Others have proposed that competing interpretations can be used in generating hypotheses to guide a further cycle of inquiry and data gathering.

5.2.3 Single-case experiments

These are known as '$n = 1$' or single-subject studies and involve the systematic evaluation of change in individual cases (e.g. the impact of an organizational merger, or the impact of a team development event, on individual participants). The aim is to record and assess specific changes attributable to specific interventions and usually involves systematic assessment before, during and after the intervention has occurred. The pre-intervention assessment provides a baseline against which subsequent changes can be gauged. Ongoing assessment carried out during the intervention displays the actual effect of the intervention, whilst post-intervention (and follow-up) assessment provides a measure of the stability of the change. This kind of research design is termed 'time-series' analysis and in its simplest form is represented by 'before' and 'after' measurement. The assumption underpinning this single-case approach to impact evaluation is that change will be meaningfully and visibly demonstrated and observed.

In the case of a team development event's impact on an individual's performance at work, it would be difficult to ascertain for sure whether the intervention itself was responsible for any changes observed, without some basis of comparison to rule out the possibility of other explanatory factors. However, impact evaluation (even in the single-case scenario) can provide some means of documenting what works in a particular situation, and to provide a source of grounded hypotheses (in the 'action research' sense) for intervention refinement and/or further (perhaps quantitative experimental or correlational) research.

5.2.4 Single-case quantitative studies

In this type of design, the aim is to use quantitative techniques to trace the unfolding over time of variables but without introducing any experimental manipulation or control over these variables as in the single-case experiment. Once again, the problem of 'contaminating' factors is raised within this type of design since it will be difficult for the researcher to conclude anything meaningful about the relative impact of a given intervention if no effort has been made to control for other contributory variables.

5.2.5 Combined quantitative/qualitative case studies

To some extent, all quantitative case studies apply a version of this approach. It may, in some cases, be meaningless to report quantitative changes without reference to more in-depth material. However, in this case, the in-depth data are used to back up or illustrate the quantitative findings. A more robust form of combined study would involve attributing equal weight to both qualitative and quantitative data in a pluralistic way.

In case-study research, the notion of combining qualitative and quantitative data offers the promise of getting closer to the 'whole' of a case in a way that a single method study could not achieve. This idea is based on the principle of triangulation which advocates the use of as many different sources of information on the topic as possible (e.g. questionnaires, observations, interviews) with a view to obtaining convergence on an issue. In practice, this can be problematic for a research project to achieve given limitations of time and resource.

5.2.6 Issues in case-study research

Despite differences in method within the case-study approach, there are some fundamental methodological issues relevant to all of them (e.g. dilemmas around generalizing from single instances, presenting case data in a succinct, yet relevant, manner and finding criteria by which to judge the validity of a case-study). These issues are outlined below:

- *Generalization*: even if it were possible to obtain a rich descriptive account of an organization or group of employees, it would be impossible to draw inferences from single-cases which could be logically applied to a broader population. It should be noted that this issue applies to any single piece of research, i.e. no one study, no matter how tightly designed will ever provide conclusive evidence which can be generalized beyond that specific research situation. It is only when a number of studies yield similar results that it can be agreed that a robust finding prevails. The logic of replication is central to systematic case-study research: ideally, the findings obtained in one case should then be tested in the next and so on. The rationale for selecting later cases is based on theoretical interest, i.e. whether they enable some feature of the emerging model to be confirmed or otherwise. Another strategy that allows the case-study researcher to bridge the gap between the specific and the general is to regard single-cases as 'exemplars' of what is possible. Logically, a single-case event can be enough to refute a theory.

- *Writing up case-study research*: there are various ways in which the case-study report can be written up. First, in the *linear analytic* frame (the standard journal format), i.e. introduction, review, method, results, discussion. Secondly, via *chronological structuring*: the application of time-series analysis to the case data or structuring material by 'stages'. With this approach, there can be a tendency to spend too long on background and not enough on outcomes. Thirdly, by *theory-building*, i.e. focusing on the theoretical implications of the findings in order to encourage subsequent research efforts and to provide them with a theoretical grounding.

- *Case-study validity*: the criteria which define a valid case-study. These include: *significance* – the case-study subject matter is of public and/or theoretical interest; *completeness* – a sense of understanding the 'whole' case is communicated; *consideration of alternative perspectives* – by drawing on the work of other researchers, or appointed 'adversaries' to the research team; *sufficient evidence is provided* – to enable the reader to make his or her own judgements as to the research findings; *sensitivity and respect is shown* – for disclosures recounted in the research report, and for the role of participants in the research process.

5.3 The correlational design

Quantitative correlational designs attempt to explore the relationships between at least two variables within a given environment. The intention is generally not to infer *causes* but to examine relationships and interrelationships between phenomena. Thus, correlational research designs are based on the assumption that reality is best described as a system of interacting and mutually causal relationships (i.e. everything affects, and is affected by, everything else). However, some methods employing correlational designs (such as path and structural equation modelling) do permit causal statements to be made (see Chapter 9 for more on structural equation modelling).

A number of approaches can be adopted within a correlational design framework: bivariate, multivariate, factor analytic and path modelling.

5.3.1 Bivariate design

Within this design, the relationship between two variables is measured. The relationship has strength and direction. The strength of relationship between the variables (how closely they are related) is expressed as a number between −1 and +1 (the correlation co-efficient). A 'zero' correlation indicates no relationship between the variables. As the correlation co-efficient moves towards either −1 or +1, the relationship increases in strength until a 'perfect' correlation is reached at either extreme.

The direction of the relationship is indicated by the sign of the correlation co-efficient. A negative correlation means that as scores on one variable rise, scores on the other decrease. A positive correlation indicates that the scores move together, both increasing or both decreasing.

For our research question regarding commitment and staff turnover, we would expect that a negative correlation would exist between the variables, since *more* committed staff would be *less* likely to leave the organization, i.e. as commitment *increases*, so turnover *decreases*.

5.3.2 Multivariate design

Multivariate correlational designs can be concerned with the degree of relationship between more than two variables or with the relative accuracy with which we are able to *predict* a target variable using more than one 'predictor' variable. Multiple regression techniques allow the researcher to examine the predictive strength of a variety of variables in predicting an outcome. If, for example, we were interested in what factors might lead to staff turnover, we could measure not only degree of organizational commitment, but also satisfaction with the job, perceived availability of alternative positions and family circumstances. By examining the degree of relationship between all of these factors, we would be able to ascertain the *most effective predictor(s)* of staff turnover.

5.3.3 Factor analytic design

This statistical procedure identifies underlying patterns of variables (Kline, 1994). A large number of variables are correlated and the presence of high intercorrelations indicates a common underlying 'factor' or construct. This technique has been used to great effect in the field of personality research in order to identify how best to conceptualize and measure personality (Kline, 1993). While it involves the application of complex statistical procedures in order to be used appropriately and effectively, Kline's (1994) treatment of the subject represents an excellent starting point for the interested researcher.

5.3.4 Path modelling

Path modelling or path analysis is used to determine which of a number of pathways connects one variable with another. It is based on the assumption of causality, i.e. that variations in one or more variables *cause* variations in the target variable, and is generally applied in the social sciences under the guise of structural equation modelling. This topic is discussed in greater depth in Chapter 9.

5.4 The experimental design

5.4.1 Introduction

Experimental research designs involve the manipulation of one variable (the independent variable) and the observation or measurement of the effects on another variable (the dependent variable), i.e. determining whether the dependent variable is, in fact, dependent on the independent variable. Such designs normally involve controlling for external variables as far as is possible (e.g. environmental conditions, differences between participants, etc).

5.4.2 The before–after design

This involves assessing the impact of an event on something by comparing outcomes before and after the occurrence of that particular event. The information obtained before the event provides baseline information against which to monitor and judge the significance of change. By comparing pre-event with post-event information, evidence for gains (or losses) can be derived which can be matched against those expected. This design is possible only if:

- You have had the opportunity to take a measurement before the commencement of the event being examined;
- It is meaningful to take measurements in advance of the event (it would be futile to measure something not yet acquired);
- It is possible to use the same measurement tool before and after the event. If there are changes in instrumentation, then the information yielded will not be comparable;
- It is feasible in terms of the resources available.

Even given the advantages of the before–after design, there is still no guarantee that the event can be assumed to be the true explanation for the observed outcome. Alternative interpretations are possible (e.g. attrition of participants from the study which would change the composition of the sample, participants mature over the course of the study, etc.). Problems can be eased to some extent if contextual information about the process and circumstances of an event can be obtained such as who and what kinds of activities are involved, what materials were used and when, what else happened during the process, who dropped out and why, whether there were any problems or difficulties that arose and so on. This information can be used to contextualize and make sense of the findings. It is important to gather this kind of information at the time rather than in retrospect, although interviewing participants after the event in order to seek explanations for the findings obtained might be argued to be better than nothing (e.g. the impact of merger).

5.4.3 Before–after (matched design)

This design is a quasi-experimental adaptation of the conventional control group design (where samples are randomly obtained and assigned to 'conditions'). In the conventional design, random assignment means that groups are equivalent insofar as a non-biased distribution of the various characteristics that might systematically influence the outcome (which might otherwise have not been considered) is assured. However, randomization is rarely possible in practice. In the adapted quasi-experimental design, the groups are assembled to be as similar as availability permits. Procedurally, it is crucial to ensure that the groups are treated in the same way except for the intervention to which the treatment group is exposed.

If some difference between the results of the two groups is obtained following the intervention, a more powerful conclusion can be drawn about its influence as long as the possibility of the groups being different in some way can be ruled out. The credibility of the findings depends on the ability of the researcher to demonstrate that the treatment and comparison groups are alike except for the intervention received. Trying to find out exactly how similar groups are is a difficult task since there are so many characteristics that can affect individuals' reactions to an intervention.

Problems can occur with this design if:

- The influence of the intervention strategy has effects which are leaked to the comparison group;
- Members of each group are aware that they are involved in an experiment of some kind which may bias their reactions to the intervention;
- The groups are treated differently in ways other than as necessitated by the intervention.

It is not feasible to use this design if:

- Comparable groups are not available or cannot be constructed;
- It is unethical to withhold treatment from one of the groups;
- There are practical constraints as regards the level of control exerted during the event.

5.5 Selecting a research design

Looking back to the research questions introduced in Chapter 3 (see pp. 40–41), it should now be possible to decide which design might be most appropriate to explore each question:

- *A significant amount of variance in staff turnover will be explained by staffs' stated level of commitment to the employing organization.* This research question is probably best answered via a correlational design, since we are examining the *relationship* between staff turnover and employee commitment.

- *The more 'transformational' the leadership style, the stronger the group bond within a given team.* An experimental or correlational design would be appropriate to answer this research question, depending in part on the operationalization of 'transformational' leadership style. The leader's style could be defined as transformational versus non-transformational, with the research thereby lending itself to an experimental group comparison design. Alternatively, the 'transformational' construct could be measured on a continuum, and if sufficient numbers of teams could be obtained, an assessment of the degree of relationship between leadership style and group bond could be obtained via a correlational design.

- *Gender of group members will interact with leadership style in determining the character of the group dynamic and performance on a standardized task.* The basic research design here is likely to be experimental in nature since there is a requirement to compare all-male and all-female groups, as well as the styles of different leaders. This will require a number of comparable groups categorized into different experimental 'conditions'.

- ***Women in dual-career families will self-report experiencing significantly more stress than women in families where only the male member is pursuing a career.*** While this research question may lend itself to an experimental design (comparing the relative experienced stress of women in dual-career versus single-career families), it may be that a case-study approach will also provide rich and useful data, particularly during the preliminary stages of research. By selecting one or two single- and dual-career women, the researcher may be able to elicit the issues most pertinent to, and characteristic of, each group. Tentative hypotheses could then be developed regarding experienced stress which could be tested via an experimental approach.

The above examples should demonstrate the potential value of all basic types of study design. For some research questions, a single approach may be seen as the most appropriate, while for others different design approaches may be equally applicable, each with their own advantages and drawbacks. It is the responsibility of the individual researcher (and his/her supervisor) to decide on the most sensible design approach given the time and resource constraints placed upon the project. In many cases, it will be worth undertaking preliminary qualitative research (perhaps using a case-study approach) in order to generate detail-rich information which can feed into a subsequent quantitative correlational or experimental design.

> Remember: the design you choose must be appropriate to the question you are asking and the type of evidence that it is necessary to elicit. It may be that several design approaches are suitable for addressing your research question. In this case, you need to think carefully about the advantages and disadvantages of each design as well as taking into account the various constraints placed on the research project in terms of time and resources.

5.6 Ethical considerations in organizational research

At this stage of the research planning process, it is of paramount importance to consider potential ethical implications of the research process. Most professional bodies representing the social sciences publish specific codes of practice and ethics for the treatment of research participants. Members of professional bodies enter into a psychological contract to uphold and abide by these ethical guidelines as a condition of their continued membership. The British Psychological Society's Division of Occupational Psychology, for example, publishes *Guidelines for Professional Practice and Conduct for Occupational Psychologists* (1996). As regards research, the guidelines include the following (BPS, 1996: 10):

Occupational Psychologists must:

11.1 make a careful evaluation of the ethical acceptability of research proposals.

11.2 undertake a careful analysis of the potential impact of the research. If there are any negative consequences, these must be ethically justified and should be explained to participants in advance of consent.

11.3 ensure that participants in research are informed of all features of the research which might reasonably be expected to influence their willingness to participate ... Consent must always be obtained in writing.

11.4 ensure that informed consent addresses both the research procedures and the publication of results.

11.5 not use any research procedure likely to cause serious or lasting harm.

11.6 ensure that research data are treated with confidence and respect and cannot be shared with others without the explicit consent of the client.

Guidelines such as these are typical of those published by academic and professional bodies throughout the social sciences. As noted by Barrett (1995), it is possible that, although a research study is feasible on practical grounds (the design is sound, the research question is specific and appropriate methods are available for its investigation), it remains unacceptable due to its ethical implications. It is key that the researcher should investigate these implications prior to embarking on a research project. When in doubt, it is always worth discussing ethical quandaries with other (experienced and disinterested) researchers, with your intended sample, with the client organization, and/or your representative academic or professional body.

Judd et al. (1991) outline a number of potentially unethical practices involving research participants, each of which will be briefly discussed below:

Involving people in research without their knowledge or consent – this possibility may arise for a number of reasons: sometimes it is impossible or impractical to inform participants; the researcher may believe that by informing participants of the research, the behaviour under investigation would be distorted. For whatever reason, if this does occur, the researcher has infringed on the participants' right to make their own decision about whether or not to participate. The researcher's ethical dilemma in such circumstances is to maximize the welfare and protection of the interests of research participants, while at the same time maximizing the validity and accuracy of research data for the benefit of the research (and more general) community. A decision as to the relative defensibility of research approaches which fail to inform individuals of their participation may be evaluated with reference to the relative 'cost' to the participant. Such costs can include imposition on participants' time, patience and physical and psychological welfare by involving them in activities in which they otherwise might not have engaged. By way of example, as Judd et al. (1991: 488) note, researchers who 'artfully disguise their confederates as injured, bloody survivors of a car wreck, seeking aid at night from rural residents, push the costs to participants to a high level.'

Coercing people to participate – in certain circumstances, a researcher may be in a position to compel or coerce individuals to participate in a project, perhaps due to the authority of an employing organization overseeing the project, or due to strong incentives being offered to employees. In such cases, the ideal of total freedom of choice is infringed. Any situation in which the individual's freedom of choice is restricted has potential ethical implications which require (a) a full explanation of the research project to be provided and (b) informed consent to be obtained (see below).

Withholding from the participant the true nature of the research – the principle of *informed consent* is crucial to much applied research. The American Psychological Society (1973, cited in Judd et al., 1991: 494) describes this principle as follows:

> Ethical practice requires the investigator to inform the participant of all features of the research that reasonably might be expected to influence willingness to participate, and to explain all other aspects of the research about which the participant enquires.

Thus, when an individual agrees to participate in a study, that individual's consent should normally be informed by knowledge about the research. This therefore precludes withholding from participants the true nature of the research.

Deceiving the participant – this may occur in order to: mask the true nature of a research programme (see above); conceal the true function of the research participants' actions; or conceal the experiences that participants will have. This is ethically unacceptable in almost all cases due to violation of mutual expectations of trust, and potential disrespect shown to research participants.

Leading participants to commit acts that diminish their self-respect – well-documented in social science research are studies which attempted to induce behaviours in participants which had the potential to diminish those participants' sense of self-respect. Such studies have attempted to induce behaviours such as lying, stealing, harming others (perhaps the best known of which are those documented by Milgram, 1965), conformity due to social pressure and failure to help when help is needed. Some participants in such studies have reported psychological distress due to engaging in behaviour which has caused them shame, embarrassment or regret, because they have violated their own moral standards, or because they have shown themselves to be less worthy and self-directed than they had previously believed. While some follow-up studies have suggested that these feelings of diminished self-worth may be temporary (e.g. Ring et al., 1970), it is clear that the ethical implications of such studies are significant and must be considered carefully when setting them against the potential wider benefits of such research.

Exposing the participant to physical or psychological distress – it is clearly questionable to expose research participants to stressful experiences without their informed consent, and is entirely unacceptable to submit them to experiences which may cause them serious or lasting harm (Judd et al., 1991: 505). The overriding goal should be for the researcher to achieve his/her objectives with the minimal exposure of participants to situations which may cause them distress.

Invading the privacy of the participant – some research designs and methods contain an implicit assumption that the privacy of participants is likely to be violated. These include: participant observation, covert observation, and questioning participants on intimate personal matters. Participants' privacy may be invaded in two main ways: by observation of acts which an individual may prefer to keep private; and by the participant being observed systematically in the absence of knowledge that this is happening. The degree to which such invasions of privacy are perceived by participants as serious are most likely to depend on the behaviours or situations being observed and on the researcher's efforts to explain and/or debrief participants on conclusion of the research. Where possible, written consent should be obtained from participants.

Withholding benefits from participants in control groups – ethical concerns around this issue are raised when researchers are fully aware of the *actual* (as opposed to potential) benefit of a particular condition to all participants, while still withholding this benefit from the control group. This is not particularly prevalent in organizational settings, but potential implications should be considered such as participant reactions on discovery of such a research design, and the possibility that control group participants may demand reimbursement consistent with the benefits provided to the experimental group.

Barrett (1995) notes a further point concerning confidentiality and anonymity of data. Most professional bodies stipulate that information obtained from a participant during a research project should remain confidential unless otherwise agreed between the parties. All participants in social science research have a right to expect that the information which they provide will be treated confidentially and that, if presented to a wider audience, will not be attributable to them. If it is not possible to guarantee such anonymity and confidentiality, participants should be informed of this prior to becoming involved in the research. In addition, as noted by the BPS (1996), all identifiable computer-based and written records in the UK now fall within the remit of the Data Protection Act 1984, which gives participants rights to access data concerning them that is stored on computer. As a researcher, collecting confidential data requires that you must register with the Data Protection Registrar and follow specific guidelines on sound practice as laid down within the Act. If working under the auspices of an educational or academic institution, it is likely that responsibilities concerning data protection will be handled by an institutional administrator. It remains the responsibility of the researcher, however, to identify this individual and to discuss any ethical implications of a proposed research venture with him/her.

Underpinning all of the above is the overriding goal of treating participants fairly and showing them consideration and respect at all stages of a research project. By ensuring that your research project abides by ethical guidelines and codes of conduct (incorporating those issues outlined above) *and by conducting research professionally*, participants are more likely to feel that they have been treated equitably and fairly. Good professional conduct can range from keeping agreed appointments with participants, through fulfilling promises and expectations (both *stated*, e.g. providing agreed incentives, and *unstated*, e.g. not compromising participants' anonymity without their consent), to delivering the personal benefits participants were led to believe they would enjoy through their participation in a study.

Depending on the nature of your target organization, you may be required to submit your research proposal to boards of ethics, or other regulatory bodies who will have the power to reject or accept your project on ethical grounds. UK healthcare trusts typically request a range of information concerning the goals of a research project, the potential impact on participants, means for managing and minimizing this impact, and means for limiting access to collected data, etc. Other public organizations, as well as larger private companies, will request this type of information from a potential researcher before allowing a research project to go ahead. Whether or not you are explicitly asked to provide this type of information, it is always good practice to include in your research proposal an outline of the potential ethical implications of your research and what measures you have put in place to ensure that ethical boundaries are not traversed.

5.7 References and further reading

Case-study design

Bromley, D.B. (1986). *The Case-Study Method in Psychology and Related Disciplines.* New York: Wiley.

Hartley, J. (1994). Case studies in organizational research. In C. Cassell and G. Symon (Eds.), *Qualitative Methods in Organizational Research.* London, UK: Sage Publications.

Hilliard, R.B. (1993). Single-case methodology in psychotherapy process and outcome research. *Journal of Consulting and Clinical Psychology, 61, 3,* 373–380.

Runyan, W.M. (1981). Why did Van Gogh cut off his ear? The problem of alternative explanations in psychobiography. *Journal of Personality and Social Psychology, 40, 6,* 1070–1077.

Correlational design

Kline, P. (1993). *Personality: the Psychometric View*. London, UK: Routledge.

Kline, P. (1994). *An Easy Guide to Factor Analysis*. London, UK: Routledge.

Tabachnick, B.G. and Fidell, L.S. (1996). *Using Multivariate Statistics* (Third Edition). New York: Harper Collins College Publishers.

Experimental design

Davis, A. (1995). The experimental method in psychology. In G.M. Breakwell, S. Hammond and C. Fife-Schaw (Eds.), *Research Methods in Psychology*. London, UK: Sage Publications.

Fryer, D. and Feather, N. (1994). Intervention techniques. In C. Cassell and G. Symon (Eds.), *Qualitative Methods in Organizational Research*. London, UK: Sage Publications.

Fife-Schaw, C. (1995). Quasi-experimental designs. In G.M. Breakwell, S. Hammond and C. Fife-Schaw (Eds.), *Research Methods in Psychology*. London, UK: Sage Publications.

Ethics

American Psychological Association (1973). *Ethical Principles in the Conduct of Research with Human Participants*. Washington DC: APA.

Barrett, M. (1995). Practical and ethical issues in planning research. In G.M. Breakwell, S. Hammond and C. Fife-Schaw (Eds.), *Research Methods in Psychology*. London, UK: Sage Publications.

British Psychological Society, Division of Occupational Psychology (1996). *Guidelines for Professional Practice and Conduct for Occupational Psychologists*. Leicester, UK: BPS.

Judd, C.M., Smith, E.R. and Kidder, L.H. (1991). *Research Methods in Social Relations: International Edition* (Sixth Edition): Chapter 20. Fort Worth, TX: Holt, Rinehart and Winston.

Milgram, S. (1965). Some conditions of obedience and disobedience to authority. *Human Relations, 18*, 57–76.

Ring, K., Wallston, K. and Corey, M. (1970). Mode of debriefing as a factor affecting subjective reaction to a Milgram-type obedience experiment: an ethical inquiry. *Representative Research in Social Psychology, 1*, 67–88.

6 Methods of Data Collection

6.1 The research process continues

You should now be at the stage of having obtained, or being *en route* to securing, organizational access, having defined and operationalized your research question, and selected a suitable design for the project (see Figure 6.1, below).

In many cases, the selection of your study's design will have suggested the use of one or more particular data collection methods. However, it is worth taking time to consider all available methods of data collection, their specific advantages and disadvantages and their suitability to your research question before setting out to collect your data. This chapter aims to describe some of the more popular methods of data collection, their advantages and drawbacks, and the ways in which they can be practically applied.

Figure 6.1, below, illustrates the continuation of the research process, from securing organizational access and selecting a study design through to final reporting and presentation of study findings. Throughout the process of data generation and collection, it may be necessary to revisit earlier stages in order to collect additional supplementary information using alternative techniques, or to simply collect more data where findings are inconclusive or stimulate further questions.

The next few chapters explore each of these stages in depth, as outlined below:

- **Chapter 6: Methods of data collection** – introduction to a number of data collection/generation techniques, including critiques and real-world examples;

- **Chapter 7: Sampling considerations** – the importance of sampling in research;

- **Chapter 9: Data analysis** – qualitative and quantitative analysis of data and how to interpret what findings mean;

- **Chapter 10: Reporting research findings** – for academic and organizational audiences.

Chapter 8 considers an issue specific to many research ventures in organizational settings: the measurement and analysis of 'performance', what this means and how it might be achieved.

Figure 6.1   The research process continues

6.2 Criteria for selecting a method

In order to select an appropriate method to explore your research question, it is worth considering the following points.

The method must be:

- Appropriate to your research objective;
- Able to elicit a form of data appropriate to testing your hypothesis/hypotheses or addressing your research question(s);
- Feasible given time, resource and organizational constraints and requirements;
- Adequately piloted;
- Ethically sound;
- Agreed and accepted by the organization;
- Used appropriately, in the context of its original formulation and development;
- One you feel comfortable with, being confident and well rehearsed in its use before you use it 'for real'.

Do not put the cart before the horse. Select the method as the means of achieving your objective rather than because you like the idea of using it or feel most comfortable with it as a methodological tool. In practice, the process of selecting a method is iterative and will in part depend on what is practical given time and resource constraints and the feasibility of using it within an organizational context.

The following sections consider data collection methods in some depth, giving background to, and guidance in the application of, the following methods:

- Interviews (including repertory grid and Q-sort approaches);
- Focus groups;
- Psychometrics;
- Observation;
- Surveys and questionnaires;
- Diary methods.

6.3 Interviews

6.3.1 Introduction

Interviewing is an extremely flexible research tool (Breakwell, 1995). It can be used at any stage of the research process: during initial phases to identify areas for more detailed exploration and/or to generate hypotheses; as part of the piloting or validation of other instruments; as the main mechanism for data collection; and as a 'sanity check' by referring back to original members of a sample to ensure that interpretations made from the data are representative and accurate. Interviews can also be readily combined with other approaches in a multi-method design which may incorporate, for example, questionnaire measures or observation. Interviewing, as with all research methods, is also open to a number of biases and shortcomings, the most critical of which is the difficulty of achieving reliable and valid results. Quantification and objectification of interview-derived data are the most powerful ways to remedy this, and highlight the importance of the researcher maintaining an objective stance throughout the research process.

6.3.2 Types of interview

Interviews can take a variety of forms depending on the type of data required to inform the research question being asked, as well as on the availability of resources.

- **Structured interviews** involve a prescribed set of questions which the researcher asks in a fixed order, and which generally require the interviewee to respond by selection of one or more fixed options. This method ensures rapid data coding and analysis, easy quantification of data and consequent comparability of responses and guaranteed coverage of the area of interest to the research. However, the approach effectively acts as an other- (as opposed to self-) administered questionnaire, with the added advantage of the interviewer being available to answer questions if the interviewee is confused. The approach constrains interviewees and does not allow for exploration or probing into further areas of interest.

- **Unstructured interviews** allow the researcher *carte blanche* to address any or all of a given number of topics which may be of interest to the research. Questions and their order are not fixed and are allowed to evolve during the interview process. Here, comparability and ease of analysis and quantification are secondary to obtaining rich, salient data from each individual using open-ended, rather than forced-choice, questions. Breakwell (1995) points out, however, that the depth of exploration in unstructured interviews may well be of the same level as that present in structured interviews, since both are dependent on the knowledge and skills of the researcher.

- **Semi-structured interviews** incorporate elements of both quantifiable, fixed-choice responding and the facility to explore, and probe in more depth, certain areas of interest. Thus, this type of interview carries with it the advantages of both approaches (generally easy to analyse, quantify and compare, but allowing interviewees to explain their responses and to provide more in-depth information where necessary) as well as the disadvantages (the temptation to spend too long on peripheral subjects, the danger of losing control to the interviewee, and the reduction in reliability when using non-standardized approaches to interview each respondent).

- **Ethnographic interviews** amount to unstructured interviews but within the context of the target research area, and extending beyond the restrictions of an unstructured interview (which still imposes the researcher's perceptions and pre-conceptions) by allowing interviewees (often termed 'informants' in this field of research) to develop their responses in their own way, using their own frame of reference. The researcher here acts more as a 'facilitator', suggesting directions for discussion rather than controlling them and, at all times, maintaining a sense of freedom and informality for the informant. However, this appearance of informality does not necessarily result in incomparable, anecdotal data which can only be reported in 'case-study' style. If the interviewer is sufficiently competent, ethnographic interviews can be *steered* through a broad range of subject matter and recorded data (note-taking is *not* advised with this approach) can be analysed via content or discourse analysis following transcription. See Spradley (1979), McCracken (1988) and Merton et al. (1990) for more information on ethnographic interviews.

6.3.3 Guidelines for the interview process

- **Design for consistency:** interviews are notoriously open to interviewer effects (interviewee reactions to interviewer characteristics, e.g. dress, manner, style, voice), so, to preserve consistency, either use the same interviewer for all interviews (all interviews will then contain error, but it will be from the same source and so can be controlled for) or randomize a group of interviewers with interviewees (in order to reduce strong effects of one interviewer and to allow examination of interviewer differences);

- **Obtain as much background information as possible**: on the sample interviewees, the setting (organization, institution, etc.), and (needless to say) the area being researched;

- **Prepare and pilot the interview in advance**: in terms of estimated running time, subject areas to cover, question content, contingency for difficult interviewees, difficult subject areas;

- **Ensure privacy and avoid interruptions**: anonymity is a key issue in much research (particularly organizational), so a private office is often a necessity; explaining to others that interviews are being conducted (via a visible sign, or notifying an organizational 'gatekeeper', e.g. secretary, should minimize interruptions);

- **Put the interviewee at ease**: inquire as to the level of knowledge the interviewee already has; explain the purpose of the interview/research programme as far as possible; explain the anonymous nature of the research; answer any initial questions;

- **Establish rapport**: avoid technical language/jargon; start slowly; establish the level of the interviewee and adapt to them;

- **Maintain control**: keep to the core areas/questions, remain relevant and directed; if necessary, steer the interviewee back to the point and avoid long discussions of peripheral material;

- **Avoid bias as far as possible**: bias may arise in terms of leading questions (all too tempting when the interview programme is well established and you feel you '*know*' what the interviewee is getting at'), social acceptability bias (on the part of the interviewer or interviewee), acquiescence bias (yea and nay-sayers), etc. If a group of interviewers is to be used, ensure that they are aware of possible biases in the interview situation and are capable of minimizing them;

- **Be objective**: never make *value* judgements about interviewees; apply the same standards to each interviewee when classifying information, even at interview stage. This is particularly important if a group of interviewers is involved in the research project: ensure that they know and understand the standards by which each interviewee is to be judged;

- **Obtain the maximum response from each question**: be a good listener and follow up questions with additional probing and exploration where an interviewee appears to have more to say (in the case of semi- and unstructured interviews); this also allows you to maintain the *flow* of the interview to avoid disjointed question-asking;

- **Be sensitive**: to the feelings and attitudes of the interviewee; avoid antagonizing the interviewee or making him/her defensive; use neutral, non-emotive language; approach sensitive issues with qualifiers, e.g. 'Would it be fair to say that...', 'Am I right in thinking that...', etc.;

- **Give yourself a chance**: allow extra time than expected for each interview as contingency; leave yourself 10–15 minutes following each interview to revisit, write up and expand notes; if you run seriously behind in your schedule (which is very possible), postpone and reschedule a complete interview to regain time and keep to the time plan.

The utility of these guidelines is illustrated in Box 6.1, which presents numerous examples of how *not* to conduct a research interview.

Box 6.1: How not *to conduct the research interview*

Interviewers can seriously limit the useability, reliability, validity and applicability of their data when they adopt one or more of the following ten 'personae':

The unprepared interviewer – wastes the early part of the interview with work that should have already been done; appears incompetent;

The talkative interviewer – overwhelms the interviewee, who consequently finds it difficult to express him/herself;

The opinionated/argumentative interviewer – cannot resist stating his/her own opinions and may encourage confrontation and conflict with the interviewee, also forcing interviewees to give an antagonistic (and perhaps unrepresentative) view of themselves;

The inattentive interviewer – writes notes and thinks ahead to the next question/interview/lunch but fails to pick up on subtle information provided by the interviewee;

The direct/leading question interviewer – prefaces questions with phrases like 'Do you ...?', 'Have you ...?', 'I'm sure you would agree that ...?', thereby leading the interviewee;

The limiting question interviewer – restricts interviewees by using forced-choice responses none of which may accurately represent the interviewee's views;

The complex language interviewer – uses jargon and professional language (either consciously or unconsciously) but rapidly loses rapport with, and the sympathy of, the interviewee;

The fraternizing interviewer – tries *too hard* to establish rapport, exposing his/her own opinions and feelings and losing his/her position of objectivity;

The captive/timid interviewer – allows the interviewee to take control and is afraid to ask potentially sensitive or embarrassing questions;

The chairman interviewer – is overconfident and regards only him/herself as having sound judgement, consequently making erroneous assumptions about interviewees rather than remaining objective.

6.3.4 Analysing interview data

1. **Keep focused** on the theoretical areas driving your research throughout the analysis process. This to some extent depends on the nature of the project (exploratory or confirmatory): if exploratory, searching for key themes from a completely empirical perspective is justifiable and in fact may be preferable to avoid bias; if confirmatory, the presence (and absence) of expected themes should drive the analysis phase.

2. **Select an analytical approach** there are several, e.g. content analysis (discussed in Chapter 9), discourse analysis and transcription analysis (involving full transcription of recorded interviews – remember that for every one hour of recorded material, seven hours of transcription are required). Choose one which best suits the data and the nature of your inquiry. Content analysis is probably the most widely used.

3. **Estimate inter–rater reliability** if more than one interviewer was used, inter-rater reliability estimations are critical. Without quantitative data (which can be obtained using content analysis) this may be difficult, but via discussions with the interviewers and analysis of transcriptions/notes, possible biases can be identified and reported. With quantitative data, direct comparisons may be made between thematic groupings by interviewer in order to uncover possible bias in interpretation or recording by different interviewers.

4. **Authenticate interpretations** by returning to a sample of interviewees with tentative conclusions from the analysis you can obtain an estimate of the conclusions' accuracy. If interpretations are inaccurate, speaking to the interviewees may help in re-shaping your ideas for re-analysis of some or all of the data.

5. **Report on the analysis** using qualitative/quantitative techniques and drawing on direct quotations where useful to elucidate particular points. Use graphical data where possible to illustrate quantitative material (e.g. theme 'counts' by group), and use statistical significance testing where appropriate.

6.3.5 Advantages and disadvantages of interviewing

Advantages:
- **Rich data** – preserving the original meaning of participants;
- **Flexibility** – interviews can be used at any stage of the research process; multi-method data collection is also possible, by including interviews with other techniques, e.g. observational and self-administered elements;

- **Interviewer availability** – due to the availability of the interviewer, interviewee questions can be answered, the interviewer is able to probe for adequate answers and can ensure that complex instructions or sequences can be adhered to;
- **Ensures co-operation** – interviews are probably the most effective way of ensuring co-operation from most populations;
- **Rapport and confidence-building** – can be ensured, both important for addressing complex or sensitive topics.

Disadvantages:
- **Cost** – need trained interviewers, logistics time-consuming, etc.;
- **Time-consuming** – due to volume of data in analysis, and to length of time needed to introduce, establish rapport, probe, debrief on completion;
- **Accessibility** – some samples (especially those which are geographically disparate or isolated) may be more accessible via other methods;
- **Open to bias** – highly reactive environment with biases from interviewer (appearance, speech, expectations, interview style) and interviewee (reaction to artificial nature of situation, adoption of role by interviewee, social acceptability bias, acquiescence bias);
- **Poor reliability** – due to their openness to so many types of bias, interviews can be notoriously unreliable, particularly when the researcher wishes to draw comparisons between data sets.

6.3.6 References and further reading

Breakwell, G.M. (1990). *Interviewing*. Leicester, UK: BPS.

Breakwell, G.M. (1995). Interviewing. In G.M. Breakwell, S. Hammond and C. Fife-Schaw (Eds.), *Research Methods in Psychology*. London, UK: Sage Publications.

Brenner, M., Brown, J. and Canter, D.V. (Eds.) (1985). *The Research Interview: Uses and Approaches*. London, UK: Academic Press.

Dunne, S. (1995). *Interviewing Techniques for Writers and Researchers*. London, UK: A. and C. Black.

Edonborough, R. (1996). *Effective Interviewing: a Handbook of Skills, Techniques and Applications*. London, UK: Kogan Page.

Fletcher, J. (1988). *Effective Interviewing*. London, UK: Kogan Page.

McCracken, G. (1988). *The Long Interview*. Newbury Park, CA: Sage Publications.

Merton, R., Fiske, M. and Kendall, P. (1990). *The Focused Interview: a Manual of Problems and Procedures*. New York: Free Press.

Minichiello, V. (1990). *In-depth Interviewing: Researching People*. Melbourne, Australia: Longman Cheshire.

Spradley, J.P. (1979). *The Ethnographic Interview*. New York: Holt, Rinehart and Winston.

6.4 Techniques for use in interview contexts

6.4.1 Repertory grids

Description: The repertory grid technique (RGT) involves three stages: the elicitation of 'elements' (i.e. the entities in the area of meaning to be investigated), the elicitation of 'constructs' (in relation to the elements), and the construction of a grid matrix of elements and constructs. Elements can be people, objects, events, or in fact anything with reference to which an individual constructs meaning. It is essential that whatever the class of element, this remains consistent within each particular grid application (e.g. all people, all events) (see Case Study 3 for more on this).

Case Study 3: Use of repertory grid technique with a nursing sample

Lee (1998) describes the use of 'critical incidents' as her class of elements in a study of nurses and their psychological contract. The psychological contract pertains to beliefs about mutual expectations in the workplace. The aim was to examine nurses' constructions of their psychological contracts.

Lee operationalized the psychological contract in terms of 'expectations' on the basis of findings demonstrating the centrality of this concept to feelings of contractual violation. She asked nurses in her sample of 25 to describe two incidents each, describing when they felt that their expectations had been unmet, adequately met, and met in more ways than expected. Each element was written on a card, shuffled and then numbered. Cards 1, 2 and 3 were then selected as the first 'triad' and formed the basis on which to elicit initial constructs. Each participant was then asked to identify the two elements which were similar and different from the third in terms of how the incidents described made them 'feel' and 'why'. They were asked to describe the nature of the similarity (at one end of the grid) and the difference (at the other end of the grid). The process was repeated until all constructs pertinent to a particular triad were exhausted.

The grid exercise yielded 352 constructs across 25 respondents (e.g. 'I felt valued by the amount of support shown, versus 'anxious because I was in a situation in which I felt out of control'; 'grateful for being offered the time to improve my quality of life' versus 'accepting of the situation and committed to the responsibility'). The grids were content analysed thematically to identify shared constructs and construct themes. Twenty-nine themes were derived, with 'working relationships' (with managers, colleagues, the team) and 'value and recognition' being the two most pertinent themes arising in connection with how the psychological contract is constructed by nurses.

Aims/theoretical rationale: The RGT originates from the work of Kelly (1955) on personal construct theory. It aims to elicit personally meaningful 'dimensions' and 'distinctions' by means of which the world is 'constructed'. The most appropriate use of the RGT is within the framework in which it evolved – i.e. constructivist philosophy. This philosophy advocates that all communication and understanding are a matter of interpretative construction, that the world which is constructed is an experiential one that consists of experiences without making claims about 'truth' or ontological reality (though it is acknowledged that reality does limit what is possible).

Procedure: The most commonly used means for eliciting constructs is the triadic method (see Case Study 3, above) which involves presenting three elements each described on cards and asking the question 'in what way are two similar' or 'how does one differ?'. The researcher presents as many triads as required to exhaust a respondent's constructs pertinent to a particular domain (usually around 20–30 constructs). Each construct is elicited in the form of a distinction (between what is similar and what is different). Once all the constructs are elicited, the grid is used as a means of comparing each element (at the top of the grid) against each construct (in rows) along a 5-point scale (i.e. measuring the extent to which each element can be regarded in terms of a particular construct).

Analysis: This can be conducted using various mathematical solutions enabling common constructs to be extracted. Alternatively, the researcher may prefer to adopt a more qualitative 'interpretative' approach (see Chapter 9 for more on content analysis, for example), as part of which the respondent may be engaged in interpretative dialogue with respect to the grid results (see Gammack and Stephens, 1994, for an example of this in an occupational context). The latter is an approach to grid analysis more in the spirit of its original use, as proposed by Kelly (1955). Gammack and Stephens (1994), however, argue that quantitative analysis imposes an 'unjustifiable metric' on the RGT.

Application: Gammack and Stephens (1994) argue that the RGT can be used to identify the distinctions and concerns relevant to working life, and in particular constructions of organizational knowledge, e.g. the construction of corporate identity, the construction of culture, or of an organizational event such as a 'merger'. They argue that the RGT offers a structure in which inquiry can proceed in the respondent's own terms. Other researchers have described the application of the RGT in an appraisal context, and to employee selection (Anderson, 1990).

Technicalities: The RGT method requires between 30 minutes and 1 hour of each respondent's time, depending on the complexity of the construct domain coupled with the ability of the respondent to articulate his/her constructs. People vary widely in the inherent level of complexity with which they construct the world, which will in part reflect the degree of experience they have had in the domain of interest. There are debates surrounding the issue of whether to *supply* or *elicit* elements. Supplied elements are unlikely to be quite so meaningful as those elicited from the respondent him or herself. Moreover, in an organizational context, supplied elements are likely to yield constructs and construct systems consistent with the 'party line'. On the other hand, supplied elements render the grid more comparable across a set of people within a group or division within an organization. A compromise scenario is to derive 'elements' from a preliminary research exercise, like a focus group forum, and then to supply organizational or group members with those which appeared to be meaningful across the board. For more technical detail on when and how to use the RGT, consult Shaw (1981) and also Neimeyer and Neimeyer (1989).

It is critical that the researcher is well practised in grid application and interviewing since the grid requires not only knowledge of the theoretical principles on which it is based, but also careful and systematic attention to design (including some pilot work) as well as skilled application and the ability to engender an atmosphere of trust and rapport during the grid interview. Use of the RGT requires a creative combination of science with artistry and also interpersonal skill. Case Study 4 concerns the use of RGT within the broader context of a research intervention exploring team identities.

Case Study 4: Team identities (Jacobs, 1988)

Introduction
Team identity and the values that help create it are critical to the way in which a team defines and perceives effective performance. Those who identify with the team and who take on its values are more likely to be perceived as more effective by the team. Team identity involves the development of 'a degree of synergy' in the accomplishment of a task on the basis of 'a similar or consensus view' of the world (Jacobs, 1988: 54). The critical issue for team development is how to promote a sufficiently positive climate in which a dynamic and constructive team dialogue about performance can be created (versus too much conformity). Teams often do not have the capacity to do this 'objectively', and avoidance of discussing emotionally charged issues means that teams may never get around to questioning their basic values, goals, performance expectations and so on.

Aim
To create 'an authentic team dialogue' by having teams examine the results of applying career self-concept theory, providing them with the language and the concepts for addressing performance issues in a meaningful way.

Method

Step 1 Individual self-concept identification using the repertory grid interview.

Step 2 Construction of team self-concept map: individual self-concepts can be compared within the team to identify the existence of dominant coalitions of the same or similar self-concept; and identification of non-conformist members.

Step 3 Construction of team assessment questionnaire: most important and relevant performance statements for the team are assembled.

Step 4 Completion of questionnaire, each member rates everyone else and self on performance statements, requiring ratings of importance, relevance, and validity of performance statements.

continues

Step 5   Analysis of data using graphical tools comparing team and individual profiles. The closer the individual is to the team, the more in touch they can be said to be with 'team reality'. The larger the gap, the more likely it is that the individual has been 'ostracized'. INGRID (a computer package for analysing repertory grids) can be used to look at the degree of consensus/agreement within the team.
Step 6   Feedback and one-to-one (confidential) counselling if required.
Step 7   Data feedback and counselling for team: 'team identity' discussed in general and then a detailed team performance profile is discussed. The relative importance of different criteria as valued by the team will be revealed. A skilled facilitator is needed at this stage. Future directions of the individual and the team are also discussed.

6.4.2 References and further reading

Anderson, N. (1990). Repertory grid technique in employee selection. *Personnel Review, 19, 3,* 9–15.

Gammack, J.G. and Stephens, A. (1994). Repertory grid technique in constructive interaction. In C. Cassell and G. Symon (Eds.), *Qualitative Methods in Organizational Research*. London, UK: Sage Publications.

Jacobs, R.C. (1988). Career anchors and team perceptions: diagnosing management team building needs. *Management Education and Development, 19, 1,* 51–67.

Kelly, G. (1955). *The Psychology of Personal Constructs*. New York: Norton.

Lee, F.E. (1998). The psychological contract of nurses in the NHS: content, violation and subsequent performance effects. Unpublished MSc dissertation, University of Surrey, Guildford, UK.

Neimeyer, R. and Neimeyer, G. (1989) (Eds.). *Advances in Personal Construct Theory*. Greenwich, CT: JAI Press.

Shaw, M. (1981) (Ed.). *Recent Advances in Personal Construct Technology*. London, UK: Academic Press.

6.4.3 The Q-sort Method

Description: The Q-sort methodology was devised by Stephenson (1936). It can be employed to assess, in a highly structured and systematic way, people's understandings of an issue (Millward, 1995), from their own unique standpoint, and has the potential to integrate qualitative and quantitative information. Individuals are invited to arrange a set of items along a scale anchored by, say +5 (e.g. most happy with) through to –5 (e.g. least happy with) within a prescribed distribution (i.e. the normal distribution). The exact number of items distributed at each point of the scale will depend on how many items are to be sorted. Thus, in a 54-item set, the distribution along which cards are to be sorted would be: 2, 4, 6, 9, 12, 9, 6, 4, 2 (see Figure 6.2). The sorting criteria are always self-referent, and domain-specific, selected depending on the aim of the Q-sort (i.e. what evidence, and with respect to what, it is designed to elicit). Each resulting Q-sort is unique to each individual; however, the process is identical for each individual and subsequently similarities and differences between people can be analysed across the sample. The number of different Q-sorts is by no means infinite (Millward, 1995) and there are likely to be similarities within each occupational group. The underlying patterning, based on communality of meaning and value, is determined by Q-analysis (see Kitzinger, 1987).

Figure 6.2   An example of a Q-sort template

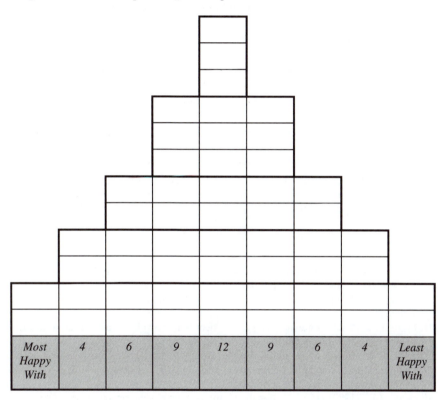

Aims/theoretical rationale: The Q-sort methodology is about capturing the way in which meaning is organized and patterned. To be implemented successfully, it must be based on a clear rationale where the domain of interest is represented fully by the items in the Q-sort (which may require some initial exploratory work to elicit).

Technicalities: The Q-sort method is enjoyable for respondents to complete so long as it is meaningful to them (or enables them to construct some meaning) and does not require too much time and concentration of effort. The respondent can be encouraged to talk aloud whilst sorting the cards along the distribution, as part of a strategy to help him or her to organize the material. The Q-sort results (i.e. the distribution) can be recorded on a grid. Each item is assigned a score depending on its assigned position along the scale. What is unusual about the way in which these data are analysed is that it is *people* who are factored rather than items. Data are input in such a way that people are the variables and the 'items' are the people. The factoring process is straightforward, requiring the application of principal components analysis as for any other type of factor analysis except that the factor contents denote groups of people rather than items (see Chapter 9 for more on factor analysis). The reader is referred to Brown (1986), for procedural and technical details on how to analyse the Q-sort.

Applications: The Q-sort can be used to ascertain shared patterns of meaning and interrelationships with other factors. Each person can be assigned a Q-Factor score for as many factors as are derived from the analysis. This means that factor meanings or shared meaning systems can be understood in terms of who it is that subscribes to the meaning represented by the factor and what other things it relates to (e.g. those who score highly on a Q-sort factor of 'personal development' as a work value might be of a particular age range, status, family status, and be more likely to leave or feel dissatisfied with an organization which does not provide them with development opportunities). In short, the Q-sort method enables group profiles to be developed in terms of shared meanings or meaning systems, and enables various hypotheses to evolve concerning the contextual basis and implications of these meanings.

6.4.4 References and further reading

Brown, S.R. (1986). *Political Subjectivity: Applications of Q-methodology in Political Science*. New Haven, CT: Yale University Press.
Kitzinger, C. (1987). *The Social Construction of Lesbianism.* London, UK: Sage Publications.
Millward, L.J. (1995). Contextualising social identity in considerations of what it means to be a nurse. *European Journal of Social Psychology, 25,* 303–324.
O'Reilly, C.A., Chatman, J. and Caldwell, D.F. (1991). People and organizational culture: a profile comparison approach to assessing person-organization fit. *Academy of Management Journal, 34, 3,* 487–516.
Sheridan, J.E. (1992). Organizational culture and employee retention. *Academy of Management Journal, 35, 5,* 1036–1056.
Stephenson, W. (1936). The inverted factor technique. *British Journal of Psychology, 22,* 344–361.

6.5 The focus group method

6.5.1 Description

The focus group is described by Millward (1995) as a discussion-based interview that produces a particular type of qualitative data. It involves the simultaneous use of multiple respondents to generate data and it is the 'focused' (i.e. on an external stimulus) and relatively staged (i.e. by a 'moderator') nature of the focus group method that separates it from other types of group interviewing strategy.

6.5.2 Aims

Used alone or in combination with other methods, the aim of focus groups is to get closer to participants' understandings and perspectives of certain issues. It is not geared to the formal testing of hypotheses in the traditional hypothetico-deductive sense, although it can be used for hypothesis formulation and/or construct development.

6.5.3 Uses

The focus group can be used either as a self-contained means of data collection (i.e. a primary research technique) or as a supplement (i.e. a supplementary research technique) to other methods, depending on how it fits into an overall research plan and also its epistemological basis (i.e. qualitative or quantitative). Used as a primary research technique, the focus group method is used as a forum in which to explore people's opinions, attitudes, beliefs, values, discourses and understandings of things, as valid in their own right. Exploration of this kind may be of particular interest to researchers operating within the qualitative epistemological tradition like discourse analysts (e.g. Lunt, 1996). Alternatively, the focus group as a primary tool may be used as a first step in the process of construct development and/or questionnaire development. Some work has also been conducted demonstrating the potential for focus groups to yield data pertinent to testing the viability of a conceptual model. Here, the emphasis was on using the theory to frame and focus the discussion rather than with offering a formal test of the theory and its validity. As a supplement to other, more traditional, methods (e.g. surveys), the focus group method may be used to provide a more in-depth exploration of the issue in question and/or to generate dialogue. Uses of the focus group for empowerment purposes, or to establish communication/dialogue between various interfacing groups, is a separate issue altogether, unrelated to its use in research.

6.5.4 Theoretical rationale

From a social psychological perspective, the focus group is 'by definition an exercise in group dynamics and the conduct of the group, as well as the interpretation of results obtained, must be understood within the context of group interaction' (Stewart and Shamdasani, 1990: 7). Two interrelated forms of evidence are therefore derived from focus groups: the group process (the way in which people interact and communicate with each other) and the content around which the group process is organized (the focal stimulus and the issues arising from it). The group process can be understood on two different levels: (i) *intrapersonal*: thoughts, feelings, attitudes and values of the individual; (ii) *intragroup*: how people communicate and interact with each other within the group. Considerations of the group process are integral to the role of the moderator who will require very different skills from those needed in one-to-one interviewing.

One advantage of using the group as opposed to the individual as the medium of investigation is its 'isomorphism to the process of opinion formation and propagation in everyday life' insofar as 'opinions about a variety of issues are generally determined not by individual information gathering and deliberation but through communication with others' (Albrecht et al., 1993: 54). Focus groups are communication events in which the interplay of the personal and the social can be systematically explored (see Case Study 5 for an example of this in an occupational context).

Case Study 5: Exploring organizational culture with focus groups

Hilder (1997) used Schein's model of organizational culture – an otherwise complex and multi-faceted construct – to frame employee discussion in a series of focus groups conducted in organizational settings.

Culture is a topic that employees may not have thought much about before, and even if they have, may not be easily able to comment on it without being provided with some kind of discussion context. The researcher is thus faced with a dilemma. If the discussion is framed using constructs from a model, there is an obvious risk of prejudicing the information obtained. Discussion cues of this kind may eliminate other avenues that would otherwise be explored by participants with respect to the topic of culture, which thus risks loss of useful information. On the other hand, participants may not know where to start or what to say, and may end up talking endlessly about quite superficial aspects of culture (or climate) which give them the greatest cause for grievance (e.g. lack of office space, poor air conditioning).

Since some kind of 'focus' is necessary and limitless time is not available, it may be more sensible, Hilder (1997) recommends, to scene-set so as to gain quality input on the preferred topic within an agreed time-span.

6.5.5 Focus group logistics

Clarifying aims: The very first step in the design and planning process is to define and clarify the issues to be investigated in terms of the exact nature of the evidence required. Both theoretical and practical considerations will influence this (see Case Study 5).

Sampling: It is not the intention of focus group methodology to yield generalizable data, so random sampling is not necessary. Nonetheless, it is important to employ a systematic strategy when deciding on group composition (read more on sampling considerations in Chapter 7). The sample should be chosen on theoretical grounds as reflecting those segments of the population who will provide the most meaningful information in terms of the project objectives. Moreover, the participants should have something to say about the topic of interest.

Recruitment strategies: These have important consequences for the degree of co-operation and commitment generated amongst respondents. The time and energy invested in meeting with 'local' people and making personal contact with potential participants at the outset can facilitate group rapport and contribute substantially to this. The general rule of thumb is that group members should exhibit at least some common characteristics (e.g. same organization, same type of job) to facilitate the sharing of experiences. Ultimately, the decision rests on determining the composition of the group which will maximize the probability of obtaining the most theoretically relevant information. It has become conventional in the marketing context to ensure that the focus group is comprised of strangers. Acquaintance of group members can indeed inhibit the flow of discussion in certain instances. Social scientists, however, would argue that there are many occasions when the existence of a shared history is of interest from the point of view of the research objectives (e.g. shared organizational history).

The focal stimuli: In the social sciences, the stimulus might be a behavioural scenario (e.g. an emergency), a concrete event (e.g. organizational change), or even a concept (e.g. culture). The range of possible stimuli is in fact quite extensive, extending to the use of projective techniques, role play scenarios, word association exercises, or 'theory'. The use of constructs to frame focus group discussion in this way can help 'translate' theory into practice.

Group size and number: A systematic perusal of recent focus group research in psychology yields an average of 9 participants per session as conventional, with a range of 6 to 12, although some would advocate between 6 and 8 participants as ideal. It is common practice to 'over-recruit' for each session by 20% since it is inevitable that not all participants will actually turn up. The group size on the day will therefore vary. The number of focus group sessions conducted will be a function of both sample and group size. Some researchers have noted that the data generated after about 10 sessions is largely redundant. The decision rests on the type of evidence required and from whom, as well as considerations of cost in terms of time and resources.

Location: Choice of location will need to balance the needs of the research with those of participants. It should set the tone of the research as professional and, where possible, on neutral ground, although there are times when the sample will be hard to reach unless the research is conducted on home territory (e.g. a hospital). Two prime considerations for participants are convenience and comfort. Once there, the room itself should be conducive to a smooth-flowing discussion and should, therefore, be comfortable (e.g. appropriate ambience of informality, availability of refreshments, nearby toilets, suitable seating and table arrangements). It is also usual to supply name badges.

Duration: Most focus group researchers agree that between 1 and 2 hours is the standard duration for each session involving adults.

Moderator style and skills: The skills of the moderator are fundamental to the effective running of the focus group. In a social science context, it is preferable for the moderator to be someone directly involved in the project who is sensitive to the research issues and the need for methodological rigour even if their group management skills are not especially polished. The issue is whether the moderator is able to obtain theoretically useful information. This will require more than just the ability to manage a group: the moderator will need to be someone who can maximize self-disclosure by balancing the 'requirements of sensitivity and empathy on one hand and objectivity and detachment on the other' (Stewart and Shamdasani, 1990: 69). In practice, people will talk surprisingly freely about a wide variety of personal topics so long as the climate is permissive and non-critical.

A good moderator guides the proceedings in an unobtrusive and subtle way, intervening only to the extent of maintaining a productive group. As well as the criterion of minimal direction, there are three additional criteria for ensuring that 'focus' is maintained: specificity, range and depth. The first requires that minute detail is sought in people's responses and reactions to the stimulus, object or event. It is the moderator's task to elicit meanings and differential responses. The second criterion concerns coverage, the issue for the moderator being one of facilitating transitions from one area of a discussion to another, and the third addresses the personal context of the response or reaction elicited by the stimulus. Eliciting in-depth responses involves expanding on responses beyond limited reports of 'positive' or 'negative', 'pleasant' or 'unpleasant' reactions. The moderator's task is to diagnose the level of depth at which participants are operating (i.e. ranging from superficial description to detailed elaboration) and where necessary to shift it towards a 'deeper' level. All these criteria can be met by the moderator who is skilled in listening and questioning techniques. Skilled use of questions also requires 'double hearing'. This means that the moderator should be able to read between the lines of a discussion in order to 'ferret out' also what is implied rather than relying totally on what is made explicit. By explicating the implied (e.g. tentatively playing it back to respondents in the form of a clarifying question), it is rendered legitimate (e.g. it is acceptable to talk about this) and respondents may thus feel better able to elaborate.

Introducing the session: Lee (1999) outlines some guidelines for focus group introductions, which can be used to set the tone for the subsequent session. Depending, in part, on the identities of the participants and on the topic for discussion, the moderator will typically introduce the session by explaining his/her role during the session, the purpose of the session, and who will see results (emphasizing anonymity and confidentiality as appropriate). In addition, the moderator should present general rules for the session: only one person speaks at a time; everyone participates; and no one dominates the discussion. Following this, the moderator will often commence the session by asking each participant to introduce themselves, providing appropriate details on, for example, job role, organizational tenure, etc. This can serve as an 'icebreaker' for the session proper, as well as providing valuable 'grouping' information on which to base subsequent data extraction and analysis.

Data extraction: Focus groups usually generate qualitative data in the form of transcripts produced from audio-tape or video-tape. By video-taping the focus group sessions, observational data can also be extracted (e.g. non-verbal communication) as well as the content of the discussion. Most researchers rely on audio-taped recordings of the discussions supplemented by a few general field notes. Whatever the type of recording used, it is crucial to first obtain the consent of the participants, having explained the purpose of the recording and having assured them of confidentiality. Once agreed, the logistics of using the tape recorders needs to be considered (i.e. how many and where best positioned). The larger the group, the less easy it is to get a clear recording using one tape recorder alone. The ground rule established at the outset that everyone should speak loudly and clearly enough to be picked up by the microphone does not always work. It has been said that the analysis of transcriptions is one of the most challenging aspects of the focus group method. If each session lasts about 2 hours, 40–50 pages of transcription are yielded. If 20 sessions are conducted, then 1,000 pages of transcription must be analysed. Transcription is a purely mechanical task. Its time-consuming and laborious nature, however, has often led researchers to analyse the content directly from the tape which entails transcribing only the most illustrative comments. Since the purpose of a focus group is to gain insight into how respondents represent a particular issue as a whole and on a collective, rather than individual, basis, it is important to capture the entire character of the discussion, 'warts and all'. Any form of editing during transcription is therefore undesirable.

Field problems: The issue of what to tell participants about the research aims is likely to become particularly salient in an organizational context where political sensitivities may arise. For example, in focus groups discussing organizational culture, the objective may be to articulate a particular model of culture, or to test an approach for eliciting employees' understandings of culture, or simply to attempt an analysis and understanding of organizational culture. In each of these cases, the topic for discussion is the organization's culture, which is made clear, but the actual objectives of the focus group may remain opaque as far as participants are concerned. Yet at the same time, participants may become suspicious and defensive, apt even to withhold information or only to say what they feel is expected of them, if they perceive that they are not being properly informed. Participants may suspect a 'hidden agenda' and will need to be reassured that this is not the case. Gaining participation in defining the nature and scope of the subject for discussion is one way of achieving a sense of group ownership of a topic (and thereby opening people up to further discussion) especially if the definition is then employed as an *aide-mémoire* throughout the session (Hilder, 1997).

The facilitator as 'organizational therapist': One of the major difficulties with focus groups taken from organizations is their desire to treat the facilitator as therapist (Hilder, 1997). Problems with the company and management are raised in the focus group, and this is particularly the case if the topic for discussion is the company itself (e.g. organizational culture, corporate identity, group commitment, etc.). Dealing with this can be a problem and presents a number of concerns: (a) Has the focus group itself precipitated this discussion, and thus opened up grievances that might have otherwise not been considered, thus creating a culture of discontent? (b) Are the problems raised relevant to the topic under discussion? (c) What are the expectations of the group in talking about the problems with you as moderator? (d) What is the state of mind of the group at the end of the discussion?

There are no ready answers to these concerns, although the following guidelines should be borne in mind. Firstly, a focus group that is managed in a truly facilitative fashion is unlikely actually to create discontent; if problem issues are raised, they can, in the main, be assumed to be real. It is, however, the facilitator's job to ensure through gentle questioning that problems raised gain adequate context and perspective. It may also be necessary to play devil's advocate, so that the session does not become a general forum for offloading. Secondly, it usually becomes quickly apparent if the problems are relevant to the topic under discussion. If they are not, firm handling and a shift back to the discussion topic is required. If they are relevant, it is still important that the discussion takes place in a positive fashion and, again, this may require firm handling. Thirdly, the group's expectations of the facilitator will have been set out at the start of the session. It may be worth reminding them at the end of the session of the aims of the focus group so that false expectations are not taken away. Equally important is the mood of the group at the close. It is important to try to wind up the focus group with a feel-good session so that the group disperses on a relative high, not a state of discontent (Hilder, 1997).

6.5.6 Organizational applications and possibilities

Advances in technology and the 'globalization' of real-time communication, in the conversational sense of the word, open up the possibility for focus groups to be run 'on-line'. Greenbaum (1998) has coined the term 'global focus groups' to describe on-line discussion groups that cross cultural, spatial and temporal boundaries. Two types of on-line global focus groups can be envisaged: real-time focus groups who log on to the network at a set time for a set period to discuss a topic or issue, and on-going focus groups whose members sign up and sign off whenever they wish, and contribute whenever convenient and/or they feel appropriate. In the real-time version, a focus group could be run in the traditional fashion with a facilitator keeping the discussion on-track and probing wherever necessary and so on. In the on-going version, a discussion is not easily managed or facilitated, the group itself being responsible for determining the shape and direction of the dialogue that ensues. Real-time 'virtual' focus groups are staged, whilst ongoing focus groups are not and exist irrespective of whether all their members are signed on at any one time. Whether the unmanaged and ongoing nature of on-line discussion groups means that they can no longer be called focus groups is yet to be contemplated.

The concept of 'global focus groups' opens up a whole realm of research possibilities but also brings with it considerable logistical problems and issues of 'virtual' facilitation. One problem is ensuring that everyone knows what time to sign up and that the timings are co-ordinated exactly across time zones. The interested reader should consult Greenbaum (1998) for more on this. One advantage of on-line discussion is that the issue of transcription is side-stepped. Greenbaum (1998) also talks about the impact of technology on focus group research in more general terms.

6.5.7 References and further reading

Albrecht, T.L., Johnson, G.M. and Walther, J.B. (1993). Understanding communication processes in focus groups. In D.L. Morgan (Ed.), *Successful Focus Groups: Advancing the State of the Art*. London, UK: Sage Publications.

Greenbaum, T.L. (1998). *Handbook for Focus Group Research* (Second Edition). London, UK: Sage Publications.

Hilder (1997). Qualitative approaches to the study of organizational culture. Unpublished research note, University of Surrey, Guildford, UK.

Krueger, R.A. (1994). *Focus Groups: a Practical Guide for Applied Research* (Second Edition). London, UK: Sage Publications.

Lee, T.W. (1999). *Using Qualitative Methods in Organizational Research*. Thousand Oaks, CA: Sage Publications.

Lunt (1996). Discourse of savings. *Journal of Economic Psychology, 17, 6*, 677–690.

Millward, L.J. (1995). Focus groups. In G.M. Breakwell, S. Hammond and C. Fife-Schaw (Eds.), *Research Methods in Psychology*. London, UK: Sage Publications.

Morgan, D.L. (1993). *Successful Focus Groups: Advancing the State of the Art*. London, UK: Sage Publications.

Morgan, D.L. (1997). *Focus Groups as Qualitative Research*. Thousand Oaks, CA: Sage Publications.

Morgan, D.L. and Krueger, R.A. (1997) *The Focus Group Kit Volumes 1–6*. London, UK: Sage Publications.

Stewart, D.W. and Shamdasani, P.N. (1990). *Focus Groups*. London, UK: Sage Publications.

6.6 Psychometric research

6.6.1 Introduction

Psychometric instruments are widely used throughout social science and applied organizational research. At both individual and organizational levels of analysis, they afford the researcher an objective, consistent and comparable method of measuring people or groups of people in various settings and to various ends. Psychometric instruments, according to Hammond's (1995) categorization, can include self-report questionnaires, objective tests (of ability, preference or personality), and normative, criterion-referenced and idiographic tests. These may be administered at an individual level (most often in the context of selection or development, but also in research, where the differences between individuals or small groups are of interest to the researcher) or at group or organizational level (most often adopting the form of an employee survey, often focusing on staffs' reactions to workplace issues; examples include job satisfaction, organizational commitment, experienced stress, work values or organizational culture).

What differentiates psychometric instruments from general scale-based instruments is that the former are constructed and validated with scientific and statistical rigour, and are based on a definite model of measurement which allows them to be standardized and normed for comparison with other populations. General survey 'scales' may address certain areas of interest from an objective viewpoint, and may provide the researcher with useable quantitative data, but they are unlikely to possess the attributes necessary to infer statistical robustness (in terms of reliability and validity), thereby restricting levels of comparability and the 'power' of the data available to the researcher. In this section, the critical issues of reliability and validity in psychometric instrument selection and development will be introduced, followed by a more in-depth discussion of the construction of organizational-level instruments for use in psychological research. Table 6.1 illustrates some of the principal types of psychometric instruments within organizational research, and gives examples of each:

Table 6.1   The use of psychometric instruments within organizational research

Type of instrument	Example
Workplace reaction	Job Involvement Scale Organizational Commitment Questionnaire Job Satisfaction Index
Ability/Attainment	Graduate and Managerial Assessments (GMA) Watson–Glaser Critical Thinking Appraisal Thurstone Test of Primary Mental Ability Raven's Progressive Matrices
Personality	Myers Briggs Type Inventory (MBTI) 16-PF NEO Five-Factor Inventory (NEO-FFI)
Interest	Vocational Interest Measure (VIM) The Strong Vocational Interest Blank Vocational Preference Inventory (VPI)

6.6.2 Reliability and validity

In order to construct and/or evaluate a psychometric instrument for research purposes, levels of reliability and validity represent a key consideration. 'Reliability' refers to the internal and temporal consistency of an instrument, that is, the degree of data consistency across a defined or undefined dimension (Suen, 1991), whereas validity may be defined as the degree to which an instrument actually represents what it *purports to* represent. Each characteristic is introduced below. The reader is referred to a number of alternative sources for a more comprehensive treatment of reliability and validity issues, as provided at the end of this section.

Reliability

In order to be able to rely on the results of a given test or psychometric instrument, a researcher must be confident that the test is consistent both internally (that is, in terms of measurement of the area of interest) and, if appropriate, externally (that is, over time and in terms of the relationship between alternative forms of the same instrument).

Internal consistency may be measured via various statistical indices including Cronbach's alpha, Guttman and split-half. Each index produces a figure ranging from 0 to 1.0 which denotes the level of consistency across the items selected, i.e. the degree to which the items selected are all 'tapping into' the target area of interest – the degree of similarity of item content within each scale. The methods vary in their approach – Cronbach's alpha, for example, examines the correlation between each item and the scale total within a sample; split-half testing involves separating scale items into two halves and examining the correlations between the halves. The reliability figure provides the researcher with an indication of the level of consistency across scale items. Different commentators have advocated different figures as indicative of lowest acceptable levels of internal scale reliability: figures ranging between 0.6 and 0.7 are generally accepted as an absolute minimum (Kline, 1986, 1993a). Also notable is the argument for an *upper* acceptable level of internal consistency reliability – some researchers have suggested that instruments reporting reliability co-efficients of 0.9 and above suggest tautology of scale items, that is, items are measuring *exactly* the same thing (limiting the *construct* validity of the scale; see below). This may be considered an issue in personality research, for example. However, in general, the higher the obtained reliability co-efficient, the better.

Temporal (generally referred to as test-retest) reliability involves administration of an instrument more than once to the same sample in order to infer that the instrument is reliable across time and situation (and therefore that measurement error within the instrument does *not* derive from situational variables such as location, time of day, fatigue levels, etc.). Reliability estimates are obtained by correlating scores from each administration, again producing a reliability co-efficient ranging from 0 to 1.0. Unlike internal consistency reliability, it is possible to state unequivocally that the higher the temporal reliability co-efficient, the more reliable the instrument. However, temporal reliability may *not* be appropriate as a measure of consistency if the test sample has experienced some sort of instrument-unrelated change between administrations. This may, for example, include learning (particularly with ability tests, where participants may have foreknowledge of test items at the second administration, thereby biasing results). Or, in the case of measures of workplace reaction administered during periods of organizational change, real changes in reaction may have occurred between test administrations which may result in wholesale differences in response unrelated to the instrument itself but affecting estimates of its temporal stability.

Validity

The concept of validity of a psychometric measure, that is the degree to which an instrument actually represents what it purports to represent, is a multi-dimensional one, comprising different forms of validity and, thus, different forms of assessment. Content validity, for example, concerns the congruence between the content of an instrument and the various areas that an investigator is attempting to research, i.e. the amount that the tool's content accurately represents the intended facets to be explored. Criterion-related validity involves setting tool scores against an independent criterion in order to indicate the level of the tool's effectiveness in predicting real-world outcomes, such as behaviour or performance. Construct validity is concerned with precisely what an instrument is measuring in terms of the underlying principles, theories or *constructs* that are being examined by the tool. A 'construct' or 'latent variable' can be defined as an aspect of human performance or behaviour which is not directly observable but which will manifest itself in some outward behaviour, e.g. neuroticism manifesting itself outwardly as the number of phobias an individual is suffering from; how badly the individual is sleeping, etc. Each of these forms of validation requires different assessment methods and produces different forms of validity estimate.

Content validity

To infer that an instrument is content valid, a thorough analysis of the target domain is required, usually drawing on expert judgement from a variety of appropriate sources. To take the example of the mathematical ability of children of a given age, domains to be investigated may include: target operations, e.g. addition, subtraction, multiplication, division; level of complexity (e.g. 'short' and 'long' versions of each operation); response type (e.g. written or spoken response); type of calculation (e.g. mental or written calculation); and presentation of items. In the context of this example, selection of experts for validation may include teachers, educational psychologists, curriculum planners, etc., with each expert being asked to produce an independent domain analysis for mathematical ability in children of the specified age. If the test ultimately developed were to contain only items of addition and subtraction, for example, without any items of multiplication or division, it would be said to have poor content validity, as the underlying construct of mathematical ability would not have been fully described. Assessment of content validity in an existing instrument depends on available explanations of the theoretical perspective(s) driving the instrument and on the way in which this theory has been used to develop items to address the area of interest comprehensively.

The ability to make an informed assessment also depends on the researcher's knowledge of the research area. Statistical assessments of content validity are not generally presented.

Criterion-related validity

As mentioned above, this type of validity pertains to the relationship between scores on a psychometric tool and external criteria which the tool is intended to predict. Criterion-related validity is usually sub-divided into 'concurrent' and 'predictive' validity. *Concurrent* validity involves the criterion and the test behaviour being measured simultaneously, e.g. a test of managerial competence being administered at the same time as actual current job performance data are obtained in order to determine how closely the two measures are related.

Predictive validity involves the criterion and the test behaviour being temporally separated. Examples include the US Scholastic Aptitude Test (SAT) being compared against 'end-of-year' grades; or a job selection tool being compared against subsequent job performance. Another use of predictive validity is in preventative intervention, where aspects of lifestyle or personality may be used to determine predisposition to, and likely future presentation of, certain types of illness or disorder, e.g. coronary heart disease. Due to the necessarily longitudinal nature of predictive validity, a concurrent substitute is often used. However, this has implications for generalizations which may accurately be drawn from a study: it may be, for example, that setting a test of management potential against an independent criterion of current achievement motivation will not in fact predict *future* achievement motivation.

Criterion-related validity can be measured and presented via a variety of methods, including correlation and regression. Where test scores and criterion measurements are continuously distributed, the correlations between the two variables can be calculated in order to determine degree of relationship between test scores and the criterion measure. In this context, the correlations are termed 'validity co-efficients'. In addition to correlational scores (usually reported as r), r^2 provides a measure of the shared or predictive 'variance' between the two variables, e.g. the relationship between an IQ test and later academic performance (r) is found to be 0.7; an estimate of the variance shared by the two variables (r^2) is thus 49%, that is, 49% of the variance in academic performance may be predicted by an individual's score on the test. Using linear regression techniques, a predictive estimation of the target criterion can then be calculated, where the 'line of best fit' can be used to predict the score on the criterion dimension by inputting an individual's score on the dimension of interest. Regression models can also be used to obtain the *relative* validity of a number of tool dimensions or scales in predicting a given criterion. By 'partialling out' the variance shared by instrument dimensions, this method can identify the best predictor(s) of the external criterion, i.e. those predictors which exhibit the greatest proportion of shared variance with the criterion. Makin et al. (1996) suggest estimates of utility according to the criterion-related validity co-efficients given in Table 6.2.

Table 6.2   Makin et al.'s (1996) estimates of relative utility of various criterion–
              related validity co-efficients

Validity co-efficient	Estimate of utility
0.5 and above	Excellent
0.40–0.49	Good
0.30–0.39	Reasonable
0.29 and below	Poor

The reader is referred to Chapter 9 for an in-depth discussion of some of these statistical techniques, their restrictions and further applications.

Construct validity
Construct validity is very closely related to theory development and testing, with an instrument being assessed while, simultaneously, its underlying theoretical concepts are being rigorously investigated. Nunnally (1978) specifies three distinct stages to successful construct validation of a psychometric instrument:

- **Clear specification** – the domain of 'observables' (items or scales) related to the construct must be clearly specified, e.g. in developing a measure of employee performance, the various behaviours to be included in the behaviour domain must be considered; thus, provision of good customer service may be included, whereas ingratiating behaviour demonstrated towards superiors may be excluded.

- **Relationship between instrument dimensions or scales** – the relationships among observables that are specified as part of the construct must be examined. This is effected by calculating correlational relationships between the observables specified in the first stage, e.g. if a subject reports similar attitudes to pay, fellow employees, company policies and the job itself, then the total score on the test is more likely to reflect a single construct; in this case, one of job attitude.

- **Relationships with different constructs** – 'convergent' validity, i.e. a direct, positive relationship, is required with other tests purporting to measure the same construct as the test under investigation. 'Discriminant' validity, i.e. a lack of relationship, should be apparent with theoretically irrelevant measures, e.g. a test of conscientiousness should not correlate highly with a test of IQ, in order for the former to be accepted as measuring a construct independent of those underlying the theory of general intelligence.

In addition to correlational analysis, principal components factor analysis can also be used to assess the robustness of tool scales or dimensions. By 'rotating' items within the instrument, it should be possible to identify 'clusters' of items which reflect the constructs underpinning the tool. For example, an instrument purporting to measure neuroticism and extroversion as independent constructs should reveal a stable factor structure when its items are rotated, with items intended to tap into neuroticism 'loading' on one factor and items intended to tap into extroversion loading on another separate factor. The factor structure of psychometric instruments is often reported by their developers. The reader is referred to Chapter 9 for further information on this analytic technique.

6.6.3 An applied example: a measure of organizational culture

The example described in Case Study 6 is based on the experience of both authors in construction and validation of an organizational-level psychometric survey tool designed to link perceptions of organizational culture to individual- and group-level performance. Each of the 'stages' involved in the validation process is outlined and is intended to illustrate 'best practice' principles in instrument development and validation.

Case Study 6: Developing a measure of organizational culture

1. **Initial research** – review of existing literature on organizational culture, databasing existing measures, theoretical perspectives and identifying areas requiring further research. Initial theoretical model developed.

2. **Item construction** – based on principles of model, scale items developed via several 'brainstorming' sessions involving culture 'experts' and the researchers, and by anglicizing and adapting existing items where necessary. See Section 6.8 on questionnaire design, for more information on the elements involved in question and item construction. Scale items tentatively combined to produce individual 'dimensions', each intended to tap into a different facet of the model.

3. **Content validation** – proposed scale items reviewed by subject matter experts in terms of mapping on to initial theoretical model and adequacy of coverage of subject area.

4. **Measurement approach** – assessment of possible measurement approaches, including forced-choice or attitude scale. Likert-type 7-point scale selected (ranging from 'strongly agree' to 'strongly disagree') due to nature of items and need for a bounded scale to show differences between organizations and other groups. See Section 6.8 for alternative questionnaire-based measurement techniques.

5. **Piloting** – on convenience sample to iron out inconsistencies of terminology, ambiguous items, use of jargon, etc.

6. **Validation sample selection** – driven by theoretical and practical criteria, including:

   - *UK-normed tool* – therefore only UK-based companies included;
   - *Inter-industry comparability* – variety of industries approached;

- *Tool comprehensibility for all levels* – all grades/disciplines within companies to be surveyed;
- *Maximum validation sample required* – only companies employing 1,000 staff or more approached;
- *Minimization of resource* – only companies within researchers' home county approached.

See Chapter 7 for further information on sampling considerations.

7. **Survey formatting** – survey formatted to be attractive and self-explanatory with free-response section included to invite comments on the questionnaire. Descriptive information section included to obtain grouping data from respondents (e.g. grade, age, tenure, etc.), varying by company; required grouping data minimized as far as possible to maximize perceptions of anonymity and thereby increase response rates and accuracy of response.

8. **Data collection** – Distribution and collection of surveys effected via existing mechanisms where possible, e.g. internal mail to central point in the company; or 'freepost' envelopes to researchers. To maximize response rates, each survey was prefaced with an explanatory letter providing details of the research, method and date for returning surveys and emphasizing the confidential nature of the research. 'Buy in' from various levels of management was also critical to reducing suspicion and increasing response rates from staff. See Chapter 4 for more on obtaining and using access to organizations.

9. **Data analysis and validation** – based on first 1,000 responses (across two organizations), validation process started, and continued until 5,000 responses secured (response totals need not be so high depending on the scope and intentions of the research):

- *Item-level analysis* to calculate percentage responses to each item (to infer comprehensibility across staff levels);
- *Internal consistency reliability analysis* for each scale 'dimension';
- *Principal components factor analysis* to examine scale structure. Both reliability analysis and factor analysis used in tandem to refine the tool, by examining the component items of each dimension, identifying items which reduced reliability or the clarity of factor structure, and marking these for deletion/refinement;
- *T-tests and ANOVA* used to infer tool's ability to discriminate between organizations and between intra-organizational groups;
- *Regressional and correlational analysis* used to examine ability of tool to predict individual-level external criteria (e.g. absenteeism, lateness, intention to leave) and group-level criteria (e.g. staff turnover, site productivity, etc.).

10. **Application of tool to new samples** – critical to ensuring that psychometric properties were generalizable and valid across samples.

6.6.4 Advantages and disadvantages of psychometric research

Advantages:
- **Cost** – speed of administration and analysis reduces costs, especially when an instrument is available in computerized form;

- **Comparability** – true comparability is afforded to the researcher where psychometric instruments have been normed and standardized following rigorous validity and reliability testing;
- **Power** – results from psychometric instruments are meaningful and powerful due to their statistical robustness. This allows researchers to draw conclusions and make predictions from obtained data.

Disadvantages:

- **Restrictive** – no facility for exploration of responses;
- **Reductionist** – by their nature, psychometric tools reduce the responses of individuals to numerical values in the most efficient way possible;
- **Reliant on understanding of population** – employees have to be sufficiently literate, articulate and able to introspect in order to complete self-report questionnaires;
- **Open to temporary bias** – anxiety, boredom, fatigue, illness, suspicion or a participant's desire to fake, acquiesce or confront can all influence and bias the way in which people respond to psychometric instruments;
- **Norm-based** – 'scoring' individuals accurately is based on the accuracy and coverage of the available norm data. Many available psychometric tools use outdated or inapplicable norm groups – *it is the researcher's responsibility to check comparison norm data **before** using a psychometric instrument;*
- **Existence of many poor psychometric tools** – many researchers and test publishers have made available tools that are not sufficiently robust for general use. They may suffer from low reliability, low validity or both. Such information may not be immediately obvious to a researcher considering selection of an instrument from a range of options, but must be sought prior to making a decision. See the sections on reliability and validity, above, for guidelines in instrument selection.

6.6.5 References and further reading

Bartram, D. and Lindley, P.A. (1994). *Psychological Testing: the BPS Level A Open Learning Programme.* Leicester, UK: BPS Books.

Cronbach, L.J. (1990). *Essentials of Psychological Testing* (Fifth Edition). New York: Harper Collins.

Hammond, S. (1995). Using psychometric tests. In G.M. Breakwell, S. Hammond and C. Fife-Schaw (Eds.), *Research Methods in Psychology.* London, UK: Sage Publications.

Kline, P. (1986). *A Handbook of Test Construction: Introduction to Psychometric Design.* London, UK: Methuen and Co.

Kline, P. (1993a). *The Handbook of Psychological Testing.* London, UK: Routledge.

Kline, P. (1993b). *Personality: the Psychometric View.* London, UK: Routledge.

Kline, P. (1994). *An Easy Guide to Factor Analysis.* London, UK: Routledge.

Kline, P. (1998). *The New Psychometrics: Science, Psychology and Measurement.* London, UK: Routledge.

Makin, P.J., Cooper, C.L. and Cox, C.J. (1996). *Organizations and the Psychological Contract: Managing People at Work.* Leicester, UK: BPS.

Murphy, K.R. and Davidshofer, C.O. (1991). *Psychological Testing: Principles and Applications.* London, UK: Prentice-Hall.

Nunnally, J.O. (1978). *Psychometric Theory.* New York: McGraw-Hill.

Rust, J. and Golombok, S. (1989). *Modern Psychometrics.* London, UK: Routledge.

Suen, H.K. (1991). *Principles of Test Theories.* London, UK: Lawrence Erlbaum.

In addition, the interested reader is referred to a comprehensive tome compiled by Cook et al. (1981). Although now around 20 years old, this volume contains approximately 250 existing psychometric measures pertaining to various areas of workplace experience, and provides references to many hundreds more. Areas covered include:

• General and specific job satisfaction;
• Alienation and commitment;
• Occupational mental health and ill-health;
• Job involvement and job motivation;
• Work values, beliefs and needs;
• Perceptions of the job, work role, job context and organizational climate;
• Leadership style and perceptions of others.

Cook, J.D., Hepworth, S.J., Wall, T.D. and Warr, P.B. (1981). *The Experience of Work: a Compendium and Review of 249 Measures and their Use.* London, UK: Academic Press.

6.7 Observation

6.7.1 Introduction

Observation is a highly skilled activity which should not be considered lightly. There are two broad types of observational activity: *participant* and *non-participant*. With participant observation, the researcher immerses him or herself in a situation alongside target participants 'in the field'. The aim here is to become an accepted member of the participant community. The observation process is unstructured (i.e. without preconceived ideas or codes or foci of investigation). The researcher observes *in toto*, writing up observations as soon as possible after they have been made. The observations may be of interest 'in the raw' or as the basis on which to formulate hypotheses. Participant observation is also often termed *ethnography* which means capturing the 'native point of view' and is mainly anthropological in thrust (see Schwartzman, 1993). In non-participant observation, the researcher stands back from the situation and observes at a distance (either *in situ* or using video material). The observation process may be guided by a set of analytical codes or checklists, or in the case of checklist development, may be completely unstructured in the first instance. In participant observation, the focus of observation is usually at the macro-level (e.g. group dynamics), whereas the non-participant kind is usually directed at the micro-level (e.g. interaction processes).

6.7.2 Aims/theoretical rationale

The aim of both types of observation is to observe and record in as objective a way as possible, target events and occurrences, using whatever unit and level of analysis is required for the achievement of the research objectives. The observation process may or may not be theoretically framed. There are many different observation systems and schedules available in the literature for researchers to draw upon, the most well known of which is that developed by Bales (1950, 1999): interaction process analysis.

6.7.3 Technical issues

It is impossible to record everything, so the researcher must be clear about what it is exactly that is of interest (e.g. the interaction process, target events, etc.). Issues to consider include:

- **Sampling:** The researcher will need to make decisions about sampling, such as when to observe, for how long and how often. The answer to these questions will depend on whether the researcher is interested in a particular event, in which case an *event sample* will be required. During the observation of an event, a decision will need to be taken regarding how often to sample and for how long – i.e. *time sampling*. The researcher may, for example, select times and durations for observations of an event on *a priori* grounds (e.g. if s/he is interested in the reaction of a group to a staged 'threat' then s/he will need to home in on the 'threat' and the immediate reaction of the group). If there are no *a priori* grounds for sampling, then the researcher may decide to sample every 30 minutes for a 5-minute period, for example.

- **Method of recording:** The way in which observations are recorded is a matter of personal preference. Researchers may develop a checklist scheme or similar observational report form on which (pre-coded) incidents can be recorded. Non pre-coded incidents may simply be recorded in the form of field notes in a designated note book. The researcher may need to invent a system of shorthand or symbols to make the recording task a little easier on the wrist!

- **Location of observer:** The location of the observer is irrelevant in participant research (although consideration should be given to the need for somewhere private where notes can be written up without arousing suspicion, particularly in a field setting), but is of crucial importance for non-participant observation. Where will the researcher sit such that their positioning is not too obtrusive yet enables them readily to see and hear all that is going on? If possible, the researcher should pilot the situation in a simulated set-up. Preparation is essential. The event being witnessed may never happen again during the time allocated for the research.

6.7.4 Application

Observation of behavioural processes is the tool-of-the-trade of the *process consultant*, and denotes a highly honed set of skills and knowledge. The research–practitioner may be interested in observing the team process prior to an intervention to identify weak spots and strong points within the team dynamic, with knowledge used subsequently as the basis for intervention design. Other situations where observation would be appropriate include: examination of interview dynamics (selection, appraisal); the dynamics of socialization in a group; interaction patterns in an open-plan office, in meetings and other group forums or events.

6.7.5 Problems/issues

Observation requires skill, time and experience at a level that is very demanding, particularly observation of the participant kind (see Waddington, 1994, for a critical review of the participant observation technique as used within an organizational setting). As part of a neatly focused research study, there is no reason why you should not endeavour to use observation as an instrument, if you feel that it is the most appropriate way to elicit the evidence you want. It is critical, however, that you pilot the technique first and become well rehearsed in its use before you need to use it to investigate the research question. You can practice using video–tape material. Check the reliability of your coding scheme by inviting someone else to observe independently and record the events of a situation and compare them with your own. Are there any substantial discrepancies of perception and interpretation in your use of coding? You will need to aim for the achievement of a substantial amount of observer agreement before you can feel confident that your application of the coding scheme is reliable. It is not possible of course to check field observations of a more macro nature derived from participation in the field. The issue arising from the unstructured observation situation pertains more to concerns about validity and reliability, insofar as there is scope for many alternative interpretations. Who is to say that your interpretation is appropriate?

6.7.6 References and further reading

Bales, R.F. (1950). *Interaction Process Analysis: a Method for the Study of Small Groups*. Reading, MA: Addison-Wesley.

Bales, R.F. (1999). *Social Interaction Systems: Theory and Measurement.* New Brunswick, NJ: Transaction Publications.

Dixon, B.R., Bouma, G.D. and Atkinson, G. (1987). *A Handbook of Social Science Research.* Oxford. UK: Oxford University Press.

Jorgensen, D. (1989). *Participant Observation.* Beverly Hills, CA: Sage Publications.

Schwartzman, H.B. (1993). *Ethnography in Organizations.* London, UK: Sage Publications.

Spradley, J.P. (1980). *Participant Observation.* New York: Holt, Rinehart and Winston.

Waddington, D. (1994). Participant observation. In C. Cassell, and G. Symon, (Eds.), *Qualitative Methods in Organizational Research: a Practical Guide.* London, UK: Sage Publications.

Wilkinson, J. (1995). Direct observation. In G.M. Breakwell, S. Hammond and C. Fife-Schaw (Eds.), *Research Methods in Psychology.* London, UK: Sage Publications.

6.8 Survey and questionnaire design

6.8.1 Introduction

Questionnaire and survey measures are probably the most widely used research tools within the social sciences (Fife-Schaw, 1995). Their low cost, minimal resource requirements and potentially large sample-capturing abilities make them an attractive research method for academics and practitioners alike. However, the construction of questionnaire/survey tools is not a straightforward undertaking and requires the researcher to consider multiple influences on the potential quality and quantity of data obtained. We will focus here on the types of response format available to the researcher developing a questionnaire tool, the issues of item construction and common wording problems, the formatting and layout of questionnaires, and the types of information a researcher can expect to obtain using these techniques.

6.8.2 Information obtained from questionnaires

Various types of information can be obtained via questionnaires, and are often combined in social science research. These types of information include: demographic/descriptive data, behavioural data and attitudinal data. Each is introduced below:

Demographic, background data: Almost all research questionnaires will require respondents to provide some background information relating to themselves. These data may be required for sampling purposes (to ensure that a representative sample of a population, whose group membership is known, has been obtained), or in order that differences or similarities between groups' responses may be examined. There are various issues attached to asking questions relating to people's backgrounds.

Firstly, the issue of sensitivity is an important one: while respondents are generally happy to answer questions relating to their sex or gender or marital status, they may be less willing to answer questions relating to their age, ethnic background or other personal details, e.g. earnings, financial circumstances, sexual orientation, etc. It is usually fairly clear which questions may cause offence or carry with them political baggage of some kind. Questions of age, for example, may be dealt with by providing respondents with age *band* option boxes, rather than asking for their specific age. However, the range of these groupings should be consistent (to maintain interval-level), and will depend on the level of detail regarding age required by the research question. The situation is similar for earnings – income bands can be presented to the respondent to reduce reactivity. Questions relating to ethnic background should be treated with caution: questions such as 'Why are they necessary to the research?', 'What will they be used to achieve?', 'What impact might they have on accuracy of response and on sample size obtained?' should be considered by the researcher. If they are necessary, the Equal Opportunities Commission suggests the use of the following ethnic groupings for UK populations:

- White
- Black African
- Black Caribbean
- Black British
- Black Other

- Indian
- Pakistani
- Bangladeshi
- Chinese
- Other

Social class/socio-economic status questions are also sensitive, but perhaps to a somewhat lesser degree. Guidelines have been drawn up with reference to UK populations and these are well known and freely available to the researcher. As Fife-Schaw (1995) suggests, the Registrar General's Classification of Occupations is among the best known and most commonly used. The issue of sensitivity will vary between individuals, and the researcher should always keep in mind the value of asking these questions – if they are critical to the research, then include them (but with care); if they are not going to form part of the analysis, exclude them.

Secondly, the issue of confidentiality is important with regard to demographic questions, particularly in organizational settings. If a questionnaire purports to be confidential, and to ensure the anonymity of all respondents, and yet a number of questions relating to individuals' group memberships are included, respondents are likely to doubt the credibility of the anonymity claim. Many respondents will be willing to provide a certain level of information, but if they feel that if someone were to cross-reference demographic details they (as respondents) would become individually identifiable, they may either fail to respond entirely or provide inaccurate (i.e. biased) answers to survey questions. It is therefore absolutely critical to balance the number of demographic questions and level of detail required with possible impacts on data quality and quantity.

Thirdly, again with respect to organizational settings, group information should be as tight and as inclusive as possible to ensure that it applies to all respondents. This requires in-depth discussion with a client organization, and a full understanding of the structure of a company in terms of hierarchical levels, departments, sites, etc. if these groupings are to be drawn upon. The culture of the company may also be crucial: in some organizations, an individual's grade is public information – everyone knows everyone else's grade and this is accepted as an informal hierarchy. In such organizations, asking an open question about grade will probably result in sensible and accurate responses. In other companies, the question of grade may be regarded as a private matter and respondents may not wish to divulge this information – bands of grades may circumvent this problem (as per age or salary), or another question, perhaps relating to terminology (e.g. senior manager, manager, supervisor, staff) may return more accurate responses. Where possible and bearing in mind the impact of asking too many detailed questions, try to obtain information of as low a level of detail as possible – it will be possible to collapse groups during analysis if necessary, but not to break them down if the information is not available.

Thus, group information can be extremely useful to a client company but must be thought through from the perspectives of applicability (to as many staff as possible), sensitivity (in terms of respondents identifying themselves) and comprehensiveness (obtaining as low level information as possible). This often requires some lateral thinking: one of the authors recently undertook a company survey where management were interested in whether staff had been recruited from overseas or from the UK to ensure that a representative sample of the target population had been obtained. This posed an interesting problem: asking the question from a nationality, residence, or ethnic background viewpoint would probably not capture the data since the UK-recruited workforce was fairly cosmopolitan. Asking the question outright would have resulted in reactivity given the friction which existed between the two groups. Ultimately, the question 'Did you receive your training in the UK?' was selected – while staff may not have fully understood the relevance of the question, it was applicable to all staff, was able to capture the level of detail required and was unlikely to cause reactivity in respondents due to the sensitive way in which it was asked.

Finally, there is an argument that descriptive information should be requested at the end of a questionnaire, rather than, as convention suggests, at the beginning. This is argued to decrease reactivity and thus increase accuracy of responses, as well as to reduce boredom early on in the survey, where mundane questions relating to one's background must be trawled through by respondents, sapping motivation at an early stage. The counter-argument to this is that by relegating descriptive information to the end of a survey, respondents may be less likely to complete this section, especially if they have responded negatively to earlier questions. In addition, failing to observe the convention of background information being requested first may serve to confuse respondents.

Behavioural information: Fife-Schaw (1995) discusses issues associated with behavioural self-report questions in some depth, highlighting the major problems of memory and social desirability as potential biases in these types of question. Clearly, respondents must have a reasonable memory of the area of interest if they are to answer a question accurately. However, even if their memory for the event or occurrence is good, they may not report its incidence accurately, if at all, if the area is sensitive, e.g. theft from work, recreational drug use. This type of bias extends beyond the reporting of undesirable acts. Sudman and Bradburn (1982) reported that social desirability bias leads to instances of over-reporting of desirable acts, such as punctuality, good performance, etc. Fife-Schaw (1995) suggests that to tackle this problem, consistency checks may be included in a questionnaire measure, or the researcher could explain to respondents that their answers will be cross-checked against real data. Clearly, this is not possible if anonymity of respondents is to be guaranteed, but may be an option in certain settings.

Attitudinal information: There are a wide variety of techniques that can be used by researchers to tap into respondents' attitudes. Among the most commonly used are 5- or 7-point attitude scales, but others include open-ended questions, semantic differential scales, diagrammatic rating, or forced-choice questions. Five- or 7-point Likert-type scales typically involve the respondent being presented with a statement to which s/he is asked to report how s/he feels about the accuracy or otherwise of the statement, ranging between the extremes of 'Strongly agree' through 'Neither agree nor disagree' to 'Strongly disagree'. An example is shown in Figure 6.3:

Figure 6.3   Example of a 7-point response scale anchored with 'Strongly disagree' and 'Strongly agree'

1 = Strongly Disagree ⟵—————————⟶ *7 = Strongly Agree*

1   2   3   4   5   6   7   DK

I feel I should be paid for any
overtime I do
(please tick appropriate box)

Note that with such scales, the inclusion of a 'don't know' (DK) option, as shown in Figure 6.3, can reveal information of importance to the research question, and can also flag up problem items, which respondents do not feel equipped to answer. A variation on this numerical rating approach involves respondents being presented with a horizontal line whose opposite ends are labelled 'Strongly agree' and 'Strongly disagree' – the respondent is asked to mark his/her response with a cross somewhere on the line. The researcher then measures the distance between one extreme of the scale and each cross, using a ruler.

Open-ended questions, as their name suggests, involve asking a question of the respondent and allowing him/her to respond as briefly, or as comprehensively, as s/he likes. Analysis of these types of question requires a particular approach to be taken, e.g. content analysis (see Chapter 9), with quantitative output being limited to frequency counts of 'thematic' data.

Semantic differential scales are 'adjectivally anchored' versions of standard response scales, where respondents are asked to report how they feel about a certain topic in terms of two adjectival extremes, as shown in Figure 6.4.

Figure 6.4   Example of a semantic differential attitudinal scale

*Now thinking of yourself as a member of your **team**, rate how you feel about this 'group membership' compared with your other group memberships and affiliations, on the following 7-point scales:*

Enjoyable	1	2	3	4	5	6	7	Unenjoyable
Positive	1	2	3	4	5	6	7	Negative
Unimportant	1	2	3	4	5	6	7	Important

Diagrammatic rating scales again present similar information but represent response options in terms of a graphical alternative. Figure 6.5 illustrates Kunin's (1955) 'faces' rating scale, a scale which purports to report interval-level data due to exhaustive validation by the researcher of hundreds of pictures of faces to ensure that the interval between each adjacent pair is equivalent to that between each other adjacent pair.

Figure 6.5   Kunin's (1955) 'faces' rating scale

*Please place a tick under the face that best expresses how you feel about your **LIFE OUTSIDE WORK**, including your home life, social life, and outside interests.*

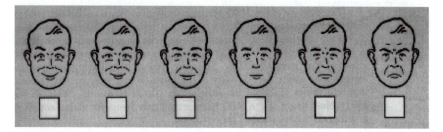

Adapted from Kunin, T. (1955). The construction of a new type of attitude measure. *Personnel Psychology, 8*, 65–78.

Forced-choice rating scales present two or more alternative statements to the respondent and ask him/her to select only one of the available options. As Fife-Schaw (1995) points out, these formats are less commonly used in psychological research since they do not provide information as to the extremity of agreement or disagreement with a statement (they also have the potential to suffer from order of presentation effects). However, 5- and 7-point standard response scales also suffer from drawbacks in that certain response sets are evident in some respondents, e.g. some people's propensity to rely on the neutral ('Neither agree nor disagree') response a little too much, while others use only extreme responses (effectively using the scale as a forced-choice design).

Finally, ranking scales can be included to elicit attitudinal information, whereby respondents are presented with a series of options and are asked to rank these in terms of importance, relevance, cost, etc.

It should be noted that all attitude measurement of this kind makes some key assumptions about the respondent. Firstly, that the respondent actually *has* an attitude about the topic in question (although this is partially addressed by the inclusion of a mid-point on a 5- or 7- point response scale), and secondly that this attitude can be adequately represented in ratings or in forced-choice judgements. It is suggested as a minimum, therefore, that attitude researchers always include an open-ended invitation to comment on any element of a questionnaire, which respondents can use to provide additional qualifying information to represent their attitudes or feelings towards an issue more adequately.

6.8.3 Wording and other problems

When constructing a questionnaire measure, question or item wording is absolutely critical to ensure comprehensibility of an item's meaning, and therefore, to accuracy of response. There are a number of ways in which respondents can be left with an ambiguous or incomplete understanding of what you are asking, such as the inclusion of:

- *Unfamiliar words* – technical or jargon words are unlikely to be understood by the respondent, unless specific to their profession/organization.

- *Ambiguous or imprecise words or concepts* – frequency response options provide a good example of ambiguity, e.g. in use of terms such as 'frequently', 'often', 'infrequently' or 'never' – options such as these must be qualified, perhaps with examples, or respondents will attempt to guess at their meaning. Imprecision can be seen in the varying definitions of certain words, e.g. 'dynamic', 'innovative', 'forward-thinking' – the more variable the definition of such words, the more error will be introduced into responses to the item.

- *Complicated wording* – questions which contain too many clauses or qualifications can be confusing. This can be detrimental to attitude questions, where a quick reaction is required from respondents, for example, 'In general at work, would you say that you were relatively satisfied or content with your relationship with your immediate supervisor, that is, your line manager or boss?'

- *Double-barrelled questions* – questions that contain more than one concept should be avoided, e.g. 'Are your parents British?', or 'Do you feel that the training programme was a good one and effective in teaching you new skills?'. Such questions should be split into their component parts and presented separately.

- *Arithmetic concepts* – percentages and proportions are regularly misunderstood by questionnaire respondents: categories such as 'All', 'More than half', 'Less than half' and 'None' may be more useful.

- *Double-negatives* can be confusing and should probably be kept to a minimum, for example 'This organization contains few staff who are not committed to the company.'

- *Leading questions* – questions that begin with such phrases as 'Would you agree that …?' contain within them implicit value judgements that will almost certainly lead to biased responses. As far as possible, questions should be neutrally worded. This is often difficult, but is particularly important with attitude questions to ensure that respondents do not try to select the 'correct' or socially acceptable response.

- *Questions with hidden assumptions* should be avoided, for example the question 'Promotion within this company is a real possibility if I put the work in' assumes that promotion is offered to all staff – this may not be the case if, for example, contract-based or part-time workers make up a significant proportion of the workforce.

- *Context effects* – these are subtle effects on response which depend in part on question order and in part on the subject matter tackled by the questionnaire. Asking the question 'Are you currently happy with your workplace?' in the context of a management-circulated employee survey, or in the context of an informal anonymous mailshot survey, may produce different responses. Similarly, questions may be influenced by their order in the survey – such effects can often be identified during piloting.

- *Sensitive questions* – these have been dealt with in detail in the context of demographic questions, but also apply to attitudinal or behavioural questions. Questions that may offend should be avoided if this is likely to bias respondents' answers to other questions. One of the authors, in carrying out a recent employee survey, was asked by the client to include a question relating to house ownership. Whilst this was of passing interest to the client, it probably did not justify inclusion given the reaction of many respondents who felt that this was a private issue and neither the concern of the survey, nor of the company's management, and may well have influenced their responses to later survey questions. There is also an argument, related to this, that sensitive questions should be included later on in a survey in order that they do not influence responses to all other questions.

In addition to issues of wording and content, questionnaire methods have several other implicit drawbacks which should be appreciated by the researcher. The first of these is social desirability, which has been touched on elsewhere. In almost all cases, except where questionnaire topics are entirely benign or superficial, or where anonymity is absolutely guaranteed and this is made clear to the respondent (e.g. in social research settings using anonymous mailshots), respondents will invariably attempt to respond in a socially desirable way that is, they will attempt to select the response option which places them in the best possible light given the context of the survey and/or question. This is a difficult effect to counter, other than by trying not to couch questions in value-laden terminology and, when using forced-choice responses, constructing equally desirable/attractive alternative options.

Secondly, any questionnaire should be customized to the level and specific characteristics of the target population. It is extremely difficult to ask questions of one sample which will not in some way condescend to, or ask too much of, another. However, the researcher should try to achieve generalizability of questions as far as is possible in order that findings are as comparable as they can be. In the case of organizational samples, it may also be necessary to slightly customize question wording to suit the company under study, for example in use of terms such as 'staff' versus 'employees'; 'Personnel' versus 'Human Resources', etc.

Finally, questionnaires, despite being beloved of many social science researchers, suffer greatly from certain technical shortcomings. Firstly, as noted earlier, people answer questions using similar response sets (some peppering the mid-point of a scale, others using only extreme points, and yet others using the full scope of a scale) and this will influence the statistical properties of information obtained using a survey measure. Reversing items or breaking long sections of questions with a different type of response scale can ameliorate this situation. In addition, 'method co-variance' refers to the use of more than one measure within a survey battery: due to the similarity of methods used to collect data from each measure and the response sets of individuals, correlations between the measures are likely to be inflated; that is, their shared variance will be unrealistically high. It is only by using alternative methods in combination with questionnaires, e.g. interviews, observation, etc., that such effects may be offset. This effect is discussed in greater depth later in this section.

6.8.4 Aesthetic issues and layout

Layout and formatting of a questionnaire or survey should not be regarded as an afterthought, since careful presentation of questions and attractive layout can significantly boost response rates and comprehensibility. Surveys which are poorly laid out and unattractive are unlikely to inspire the respondent to complete them no matter how well-piloted the content – it is imperative, therefore, that the researcher spends time and effort producing a professional-looking survey. Even with very limited resources, this is perfectly possible given the increasingly user-friendly software packages now available to computer users. Issues particularly worthy of consideration include the following:

- *Respondent instructions and covering letter* – in order to promote respondent motivation, instructions should always be provided for self-report questionnaires. In addition, and particularly for organizational samples, covering letters can be very useful in elevating response rates. By explaining some of the background to the research, the aims of the research, and the crucial role of the respondent in achieving those aims, motivation can be heightened. The issues of confidentiality and anonymity cannot be overemphasized – by ensuring that respondents are aware of the confidential nature of the research, their help with the research is far more likely to be secured. Phrases such as 'the answers that you give will be used for research purposes only and will **at all times remain completely confidential',** and 'please be assured that you cannot be identified, nor can your views and comments be directed back at you. We are interested in **what was said, not who said it**' can be helpful in effecting this.

- *Questionnaire length* – Fife-Schaw (1995) cautions the researcher against developing questionnaires which are either too long or too short. He includes in the former category those surveys that take more than 45 minutes to complete, arguing that extremely high motivation would be required of the respondent to complete a questionnaire of greater length than this. On the other hand, questionnaires of two pages or less in length, while quick to complete and analyse, are rarely taken seriously by respondents since such a short questionnaire is unlikely to address any substantive research area.

- *Question order* – as mentioned above, background/descriptive information can be located either at the beginning or the end of a questionnaire. Arguments exist for each approach. Sensitive questions are rarely included at the front end of a survey since respondents need time to 'get accustomed' to question-answering, and be put at ease by early questions. They may, therefore, find it difficult not to react to questions relating to sensitive issues and these are therefore generally placed towards the end of the questionnaire.

- *Spelling/grammar* – although this may seem like a minor issue, accurate spelling and grammar are, in fact, critical to respondents' perceptions of a researcher's competence and professionalism, and therefore to perceptions of credibility of the research itself. Poor spelling and grammar suggest a slapdash approach to questionnaire construction (particularly in today's world of computerized spelling/grammar checking packages) and detract significantly from their content. Respondents in some professions (engineering in particular springs to mind) are particularly prone to being distracted from a questionnaire's content by such seemingly minor errata.

- *Font type and size* – wherever possible, readable, sufficiently large type should be used. Point size 10–12 has been shown to be a reasonable size for readability. 'Novelty' fonts should be avoided for the questionnaire itself – quick responses to questions are required and anything which distracts from, or interferes with, the readability of questions should be avoided.

- *Layout density* – cramming as many questions as possible on to a page simply to reduce the total number of pages of a questionnaire is not advised. Again, readability and legibility are paramount and any device that can be used to assist the reader in responding to questions should be employed. This includes tabulating questions to assist the respondent in tracing across from question to answer box (shading alternative rows can also be a good idea to aid the navigability of the questionnaire), 'grouping' forced-choice response options by leaving space between questions, etc.

- *Provision of sufficient space for responses* – if open-ended questions are included in the questionnaire, respondents should be provided with sufficient space in which to answer. Always provide more space rather than less.

6.8.5 Common method variance

As noted by Podsakoff and Organ (1986), one of the principal problems that may arise from the use of self-report questionnaire measures within organizational research is that of common method variance (Campbell and Fiske, 1959). This refers to the conflation of response-response correlations when all data derive from the same source, i.e. from each questionnaire respondent. Podsakoff and Organ (1986) note a number of *post hoc* statistical procedures which may be used to address this problem following data collection, including Harman's (1967) one-factor test, social desirability partialling (Edwards, 1970) and scale 'trimming' (Birnbaum et al., 1986). However, each of these procedures contains its own drawbacks and none has gained overwhelming popularity within the research community. However, there remains the possibility that the self-report researcher may introduce mediating measures at the *design* stage.

Several design alterations may be made to questionnaire-based approaches to address the problem of common method variance. The first is the use of multiple methods, as advocated by Rousseau (1990). This approach involves the combination of various methods of data collection in obtaining data on a single topic. In the case of individual-level data, this would involve, for example, interviewing respondents to explore their responses in more depth and ensure that their views were adequately represented by the survey, or eliciting critical incidents from respondents to enrich the numerical data provided by the survey.

In addition, it is possible to separate sections of a questionnaire-based tool into distinct areas of investigation, each prefaced with a title and short introductory paragraph. In this way, acquiescent and global satisfaction/dissatisfaction response sets may be mediated to some degree in that respondents are encouraged to consider each section of the questionnaire as referring to a fresh area for exploration. As such, they are required to think differently about their own attitudes and appropriate responses.

6.8.6 References and further reading

Questionnaire and survey design

Edwards, J.A., Thomas, M.D., Rosenfield, P. and Booth-Kewley, S. (1996). *How to Conduct Organizational Surveys*. London, UK: Sage Publications.

Fife-Schaw, C. (1995). Questionnaire design. In G.M. Breakwell, S. Hammond and C. Fife-Schaw (Eds.), *Research Methods in Psychology*. London, UK: Sage Publications.

Furnham, A. and Gunter, B. (1993). *Corporate Assessment: Auditing a Company's Personality*. London, UK: Routledge.

Gaskell, G., Wright, D. and O'Muircheartaigh, S. (1993). Reliability of surveys. *The Psychologist, 6, 11,* 500–503.

Kunin, T. (1955). The construction of a new type of attitude measure. *Personnel Psychology, 8,* 65–78.

Oppenheim, A.N. (1992). *Questionnaire Design, Interviewing and Attitude Measurement*. London, UK: Printer Publishers.

Sudman, S. and Bradburn, N.M. (1982). *Asking Questions: a Practical Guide to Questionnaire Design*. San Francisco, CA: Jossey-Bass.

Common method variance

Birnbaum, P.H., Farh, J.L. and Wong, G.Y.Y. (1986). The job characteristics model in Hong Kong. *Journal of Applied Psychology, 71,* 598–605.

Campbell, D.T. and Fiske, D.W. (1959). Convergent and discriminant validation by the multitrait-multimethod matrix. *Psychological Bulletin, 56,* 81–105.

Edwards, A.L. (1970). *The Measurement of Personality Traits by Scales and Inventories*. New York: Holt, Rhinehart and Winston.

Harman, H.H. (1967). *Modern Factor Analysis*. Chicago, IL: University of Chicago Press.

Podsakoff, P.M. and Organ, D.W. (1986). Self-reports in organizational research: problems and prospects. *Journal of Management, 12,* 4, 531–544.

Rousseau, D.M. (1990). Assessing organizational culture: the case for multiple methods. In B. Schneider (Ed.), *Organizational Climate and Culture*. San Francisco, CA: Jossey-Bass.

6.9 Diary methods

6.9.1 Introduction

Burgess (1982) suggests that a diary provides a first-hand account of a situation to which a researcher may not have direct access. Any form of personal log of events, generically described as a diary, then, may provide the researcher with an insight into issues and events which would not be accessible via other means, such as interview, questionnaire or observation methods. At their heart, diary methods draw on the subjective interpretation of events by individuals in particular situations to contextualize reported experience, and place this within a continuous temporal framework. Transient feelings, unobservable and unmeasurable, can be logged using diaries. Seemingly trivial, inconsequential events can also be analysed for pattern and meaning. Within the context of organizational research, diary methods can be used to any number of ends: for example, to log communications between team members in a given department; to chart employees' reactions to an organizational merger or takeover on a day-to-day basis; to record the effects of shiftwork on workers' psychological health; or to study the behaviour and attitudes of new recruits over their first few months' tenure within an organization. Diaries can be recorded using traditional journal entries, via computerized or other multimedia recording systems (e.g. photographs, audio-tapes, written logs, etc.), or via specifically designed questionnaire-style input sheets.

6.9.2 The method

Breakwell and Wood (1995) summarize the critical issues in using diary techniques as follows:

- *Select an appropriate medium* – written diaries are only appropriate for literate participants. Audio-taping may be suitable for participants not at ease with the written approach.

- *Provide clear instructions* – participants should understand the background to, and aims of, the research and their role in the research process, and should have issues involved in diary research explained to them, e.g. the problem of memory (and so the need for regular diary entries), the importance of accuracy and the correct use of any *pro forma* provided. An example is also often provided of a completed diary entry.

- *Ensure usability of the diary format* – as with questionnaire layout (see Section 6.8 above), issues of aesthetics and usability are important in diary research. Ensure that enough space is provided for open-ended comments if required, and that the layout of the diary minimizes errors and encourages speed of entry as far as is possible.

- *Incentivize the research* – diary studies may be long term and, as such, may require a continuation incentive to be provided to participants (in the form of a lottery/raffle system, small payment, etc.).

- *Remain available* – researchers should remain available and accessible, particularly during the early stages of the research, to ensure that participants' questions can be answered regarding category definitions, level of detail required, etc.

- *Keep it short initially* – shorter diaries have been shown to be more effective than longer diaries during initial stages of the research to reduce sample mortality. Once introduced to short diaries, longer ones can be introduced to participants more effectively.

Case Study 7 summarizes Furnham and Gunter's (1993) applied use of diary techniques in recording communication between departmental members in order to develop a communicogram – an illustration representing the flow of information between group members in a target setting.

Case Study 7: Communicograms: applying diary methods

Furnham and Gunter (1993) describe the use of diary methods in developing a communication chart, or communicogram, of interactions between members of a department, to identify patterns of communication and the role of each departmental member in the communication process. An emphasis was placed on mutually perceived interactions, i.e. those cases where there was mutual agreement between each party involved that the communication had occurred and when it had occurred. This research issue, then, seems to lend itself well to diary methods. A temporal, subjective record was needed of all interactions taking place between all departmental members over a given period.

The researchers report that diaries were kept by each participant over a two-week period, with each participant required to make a diary entry twice daily, noting face-to-face and telephone interactions in which s/he took part as far as s/he remembered them. Written communication was excluded from the process due to the difficulty of inferring mutual perceptions between parties. Diary entry times were formalized on the premise that if participants were able to remember interactions, the interactions were more likely to have been important to them. Participants were asked to record the topic of each interaction, its nature, their impressions of it and the other party or parties involved. Thus, each diary entry required the following information on each interaction:

- With whom the communication took place;
- The topic of the communication;
- Whether the communication was by telephone or face-to-face;
- The initiator of the communication;
- The type of communication;
- Identification of the main role player;
- Rating of the importance of the communication;
- Rating of the success of the communication;
- Whether a decision was required or not;
- Whether a decision was made or not;
- Identification of the decision-maker;
- Rating of preference for the decision that was made;
- Rating of satisfaction with the decision that was made.

Diary data were analysed by computer, following coding, to report:
- Average number of interactions per person, per day, per day of participation in the research;
- The proportion of all potentially mutual interactions which were mutually perceived;
- The characteristics of the interaction (initiator, type, etc.), with separate figures for mutual, non-mutual and total interactions;
- The extent of consensus as to the characteristics of mutual interactions.

The example illustrates the advantages of diary techniques in eliciting data which would otherwise be extremely difficult to tap into, given time and memory constraints and the subjective nature of perceived mutuality of communication.

6.9.3 Advantages and disadvantages of diary methods

Breakwell and Wood (1995) summarize the various advantages and disadvantages of diary techniques as follows:

Advantages:
- *Familiarity* – participants will be familiar with the diary concept and with the idea of recording events within a temporal framework.
- *Cost-effective information sampling* – if information is required over an extended period, with a little incentivizing where necessary, diary methods can be used to great effect with very little resource requirement.
- *Sequencing data* – information is framed in temporal space and can readily show changes and developments over time.
- *Sensitive information* – intimate information can be obtained using diary methods, although such information is more likely to derive from existing diary accounts that from entries elicited for the purposes of research. Existing diaries can also be useful as historic, spontaneous accounts of past events. This is of less relevance to the organizational researcher, unless perhaps s/he is working within a comparative historical theoretical framework.

Disadvantages:
- *Control of content* – this is often minimal, regardless of the quality of instruction, training and feedback given. Participants will invariably mis-remember information, either consciously or not, and will also self-select material depending on their motivation.
- *Mortality* – diary methods suffer greatly from a high dropout rate. Incentivizing the research can go some way to ameliorating this, but it must be remembered that the eventual result of high dropout from a very specific group of people (i.e. those agreeing to participate in the research in the first place) may well be a severely restricted (and biased) sample.
- *Verification* – verification of diary entries is extremely problematic. Breakwell and Wood (1995) suggest tandem use of interview techniques to act as a verification check for diary entries.
- *Reactance* – finally, it should be noted that the very act of completing a journal log of events or feelings may alter perceptions, attitudes or even behaviours which may, in turn, impact on data obtained.

6.9.4 References and further reading

Breakwell, G.M. and Wood, P. (1995). Diary techniques In G.M. Breakwell, S. Hammond and C. Fife-Schaw (Eds.), *Research Methods in Psychology*. London, UK: Sage Publications.

Burgess, R. (Ed.) (1982). *Field Research: a Sourcebook and Field Manual*. London, UK: Allen and Unwin.

Burgess, R. (1984). *An in the Field Introduction to Field Research*. London, UK: Allen and Unwin.

Furnham, A. and Gunter, B. (1993). *Corporate Assessment: Auditing a Company's Personality*. London, UK: Routledge.

Hammersley, M. and Atkinson, P. (1991). *Ethnography: Principles in Practice*. London, UK: Tavistock.

Plummer, K. (1983). *Documents of Life*. London, UK: Allen and Unwin.

7   Sampling Considerations

7.1 Introduction and definitions

For practical and cost reasons, it is often not possible to collect information about the entire population in which a researcher is interested. Therefore, a subset or sample of the population is usually selected for study in its place. A sample is a selection of individuals drawn from the target or parent population which is intended to reflect this population's characteristics in all significant respects. The main criteria of sample selection, then, are:

- Ensuring that a sample provides a faithful representation of the total population from which it is selected;
- Knowing as precisely as possible the probability that a sample is reliable in this way.

Randomization meets these criteria since it protects against bias in the selection process and provides a basis on which to apply statistical theory, thus allowing an estimate to be made of the probability that conclusions drawn from the sample are generalizable to the population. The term 'sampling error' is used to describe the amount by which the sample's characteristics deviate from the population's characteristics and can be described in terms of the 'standard error' statistic. A 'sampling frame' describes the list of members from a given population from which the sample may be drawn. Random or 'probability' sampling (where each person in the population has an equal probability of being selected) requires a complete and accurate list of the target population. 'Non-probability' sampling involves some people in the population being more likely to be selected than others for some reason.

Before introducing different sampling strategies available to the researcher, some of the potential problems and drawbacks touched on here will be further described in terms of a hypothetical organizational survey (see Case Study 8).

Case Study 8: Sampling problems with an organizational survey

A major engineering company (with 1,200 employees) was interested in staff attitudes (across the organization) towards the company's recent buyout by a US multinational. They approached a research consultancy who agreed to undertake a company-wide survey of staff attitudes. The consultancy worked hard to produce a customized measure of staff attitudes, drawing on the areas suggested by the company's management for inclusion. The consultancy then provided the company with a final version of the survey, since the client had agreed to copy, distribute to, and collect the surveys from, staff. Two weeks later, the consultancy had received 155 completed surveys (a 13% response rate), 80 of which had been completed by middle managers (who actually represented only 20% of the total workforce) and 120 of which had been completed by HQ staff (who in total represented 15% of the workforce). The client was already requesting a draft report on findings. The consultancy realized too late that they had not addressed the sampling issues relevant to the client organization. Following further discussions with the client, the consultancy discovered that:

1. The breakdown of the workforce was as follows: 120 senior management, 240 middle management; 240 supervisory; 600 staff level employees; 180 HQ-based, 1,020 site-based employees.
2. All staff and supervisors worked on site, many in remote parts of the country. There was no internal mail distribution system and surveys had been distributed in a haphazard way to sites. Distribution throughout the company's central office, however, had been effective.
3. Many staff had complained about the level of language used and had claimed to be unable to understand some questions.
4. No explanation of the survey had been given to employees at staff or supervisory grade outside the company's HQ; middle managers had, however, been fully briefed by their superiors.

By failing to gather all the necessary information relating to the target sample prior to running the survey, the consultancy had obtained a sample which was wholly unrepresentative of the population. While they were able to report quite comprehensively on HQ-located middle managers' and support staffs' views on the buyout, all other staff were severely under-represented, if indeed represented at all. To have circumvented this problem, the consultancy could have:

*   Identified staff level groupings at the outset and aimed to obtain a representative sample of staff by site and by grade, i.e. 15% responses from HQ, 85% responses from site; 10% responses from senior managers, 20% from middle management and supervisors respectively and 50% from staff grades.
*   Obtained staff lists for all grades and locations and have selected a representative proportion of employees according to each group.
*   Ensured that language was accessible to all employees and that all employees (and not just middle managers) were forewarned of the survey and of its purpose.
*   Ensured that distribution and collection mechanisms were as uniform as possible, e.g. survey distributed to all staff with wage slip together with reply-paid envelope.

7.2 Probability sampling

A probability or random sample describes a sample selected in such a way that all members in the population have a known chance of selection. Probability samples are preferable because they are more likely to produce representative samples and also enable estimates of the sample's accuracy to be made. Types of probability sampling approach are described below.

7.2.1 Simple random sampling (SRS)

This involves completely random selection of individuals from the total population and assumes the availability of a complete list of population members. Whilst this may be available for some groups/organizations (e.g. unions, schools, some organizations), depending on the type of research intended, SRS may remain inapplicable. Since SRS is likely to identify some sample members who are geographically disparate, particularly in nation-wide surveys, for anything other than mail- or telephone-based research the technique is not cost-effective. Research based on *interviewing* sample members, for example, would rapidly increase in cost with the addition of one or two remotely located workers. Overall, SRS is best used when a good sampling frame exists and when the population is geographically concentrated or the data collection technique does not involve travelling.

7.2.2 Systematic sampling

Systematic sampling is a very similar technique to SRS, differing only in that it does not rely on the generation of random sample members but instead involves the researcher selecting a suitable 'sampling fraction' (e.g. 10% of the total population) and from the population list, selecting every n^{th} sample member (e.g. every tenth sample member). This approach offers the same advantages and limitations as SRS other than the additional problem of *periodicity of the sampling frame*. That is, a certain type of person may reappear at regular intervals within the sampling frame, but only if the sampling frame has been generated in a cyclical way which maps directly on to the sampling fraction.

7.2.3 Stratified sampling

This method builds on SRS and systematic sampling techniques in order to generate a more representative sample, but employs a slightly more complex procedure, similar to that suggested in Case Study 8, above. In order to be representative, the proportions of various groups in a sample should be the same as in the population, but due to chance (sampling error) this will not always be the case. The researcher first needs to select a grouping or stratifying variable on which s/he wants to ensure correct representation (grade or location in the Case Study 8 example). Having selected this variable, the researcher orders the sampling frame into groups according to the category of the stratifying variable, and then employs an SRS or systematic sampling approach to select the appropriate proportion of people within each stratum.

7.3 Non-probability sampling

There are often situations where probability sampling techniques are either impractical or unnecessary and in these situations, cheaper, less resource-intensive, non-probability techniques may be used. Suitable situations include those where a sampling frame is unavailable, where the population is so widely dispersed that probability sampling would be inefficient, or during the preliminary stages of research (e.g. questionnaire piloting, hypothesis generation or preliminary examination of range or variety of response to a research question) where generalization to the population is not important.

7.3.1 Purposive sampling

Individuals are selected from a population according to an underlying interest in particular groups. For example, a study of union attitudes in a workforce might, in the absence of a clearly defined sampling frame or population, select some *typical* members from a number of *typical* work groups. This form of sampling may not be representative, but will probably yield useful information all the same. Political polling often uses this technique: by selecting electoral constituencies that have previously been shown to predict the outcome of national elections, or selecting key constituencies which generally reflect the national pattern (i.e. 'typical' constituencies), purposive sampling techniques are employed, and, while not based on probabilistic sampling theory, are often shown to be extremely effective in predicting outcomes.

7.3.2 Quota sampling

Using this approach, researchers are required to find individuals with particular characteristics, on the assumption that these different characteristics are distributed systematically throughout a population and so selecting the correct *quotas* of people displaying variations of the characteristic will ultimately result in a representative sample. Characteristics on which to base quotas can be simple, e.g. age, or can combine characteristics, e.g. age, sex, marital status, car ownership, with different quota targets identified in each combined characteristic group. Quota sampling, while appearing useful and usable from a theoretical (if pragmatically driven) point of view, suffers from the drawback that individuals who are most easily accessible to the researcher and who fulfil the characteristics required, e.g. friends, family, etc., are most likely to be selected for inclusion. In addition, the researcher also requires knowledge of the proportion of each characteristic present in the target population. As with all non-probability sampling approaches, it is also impossible to calculate standard error estimations with quota-sampled data.

7.3.3 Convenience sampling

While a widely used approach, particularly in student circles, convenience or availability sampling must only be used with caution and restricted to use in specific situations. This approach, as its name suggests, involves the researcher obtaining data from anyone 'convenient' (friends, family, work colleagues, etc.). While the technique can produce quite large samples relatively quickly and cost-effectively, size does not compensate for unrepresentativeness. Such approaches should really be restricted to exploratory research or to piloting questionnaire- or survey-based tools where the make-up of the sample is fairly irrelevant. Even in these cases, however, the biased nature of the sample may lead the researcher to erroneous conclusions, e.g. in the case of an all-student convenience sample used for piloting a work-attitude questionnaire, the researcher may be led to believe that all the items contained within his/her questionnaire are understandable and contain no jargon, but when introduced to a non-student population, problems may arise in respondent understanding, not identified during the pilot phase due to the unrepresentative nature of the sample.

7.3.4 Snowball sampling

Snowball sampling represents the loosest possible definition of a sampling approach, since it involves including members of the target population by drawing on existing contacts and on their contacts. Initial participants in the research are asked to provide further contacts, hence the term 'snowballing', although only if the researcher is particularly persuasive or participants extremely co-operative. This approach is most applicable in small populations which are difficult to access due to their 'closed' nature, e.g. secret societies, organizational 'cliques', inaccessible professions, etc. Clearly, generalizability will be minimal, but the type of research conducted with such samples would be unlikely to have generalization to a wider population as an underlying aim, e.g. ethnography, participant observation, etc.

7.4 Limitations of sampling approach on analysis

The size and content of any research sample will affect the type, level and generalizability of analysis that can be undertaken. If one of the research programme's aims is to apply statistical analyses to the data, total sample sizes will significantly influence the accuracy of results reported by statistical tests. This is due to the statistical 'power' required to report significance or non-significance accurately, taking into account type of statistical test, effect sizes observed by the research, significance level employed and sample size. Table 7.1 illustrates the group sample sizes required for different types of statistical tests, depending on the mean effect size observed in the research (large or medium), in order for statistical power to be 0.8; that is, for the null hypothesis to be correctly rejected 80% of the time (Cohen, 1988, 1992) – an acceptable level of power. See also Kraemer and Thiemann (1987) and Sedlmeier and Gigerenzer (1989) for further discussions of statistical power. See also Chapter 9 for more information on the selection of appropriate statistical tests.

Table 7.1 Participants required per condition according to effect size and statistical test in order for adequate statistical power to be achieved

Test	Participants *per condition*	
	Large effect size	Medium effect size
Independent samples t-test	26	64
Product moment correlation co-efficient	28	85
Binomial and sign tests	30	85
Chi-squared test (degrees of freedom = 1)	26	87
Chi-squared test (degrees of freedom = 2)	39	107
Chi-squared test (degrees of freedom = 3)	44	121
Chi-squared test (degrees of freedom = 4)	48	133
One way ANOVA (2 groups)	26	64
One way ANOVA (3 groups)	21	52
One way ANOVA (4 groups)	18	45
One way ANOVA (5 groups)	16	39
One way ANOVA (6 groups)	14	35
Multiple regression (2 independent variables)	30	67
Multiple regression (3 independent variables)	34	76
Multiple regression (4 independent variables)	38	84
Multiple regression (5 independent variables)	42	91
Multiple regression (6 independent variables)	45	97
Multiple regression (7 independent variables)	48	102
Multiple regression (8 independent variables)	50	107

It is possible to make decisions as to required sample sizes according to this rationale prior to collecting data. The difficulty with this, however, is that the researcher must know beforehand what likely observed effect sizes are going to be and these are difficult to predict. Nevertheless, Table 7.1 gives some indication to researchers as to the sample size they are likely to need in order to infer accurate conclusions from various statistical tests.

In addition to sample size, the level of representativeness of a sample, i.e. how closely the sample represents its original population, will limit the applicability and generalizability of findings. If a complete population is sampled, or a representative sample is obtained via SRS or other forms of probability sampling, findings will be generalizable to the population, i.e. it will be accurate to say that the sample's results are probabilistically likely to be similar to the total population's results were it possible to assess the total population. However, non-probability sampling approaches will limit the level of representativeness and observed effects in the research may thus be due to sampling error (although, of course, it is not possible to quantify this possibility using non-probability sampling). Ultimately, unequivocal conclusions about the target population cannot be drawn from findings deriving from samples obtained using non-probability approaches.

7.5 Conclusion

The type of sampling selected for a given research project will be dependent on the research method selected, the goals of the research and the availability of population-specific information. Simple random or stratified sampling are real possibilities in organization-wide survey-based research. Indeed, in the case of such studies, sampling may not even be required as the entire organizational population may be made accessible. In general, interview-based techniques will require some form of stratification or narrowing of the population to achieve a representative, yet workable, sample. Research methods which require access to a specific, restricted sample or whose goals do not necessitate accurate representation of the population (e.g. questionnaire piloting, exploratory research or hypothesis generation) may be suited to non-probability sampling techniques. In all cases, however, the nature of a study sample and the method via which it was obtained should always be reported by a researcher, together with the implications of these factors for any conclusions or generalizations which the researcher wishes to make about the data. In this way, any restrictions of the sampling approach can be explained to the reader and applicability and generalizability of the findings can be assessed by the reader on this basis.

7.6 References and further reading

Cohen, J. (1988). *Statistical Power Analysis for Behavioral Sciences* (Second Edition). Hillsdale, NJ: LEA.

Cohen, J. (1992). A power primer. *Psychological Bulletin, 112*, 115–159.

Fife-Schaw, C. (1995). Surveys and sampling issues. In G.M. Breakwell, S. Hammond and C. Fife-Schaw (Eds.), *Research Methods in Psychology*. London, UK: Sage Publications.

Furnham, A. and Gunter, B. (1993). *Corporate Assessment: Auditing a Company's Personality*. London, UK: Routledge.

Judd, C.M., Smith, E.R. and Kidder, L.H. (1991). *Research Methods in Social Relations: International Edition* (Sixth Edition). Fort Worth, TX: Holt, Rinehart and Winston.

Kalton, G. (1983). *Introduction to Survey Sampling*. Beverley Hills, CA: Sage Publications.

Kraemer, H.C. and Thiemann, S. (1987). *How Many Subjects? Statistical Power Analysis in Research*. London, UK: Sage Publications.

Sedlmeier, P. and Gigerenzer, G. (1989). Do studies of statistical power have an effect on the power of studies? *Psychological Bulletin, 105*, 309–316.

8 Assessing Performance in Organizations

8.1 Performance, effectiveness and productivity

The 50-year-old statement of Bechtoldt (1947: 357) that there is 'no subject of greater importance than the criterion to be used in evaluating performance' remains as salient today as it ever was. Schneider and Schmitt (1986: 77) define performance criteria as 'those behaviors and outcomes at work that competent observers can agree constitute necessary standards of excellence to be achieved in order for the individual and the organization to both accomplish their goals.'

A similar definition of performance is provided by Campbell et al. (1970) as indicative of the value attributed to particular behaviours by an organization that leads to the attainment of important organizational goals. Campbell et al. stress that performance is thus more than simply behaviour, it is behaviour imbued with significance and value by an organization because of what it leads to. Performance occurs in the context of a job, position or role in an organization and, they argue, can be differentiated from the outcomes of performance. Performance is not the consequence or result of job behaviour, it is *the act itself* (e.g. preparing a tender document). The consequences of performance may not ultimately reflect the unique contributions of one particular employee (e.g. the tender document). Many factors influence performance outcomes, some of which are not under the control of the individual employee (e.g. lack of appropriate tools or resources, financial considerations).

The distinction between performance and performance outcomes may, in many respects, appear problematic since the act of performing may not necessarily be observable (e.g. information-processing and decision-making) and thus may only be evident in its effects. Campbell (1990) is adamant, however, that performance is a process of behaving that can be assessed independently of its outcomes, irrespective of whether it is directly observable. Thus, decision-making processes can be operationalized independently of the final decision and also the outcome of that decision. Campbell (1990) also differentiates performance from effectiveness and productivity. *Effectiveness*, he says, refers to an 'evaluation of the results of performance', whilst *productivity* is defined as 'the ratio of effectiveness to the cost of achieving that level of effectiveness' (p.705).

These differences in definition illustrate the various difficulties inherent in assessing performance and performance outcomes in organizations, i.e. the *criterion* used to evaluate performance.

8.2 The criterion issue

Much organizational research is concerned (at least in part) with the notion of 'performance', whether at the individual, group (e.g. team or department) or organizational level of analysis. It is often critically important to the organization participating in a research venture that a 'bottom-line' assessment of performance is provided as one of the project outcomes or deliverables. Within many of the applied social sciences, too, prediction of performance and performance outcomes can demonstrate the *practical value* of research findings. Each of the following research questions contains the implicit assumptions that performance/outcome criteria are available, accessible and usable:

- The degree of cohesiveness reported by any given team will lead directly to that team's effectiveness within an organizational setting;
- Adopting a participative management style will lead to improved employee performance at departmental level;
- Salespeople reporting a greater degree of extroversion will achieve a higher proportion of sales conversions over a given time period;
- Organizations employing progressive HRM policies will gain greater market share over a 5-year period within the IT industry;
- Employee integrity is directly related to employee reliability (i.e. lateness and absence from work).

These examples demonstrate that performance/outcome research can take place at different levels of analysis, i.e. individual employee, team or group, and at macro organizational levels. There exist various ways and means of evaluating 'performance' at each of these levels and each brings with it its own inherent shortcomings and 'contaminants'. Herein lies the criterion problem.

Table 8.1 provides some examples of performance/outcome criteria pertinent to each level of organizational analysis.

Table 8.1 Typical performance/outcome criteria at various levels of analysis

	Individual	Group/team	Organizational
Performance/ outcome criterion	Sales achieved Absence rate Lateness Supervisor rating	Cohesiveness Adaptability Use of resources Production output	Sales volume Market share Return on investment Profit

As can be seen from Table 8.1, many of the criteria selected could fall into more than one category, e.g. sales achieved could be equally relevant at the individual, group or organizational level. Absence and lateness rates could also be assessed at all three levels. Supervisor ratings, too, could be used at the individual and team levels.

In order to assess whether any given criterion of performance/outcome is useful at a particular level of analysis, it should be subjected to the following critical analysis:

- **Objectivity** – the score on a criterion should be the same whoever measures it;
- **Reliability/validity** – the score on a criterion should be related to performance and performance alone, i.e. it should be indicative of performance at work (valid) and should not be affected by factors other than performance (reliable);
- **Discriminability** – the criterion should be able to discriminate *fairly* between different levels of performance;
- **Accessibility** – the criterion should be readily available and accessible.

For many of the criteria listed in Table 8.1, however, upholding these principles is not as straightforward as it might seem. Take, for example, absenteeism as a criterion of effectiveness. As a criterion, absenteeism should be **objective**, as long as the process for recording absenteeism is sound and not open to error. However, absenteeism is unlikely to be a **reliable** indicator of effectiveness since it can be affected by influences outside of 'performance' or 'effectiveness', such as sickness, training or study time, holiday or compassionate leave. This, of course, leads to questions being raised as to the criterion's **validity** – if absenteeism can be affected by these external factors, is it really measuring effectiveness and effectiveness alone? Again, this would depend on the system used to collect that information. Absenteeism, if data are collected fairly and objectively, should represent a criterion which is able to **discriminate** between different levels of effectiveness, e.g. one employee taking 25 absent days per year (low effectiveness), compared to one taking zero absent days in that same year (higher effectiveness). Finally, absence data may be fairly easily **accessible** to the researcher, via personnel records. However, if the researcher is collecting confidential information from project participants, whose anonymity is therefore guaranteed, cross-referencing these data with absence levels will be more difficult.

Supervisory appraisal ratings provide another example. Such ratings are unlikely to be **objective**, since different supervisors may exhibit different biases when appraising staff (e.g. 'halo' effect – for more on this, see Section 8.3.2, below). Because of this, appraisal ratings may not be **reliable**, since other influences (e.g. supervisors' perceptual biases) are affecting judgement on the criterion. **Validity** may, therefore, not be guaranteed since the rating may not be a true and accurate representation of performance. Finally, it may be that the scale on which the employee is appraised is so restrictive as to minimize the capacity of the scale to **discriminate** between employees. All of these drawbacks can be overcome if a high-quality appraisal system is in place. Objectivity can be achieved by training supervisors in the appraisal process, providing objective 'behavioural anchors' against which to judge employee performance. Reliability can be improved again by training supervisors to be aware of the various contaminating biases which can creep into the appraisal process. With a more objective and reliable appraisal system which maps directly on to job success by linking the appraisal with a thorough job analysis, the validity of the rating as an indicator of job performance is likely to increase. Finally, by providing objective behavioural anchors against which to judge success, the rating is more likely to discriminate fairly between employees. Section 8.3.2, below, discusses these issues in greater depth.

These examples illustrate the importance of the *quality* of performance/outcome data made available to the researcher. Without investigating how certain indicators of performance/effectiveness are measured and reported, it is impossible for the researcher to determine whether or not those indicators are useful criteria against which to judge individual, group or organizational performance/effectiveness. The following sections outline some of the advantages and disadvantages of assessing performance/outcomes at each level of analysis – individual, group and organizational.

8.3 Individual performance

8.3.1 Objective measures

Dipboye et al. (1994) report that objective measures of performance/effectiveness are commonly regarded as the most useful, and the least contaminated by error. They cite examples such as a typist's typing speed (number of words typed per minute), a forester's speed of felling trees (number of trees felled per hour) and a salesperson's financial sales per unit time as examples of 'objective' outcome measures of performance.

In IT-led industries, there is now an increasing use of technology to collect objective individual-level performance outcome data routinely. For example, in the call-centre industry, information can be collected on the amount of time a telephone agent spends at different stages of the calling process, e.g. time spent on the call itself, time spent writing up notes on the call, and time spent out of the system for breaks, etc. These data may be collected and collated by computer, are fed back to management and, via the appraisal process, to telephone agents themselves. It could be argued that the collection of such rich and complex data represents true assessment of the 'process' of performance, since an individual's behaviour at each stage of the job task can be objectively assessed and built up into a picture of specific, as well as overall, performance.

However, whilst such data are quantitative (making statistical analysis more straightforward for the researcher), there are some significant drawbacks to the use of certain criteria. These drawbacks should lead the researcher back to the four-point criterion evaluation checklist presented above, whenever a criterion is required as part of a research project. The researcher should be sure that a criterion is, as far as possible, collected **objectively**, is **reliable** and **valid**, **discriminates** fairly between employees and is **accessible** for analysis.

Detailed performance and performance outcome data, as collected routinely within many IT companies, may raise ethical issues for the researcher, since obtaining this level of information on the behaviour of individuals at work could be argued to constitute a contravention of human rights. It is also important that the researcher is sure precisely how a specific criterion, e.g. average call length for a call-centre telephone agent, is related to the 'performance' of the individual. For example, depending on the context of the job, it may be that average call length is regarded more positively or more negatively as a criterion of performance. If, as is the case for some companies (e.g. Directory Enquiries), average call length is to be reduced to a maximum of, say, 30 seconds per call, the lower the average call length, the higher the 'performance' of the telephone agent. In another part of a call-centre, where agents are required to troubleshoot computer problems, for example, average call length would not be a useful indicator of performance since a shorter call would not necessarily equate to better performance (the caller's problem may not have been solved in the time available). In fact, it could even be argued that call length is not a particularly *reliable* assessment of even the Directory Enquiries telephone agent's effectiveness, since there are likely to be a number of factors outside the control of the agent which will contribute to total call time (competence of caller in asking for information; availability of information via computer system; differences in speed of callers' natural speaking styles, etc.). Again, the researcher must refer to the criterion checklist outlined in Section 8.2 to ascertain the utility of the available criteria.

Certain objective performance/effectiveness criteria are fairly commonly used. These include absenteeism and sales criteria. According to Hammer and Landau (1981), however, three problems beset absenteeism measures:

- **Criterion contamination:** e.g. absence can be voluntary or involuntary;
- **Instability:** i.e. organizational factors can influence absence rates differently for different employees with the result that absence measures are highly unreliable;
- **Skewing of distributions:** e.g. there are often many employees with no or only a few absences across the year, resulting in reduced power for significance tests.

As noted in Section 8.1, then, absenteeism as a measure of performance effectiveness is problematic, particularly in terms of its reliability and validity (does a measure of absence assess effectiveness and effectiveness alone, or are other factors involved?). The problem of anonymity (i.e. cross-referencing a project participant's confidential responses to a questionnaire with his/her personnel files) can be overcome by asking participants to self-report their absence levels over a given time period. Clearly, however, this introduces a number of additional sources of error, including, amongst others, social desirability (most employees want to present themselves in the most positive light possible and may therefore underestimate their true absence rate) and memory (participants may not be able to recall their absence rates accurately over a 6- or 12-month period), again throwing into question the reliability of this source of performance data.

Sales criteria are outcome measures with much appeal, but are again open to a number of contaminants. Sales success is a function of both *individual* skill and *environmental* factors, suggesting their unreliability as outcome measures. Because of this, it may be very difficult to compare sales achieved across individuals if external factors (e.g. geographical location – comparing sales representatives operating in London and the far south-west of England, for example) have a marked effect on the criterion.

8.3.2 Subjective measures

Because of the problems outlined above as regards objective measures, organizations often rely heavily on appraisal *ratings* in order to assess the performance and effectiveness of their employees (Dipboye et al., 1994). However, these are inherently subjective measures and, as will be shown, are also open to a wide range of contaminants. Graphic rating scales, an example of which is shown in Table 8.2, represent the most common usage of ratings for supervisory or managerial appraisals. Indeed, Crites (1969) reported that 60% of organizations used rating systems to assess individual employee effectiveness. Table 8.2 presents a number of 'criteria' purporting to assess the effectiveness of a trainer. Each criterion (e.g. 'organization', 'knowledge', 'enthusiasm', etc.) may be rated by the appraiser according to the 5-point scale provided (which ranges from 'Poor' to 'Outstanding').

Table 8.2   Example of a graphical rating scale for evaluating training effectiveness

	Poor	*Marginal*	*Average*	*Above average*	*Outstanding*
Organization	1	2	3	4	5
Responding to questions	1	2	3	4	5
Knowledge	1	2	3	4	5
Enthusiasm	1	2	3	4	5
Use of teaching aids	1	2	3	4	5
Encouragement	1	2	3	4	5

A number of significant drawbacks exist in the use of such graphic rating scales, which can undermine their objectivity, reliability, validity and ability to discriminate. Some of these shortcomings will be introduced below. There are methods available, however, which permit more reliable, valid, objective and fair judgements of employees' performance and effectiveness to be made using rating scales.

A number of 'rating effects' exist which limit the utility of rating scales unless used with great care. These rating effects include:

- **Halo** – occurs when the rater tends to give the same level of rating across all criteria (e.g. in the Table 8.2 example, the same rating would be given across 'enthusiasm', 'encouragement', 'responding to questions', etc.). In many cases, this effect represents an error on the part of the rater in generalizing from a certain level of performance/effectiveness on one criterion to the remainder. It may be, as noted by Cooper (1981), that similar ratings on all criteria may represent a *true* appraisal of performance/effectiveness, and this requires a distinction to be made between '*true* halo' and 'halo *error*'.

- **Central tendency, severity and leniency** – it is often the case that a rater will use only part of a rating scale due to personal preference. For example, some raters may tend to use the central portion of a scale (central tendency), while others restrict themselves to the more positive ratings (leniency) or to the more negative ratings (severity). This leads to reduced objectivity, since ratings cannot be argued to measure criteria in the same way regardless of who is doing the measurement. This source of error also influences the capacity of the scale to discriminate between employees if raters are restricting their judgements to only a narrow range of ratings.

- **Context** – this source of error refers to differences in individual ratings of employees when alone, or when in a group setting. Depending on the relative performance/effectiveness of the group, *contrast* effects could influence the rating attributed to an individual employee. For example, if two individuals receive moderate–good appraisals when appraised alone, placing one in a poorly–performing group and the other in a high-performing group may result in the rater contrasting those individuals with the rest of the group and reporting inaccurately high or low group-level appraisals respectively for these employees. This effect may undermine the reliability (and also validity) of the rating process.

- **Similar-to-me** – these effects, which impact on the reliability and objectivity of rating scales, involve the rater making judgements as to the similarity or dissimilarity of the ratee to him/herself and allowing these comparisons to affect judgement of performance or effectiveness, e.g. reporting more positive judgements of those employees with similar backgrounds or political beliefs, or who attended the same educational institutions, etc.

Despite these various rater effects, it is possible to improve the utility of subjective rating scales markedly via a number of means, outlined below:

- **Provide a comprehensive definition of the criterion for judgement**. For example, rather than relying on 'enthusiasm' as a criterion for judging trainer effectiveness, this could be extended to 'Enthusiasm of the trainer in communicating course material to delegates; ability of the trainer to enthuse and 'energize' delegates with his/her presentation of material.'

- Linked to this, the **rating scale** (i.e. the 1–5 rating value and associated descriptors, e.g. 'Outstanding') **can be redesigned to be 'behaviourally anchored'**. This means that, instead of relying on single word descriptors to assess performance, the rater can be provided with a more comprehensive definition of each level of effectiveness and the *behavioural* indicators associated with each. For example, in addition to using the definition 'poor', the scale could include example behaviours such as *'Shows little interest in the training material. Does not vary pitch of voice, or use gesture to enliven presentation. Makes little effort to engage directly with delegates in order to catch their interest.'* At the opposite end of the scale, behavioural descriptors of 'Outstanding' could include *'Makes repeated efforts to engage delegates' interest at group and individual levels as appropriate. Uses a variety of verbal and non-verbal techniques (e.g. gesture, movement, appropriate tone) in presenting material. Appears to have, and communicates, a genuine interest in the material.'*

- Ensuring that **all raters are trained** using the same material, and are periodically appraised in their use of rating scales by third party observers;

- **Drawing on existing job incumbents to develop scale definitions, descriptions and behavioural anchors**.

Given that many forms of subjective rating scale currently in use in organizations do not uphold all (or perhaps any) of the above guidelines, the researcher must remain aware of the limited utility of these data when attempting to assess performance or effectiveness at the individual level.

8.4 Group performance

8.4.1 'Groups' and 'teams'

Schein (1988) defines a group as any number of people who (1) interact with one another; (2) are psychologically aware of one another; and (3) perceive themselves to be a group. Groups are a way of structuring roles and activities to achieve organizational goals. This assumes that many organizational goals cannot be achieved by individuals acting alone.

A group does not, however, necessarily operate as a **team**. The word 'team' describes a *dynamic* operating within a group which may exist within a range of organizational contexts. The term has become widely used within applied social

,ciences literature, particularly over the past 10 years. Current pressure to downsize organizations, resulting in a flattening of organizational structures and a focus on more flexible forms of working, arguments about the empowerment of employees and the interdependence between individuals which is said to characterize most modern, semi-automated work has brought about an emphasis on the work of the team.

Adair (1986) has described work teams as a collection of people who share most, if not all, of the following characteristics:

- A definable membership;
- Group consciousness;
- A sense of shared purpose;
- Interdependence;
- Interaction;
- Ability to act in a unitary manner.

Whether the researcher is interested in the performance or effectiveness of work 'groups' or 'teams', assessing performance at this level brings with it a range of methodological considerations.

8.4.2 Conceptualizing performance and effectiveness

At group or team level, performance and effectiveness have been conceptualized in a variety of ways, each of which has important implications for methods used to assess performance.

Poulton and West (1993) developed a model of team effectiveness built on the concepts of *performance* and *viability*. Team *performance* is defined as the achievement of agreed extrinsic targets in combination with consumer acceptability of the team product or service. Team *viability* refers to *internal* team health and efficiency, team spirit, confidence, trust, communication and support, and comprises the following factors:

- **Team vision and objectives** refer to the focus and direction of the team. Do team members all aspire to one goal? Are they all motivated to achieve this goal?
- **Participative safety** refers to two things: a democratic style of decision making and management and a co-operative team culture. A democratic management style signifies information sharing, regular interaction and influence over decision making. A co-operative team culture will be experienced as supportive and non-threatening.
- **Commitment to excellence** refers to a shared concern for quality of task performance and service. This involves individual and team accountability for setting and monitoring performance/service standards, constructive debate and explicit commitment to a quality service or performance level.

- **Support innovation** refers to the encouragement of initiation and development of new ideas and ways of working. This may translate into support for continuing education or professional development, and allowing the development of specialist interests amongst team members.

In an alternative conceptualization of team effectiveness (but one which shows some overlap with Poulton and West's 1993 model), Harper and Harper (1991) suggest ten key elements of high-performing teams:

- Goals are understood and committed to;
- A climate of trust;
- Open and honest communication among members;
- A sense of belonging and pride in accomplishments;
- Diversity of opinions and ideas is encouraged;
- Creativity and risk-taking are encouraged;
- Team is constantly learning and improving itself;
- Procedures are developed to diagnose, analyse and solve problems;
- Participative leadership is practised;
- Decisions are supported and made together.

Finally, Woodcock (1989) suggests a number of 'building blocks' for effective teamwork, including:

- Balanced roles;
- Clear objectives and agreed goals;
- Openness;
- Support and trust;
- Co-operation;
- Sound procedures and processes;
- Appropriate leadership;
- Regular review and evaluation;
- Individual development;
- Good inter-group relations;
- Good communication.

As suggested by Poulton and West (1993) with their assessment of team 'performance', it is clearly possible to assess team effectiveness in terms of 'bottom-line' output or results, depending on the nature of the team and the tasks its members are required to undertake on a daily basis. Sales teams, for example, could be assessed in terms of total sales revenue generated over a 3- or 12-month period, for example. Production teams could be assessed in terms of unit output per day or week. Design teams could be assessed in terms of the quality and quantity of designs generated over a given period. In all these cases, however, the four critical criteria for evaluating performance/effectiveness indicators must be considered.

8.4.3 Measuring group performance and effectiveness

The previous section outlines some alternative attempts to conceptualize team performance in the workplace. A wide variety of methods for assessing performance outcomes and effectiveness at the group level is available to the researcher and a selection is outlined below, together with their associated advantages and drawbacks.

Self-report questionnaires
These can be used to assess various elements of team effectiveness and are usually administered to all members of a team independently of one another. Moxon (1993) lists various self-report questionnaires for: assessing group and team effectiveness; interpersonal processes; team 'climate'; effectiveness of team meetings; and team leadership. Guzzo et al. (1993) developed a self-report measure of team 'potency', comprising items similar to those listed below:

- This team believes it can produce high-quality work;
- This team feels it can solve any problems it encounters;
- This team has little confidence in itself;
- This team believes it can be very productive;
- Some tasks are too tough for this team;
- This team can get a lot done when it works hard;
- This team does not expect to have a lot of influence;
- This team has the capability to work well together.

Whilst self-report measures such as these can provide useful insights into team effectiveness in all sorts of areas, as with all self-report measures there are various drawbacks to their use. Firstly, they rely on the ability of the respondent to introspect and to reflect on the area of questioning. Secondly, they are open to a wide range of response biases including leniency, severity, social desirability, central tendency, etc. Thirdly, when providing an overall assessment of a team, it is common to report **aggregated** performance ratings by taking mean ratings across all respondents. This is unlikely to represent the views of all team members accurately and can reduce findings to an unrepresentative amalgam of very disparate views from within the team.

A separate issue also needs to be considered when adopting an **evaluative** approach to team-based research (particularly if comparing team members' ratings of a specific element of effectiveness both before and after an organizational event or intervention). This involves the difference between alpha, beta and gamma change:

- **Alpha change** is the shift in numerical rating that reflects real change in the target of the intervention;
- **Beta change** is a 'recalibration' of the scale in the light of new experience gained from the intervention;
- **Gamma change** is the redefinition of the construct underlying the scale.

By way of example, a team could be asked to evaluate a team-building intervention designed to improve openness of communication between team members, using a rating scale ranging from 1 (very closed) to 7 (very open). If the pre-intervention rating was 6 and the post-intervention rating 4, what does this tell us about the relative success of the intervention?

- If the shift reflects an **alpha change**, the team would perceive that its previous openness had been lessened due directly to the intervention itself;

- However, if the shift reflects a **beta change**, the team could have redefined the scale in the light of new knowledge and experience. Whereas they had perceived their openness as fairly high before the intervention, their experience during the intervention had led them to the conclusion that their openness was, in fact, low pre-intervention (maybe a rating of 2) and that they had now improved from that recalibrated score to 4, but still had some way to go.

- If the shift reflects a **gamma change**, the group may have previously conceived of openness in communication as providing information when asked. The team saw itself as a 6 in this area. On completion of the intervention, the team had redefined its entire conceptualization of 'openness' as comprising a wider range of behaviours, with a less positive overall rating as a result.

Organizational researchers using self-report measures to assess performance at group or team level should remain vigilant for the appearance of these possible sources of error.

Observation

An observational method for evaluating team effectiveness is 'interaction process analysis' (Bales, 1950). IPA was designed for the observation and analysis of group, or team, interaction. Interaction is broken down into 'acts', e.g. what is said and how it is said. Bales identified twelve mutually exclusive categories of 'act' (see below), covering verbal and non-verbal behaviours and sub-divided into socio-emotional and task-oriented functions. When a group is observed, he argues, it is possible to create an interaction profile indicating the percentages of time spent engaged in each different category of behaviour. Bales and others have argued that teams which focus their time and effort on *both* socio-emotional and task-oriented issues are likely to be the most effective.

Socio-emotional: positive reactions
1. *Shows solidarity*: raises the status of another group member, provides help and reward
2. *Shows tension release*: laughs, jokes, shows satisfaction
3. *Agrees*: shows passive acceptance, concurs, complies

Task: attempted answers

4. *Gives suggestion*: direction, implying autonomy for the other
5. *Gives opinion*: evaluation, analysis, expresses feelings or wish
6. *Gives orientation*: information, repeats, clarifies, confirms

Task: questions

7. *Asks for orientation*: information, repetition, confirmation
8. *Asks for opinion*: evaluation, analysis, expression of feeling
9. *Asks for suggestion*: direction, possible ways of action

Socio-emotional: negative reactions

10. *Disagrees*: shows passive rejection, withholds help
11. *Shows tension*: asks for help, withdraws out of field
12. *Shows antagonism*: deflates others' status, defends or asserts self

As the example of IPA suggests, observational analysis of groups and teams can be extremely intensive for the researcher and may require more than one observer to be tenable. In addition, analysis of observational data is very much open to unreliability and low objectivity due to differences in the way in which different observers categorize data. Chapter 6 outlines some measures for improving reliability and objectivity of observational designs, including the development of a robust coding scheme (similar to that shown above for IPA) and piloting the observational situation as far as possible prior to running the study proper.

Supervisor/managerial ratings

A fairly accessible method for evaluating team performance or effectiveness is that of supervisory/managerial ratings. These methods were discussed in depth in Section 8.3.2, above, with regard to individual performance. Many of the same potential sources of error are present when managerial ratings are applied to team performance, including halo effects and response biases (leniency, severity, central tendency). The presence of particular individuals within teams may also bias the rater into making inaccurate judgements of a team's *overall* effectiveness or performance on any given criterion.

'Bottom-line' performance

'Bottom-line' measures of team performance (e.g. financial indices of effectiveness, production rates, etc.) may appear intuitively attractive as performance criteria since they are likely to yield quantitative data. However, they are open to a range of contaminants. The problem of unreliability can be particularly marked, especially when external factors are able to affect the criterion (e.g. geographical location affecting number of potential leads for a sales team, leading to unfair comparison of teams' overall sales effectiveness). It is crucial, then, for teams to be as similar as possible (thereby controlling for contaminating factors) when comparing them on bottom-line effectiveness.

Production rates, for example, afford a compelling bottom-line index, but much caution and care are required if these are to be used to compare groups or teams. If the following elements are held constant, it may be possible to use such measures to assess differences in level of team effectiveness:

- Opportunity to achieve a certain production level (without locally influenced constraints);
- Representative time-frame (it may be that a 1-month or 3-month period is unrepresentative of production across all comparison groups);
- Level of experience of team members (e.g. teams with new members may exhibit artificially suppressed production rates until a certain level of competence is achieved).

Asking **the team**

Meyer (1994) points out that the best source of data on team effectiveness may well derive from team members themselves. By discussing with team members how performance should be conceptualized and measured, it is likely that a rich source of knowledge will be opened up. This is likely to have the added advantage of gaining 'buy in' from the team to the overall research process. However, such an approach must be handled with sensitivity in order that management is not undermined and that the criteria selected by the team are as robust and measurable as practicable.

8.5 Organizational performance

8.5.1 Linking organizational culture to performance

The various issues surrounding the conceptualization and measurement of performance and effectiveness at the corporate or organizational level are well illustrated with reference to management, sociological and applied psychological research on organizational *culture*.

Organizational culture has gained much management and research interest in the past 20 years. To some degree, this interest reflects contemporary workplace focuses on people and performance. Whilst managers are keen to address 'soft' people issues by introducing intervention programmes such as personal and career development, participative management, team-building, etc., these areas may only be regarded as worthy of attention if they can be shown to *make a significant and measurable difference* to the performance of the organization itself. As a result, many organizational and management specialists have conducted research to address the question of the link between organizational culture and performance. It is widely agreed that organizational performance may manifest itself in a number of ways, dependent on the organization/industry of interest. These indicators have included:

- Staff turnover;
- Staff absenteeism;
- Volume of sales/product;
- Profit;
- Market share;
- Return on investment.

There is a distinction here between commercial and 'people' measures at the organizational level of analysis. While it is true that commercial or fiscal measures are the most commonly used indices of performance for financiers, accountants, bankers and investors, staff measures also provide a useful indication of the state of the workforce and may flag up possible problems looming on the horizon.

Some researchers have attempted to frame organizational culture in terms of 'cultural types' when considering performance in the marketplace (Deal and Kennedy, 1982; Peters and Waterman, 1982). Specific companies have been held up as prime examples of 'successful' and 'high-achieving' organizational cultures. This apparently straightforward relationship was questioned by Ernest (1985), who stated that effective business planning requires an understanding of not only the external competitive environment but also the internal corporate culture, suggesting that there must be a 'fit' between planning and the beliefs, values and practices within the organization. Ernest argued that there is no single cultural 'type' which leads to success, but that organizational plans are often ineffective because of the incompatibility of those plans with organizational culture(s).

Many studies undertaken in the 1970s and early 1980s were keen to develop taxonomies of culture 'types' to describe the components present within companies in the hope of linking those components with organizational outcomes such as performance. Harrison (1972), Deal and Kennedy (1982) and Schein (1985) all produced interesting accounts of culture types, with appealing descriptions of the types of behaviour associated with each:

Deal and Kennedy (1982):
- Tough-guy macho culture;
- Work hard/play hard culture;
- Bet-your-company culture;
- Process culture.

Harrison (1972); Schein (1985)
- Power culture;
- Role culture;
- Achievement culture;
- Support culture.

However, as noted by Furnham and Gunter (1993), these posited cultural systems have proved little more than interpretative intuitions which have yet to be validated.

More recent research has questioned this typological approach and has focused increasingly on the *multi-dimensional* nature of organizations' cultures, and how separate 'dimensions' of culture may be related to organizational performance. Marcoulides and Heck (1993), for example, examined a number of elements of over 30 US organizations' cultures, including product and service organizations of various sizes, resource types (capital or labour intensive), from both public and private sectors. They found that, when taken together, the cultural dimensions listed below measured at organizational level could predict over 50% of the following performance indicators:

- Volume (gross revenue: product value);
- Share (extent of penetration into potential customer base);
- Profit (revenue: costs);
- Return (profit: assets and equity invested).

The cultural dimensions together predicting these elements of performance included:

- Propriety of criteria for, and distribution of, remuneration;
- Managers taking an interest in employee welfare and performance;
- Attitudes of staff towards loyalty and commitment;
- Extent to which staff believe management involve them in decisions;
- Degree of communication flow across the organization;
- Pressure imposed on staff;
- Means for evaluating employee performance.

Zamanou and Glaser (1994) measured six dimensions of organizational culture (teamwork, supervision, morale, involvement, information flow and meetings), before and after a 2-year intervention to improve teamwork, participation and communications training across the company. They found that all six dimensional scores improved significantly pre- and post-intervention, as did the following: sick leave reduced from 35,000 hours to 24,000 hours (32% reduction); associated cost of absenteeism reduced from $349,000 to $254,000 (27% reduction), despite a 4% increase in the number of employees (311 to 322).

8.5.2 Measuring performance at organizational level

The above example of organizational culture and performance illustrates some of the means used to operationalize performance at the organizational level. Commonly selected criteria include turnover, absence, sales, profit and market share. As with all measures of performance, if the researcher is to draw on a particular criterion, s/he must be satisfied that that criterion is objective, reliable, valid and is able to discriminate fairly between organizations. The principal problems of analysing organizational performance stem from poor reliability (the influence of external factors on the criterion), limited sample sizes, and the associated problem of limited comparability of organizations. Some commonly used measures of performance (together with their advantages and disadvantages) are introduced below.

Turnover

Staff turnover, initially at least, appears to be an important and potentially useful criterion against which to judge organizational effectiveness or performance, due to the high cost of replacing and training new personnel. Moreover, turnover, particularly of key people, can be disruptive at the organizational level. However, the researcher needs to be aware of the various factors at work when considering staff turnover as a possible criterion of organizational effectiveness:

- **External job market** – this varies over time, becoming more or less buoyant in line with other economic factors. The relative availability of other positions in particular industrial sectors will impact on the extent to which staff leave a particular company over a given time period. Clearly, this throws into question the reliability of staff turnover as a criterion unaffected by external factors.

- **Contemporary workplace** – it could be argued that in today's workplace, with the changes in perceived expectations of employees and employers, turnover may become less salient and valid as an indicator of organizational performance. Since many employees are becoming increasingly focused on managing their own careers in the absence of a 'job for life', natural turnover is likely to increase. This does not preclude employees who intend to leave the company from performing highly effectively during their tenure, and so restricts the validity of turnover as a criterion measuring much more than cost associated with recruitment and training.

- **Differences in reporting turnover** – the researcher should also be aware of the variations in how turnover is reported depending on the policy of the organization. This should be identified prior to analysis of organizational performance data to ensure comparability of data.

- **Identity of leavers** – the identity of those leaving an organization will have a varied impact on the overall effectiveness of the firm. Clearly, the loss of less-effective employees will have a less-damaging effect on overall organizational effectiveness than the loss of high-performing and also more senior staff. The loss of senior staff can have a significant disruptive effect on the organization's operation, with a knock-on effect felt from top to bottom of the organization, as noted by Cannella and Hambrick (1993).

Absence

Absence rates, when aggregated to organizational level, can tell the researcher something about the effectiveness of the organization in retaining a certain level of staff resource over time. Clearly, if staff are absent from work, they are unable to contribute to the performance of the organization, making absence rates a fairly valid indicator of effectiveness. However, as with staff turnover, differences in recording absence rates can reduce reliability of the measure (whether or not an organization takes into account sickness, maternity and compassionate leave, and training when assessing absence rates), as can differences in the historical attitudes and 'culture' of organizations in their relative levels of acceptance of a certain amount of unauthorized absence from work (as discussed in depth by Nicholson and Johns, 1985). However, absence data may well be able to provide the researcher with a valuable index of organizational effectiveness as long as care is taken in ensuring that reporting systems (and organizations themselves) are comparable.

Fiscal indicators

Profit, financial turnover of organizations, and other fiscal indicators (e.g. return on investment, market share, etc.) are clearly open to an enormous range of external factors, making them problematic as 'pure' indicators of organizational effectiveness. As Eccles (1991) states, 'the leading indicators of business performance cannot be found in financial data alone.' (appearing in Eccles, 1998: 25). Differences in economic conditions, competition in different sectors, rates of exchange, mergers and acquisitions, and accounting procedures, for example, can all impact enormously on the 'bottom-line' financial performance of an organization. It may be possible, however, to control for some of these external factors by ensuring that financial data are directly comparable from organization to organization (e.g. by making statistical adjustments for differences in end-of-year dates, omitting data on major acquisitions, ensuring that accounting procedures are comparable, etc.). It is important that the researcher is confident of the comparability of such data in order to include them as indicators of performance or effectiveness.

Perceptions of corporate performance

Various writers (Dess and Robinson, 1984; Venkatraman and Ramanujam, 1987) have found that *perceptions* of corporate performance by top management teams are highly correlated with actual financial performance data. This suggests that it may be possible to obtain subjective perceptual data on corporate effectiveness with some confidence, if this information can be obtained from a trusted and reliable source (e.g. senior management).

The 'balanced scorecard'

It is becoming increasingly widely accepted, at least within management research, that 'performance' at the organizational level should take in a variety of disparate indicators in order that a comprehensive understanding of an organization's behaviour and success may be obtained. Chakravarthy (1986),

Dess and Robinson (1984) and Eccles (1991) all concur with this view, which has been described as the 'balanced scorecard' approach (Kaplan and Norton, 1996) to assessing performance at the organizational level of analysis. Such approaches see a variety of measures, including 'bottom-line' indicators such as return on investment or market share, as well as more subjective criteria such as perceptions of customers/shareholders of service quality, employee views of the culture of the company and ratings of the effectiveness of organizational processes, being used *in combination* to provide a broad overview of organizational effectiveness. Of course, the breadth of such an approach should in no way detract from the rigour required to assess the utility of available criteria. Once again, the researcher must remain vigilant for evidence of objectivity, reliability, validity and ability to discriminate fairly in criteria obtained within a balanced scorecard framework.

8.6 Conclusion

Performance, then, is a critical issue within organizational settings, for both academic researchers and for client organizations. This section is intended to provide the prospective researcher with a brief introduction to the performance criterion issue within organizational settings. It is hoped that the introductory treatment of each level of performance measurement (individual, group, organizational) will provide a starting point for those researchers wishing to incorporate performance measures into their research designs. In order to obtain a more in-depth treatment of these issues, the reader is referred to the texts presented in Section 8.7.

8.7 References and further reading

The performance criterion issue

Bechtoldt, H.P. (1947). Factorial investigation of the perceptual-speed factor. *American Psychologist, 2*, 304–305.

Borman, W.C. (1991). Job behavior, performance, and effectiveness. In M.D. Dunnette and L.M. Hough (Eds.), *Handbook of Industrial and Organizational Psychology, Vol. 2* (Second Edition). Palo Alto, CA: Consulting Psychologists Press.

Campbell, J.P. (1990). Modeling the performance prediction problem in industrial and organizational psychology. In M.D. Dunnette and L.M. Hough (Eds.), *Handbook of Industrial and Organizational Psychology, Vol. 2* (Second Edition). Palo Alto, CA: Consulting Psychologists Press.

Campbell, J.P. and Campbell, R.J. (1988). *Productivity in Organizations: New Perspectives from Industrial and Organizational Psychology*. San Francisco, CA: Jossey-Bass.

Campbell, J.P., Dunnette, M.D., Lawler, E.E. and Weick, K.E. (1970). *Managerial Behavior, Performance and Effectiveness*. New York: McGraw-Hill.

Schneider, B. and Schmitt, N. (1986). *Staffing Organizations* (Second Edition). Glenview, IL: Scott, Foresman.

Individual performance/effectiveness

Cooper, W.H. (1981). Ubiquitous halo. *Psychological Bulletin, 90,* 218–244.

Crites, J.O. (1969). *Vocational Psychology.* New York: McGraw-Hill.

Dipboye, R.L., Smith, C.S. and Howell, W.C. (1994). *Understanding Industrial and Organizational Psychology: an Integrated Approach.* Fort Worth, TX: Harcourt Brace.

Hammer, T.H. and Landau, J.C. (1981). Methodological issues in the use of absence data. *Journal of Applied Psychology, 66, 5,* 574–581.

Group performance/effectiveness

Adair, J. (1986). *Effective Teambuilding.* Aldershot, UK: Gower.

Bales, R.F. (1950). *Interaction Process Analysis: a Method for the Study of Small Groups.* Chicago, IL: University of Chicago Press.

Guzzo, R.A., Yost, P.R., Campbell, R.J. and Shea, G.P. (1993). Potency in groups: articulating a construct. *British Journal of Social Psychology, 32, 1,* 87–106.

Harper, B. and Harper, A. (1991). *Succeeding as a Self-Directed Work Team: 20 Important Questions Answered.* Croton-on-Hudson, NY: MW Corporation.

Meyer, C. (1994). How the right measures help teams excel. *Harvard Business Review, 72, 3,* 95–97.

Moxon, P. (1993). *Building a Better Team.* Aldershot, UK: Gower.

Poulton, B. and West, M. (1993). Effective multi-disciplinary team work in primary health care. *Journal of Advanced Nursing, 18,* 918–925.

Schein, E.H. (1988). *Organizational Psychology* (Third Edition). London, UK: Prentice-Hall.

Woodcock, M. (1989). *Team Development Manual* (Second Edition). Aldershot, UK: Gower.

Organizational performance/effectiveness

Cannella, A.A., Jr and Hambrick, D.C. (1993). Effects of executive departures on the performance of acquired firms. *Strategic Management Journal, 14,* 137–152.

Chakravarthy, B.S. (1986). Measuring strategic performance. *Strategic Management Journal, 7, 5,* 437–458.

Deal, T. and Kennedy, A. (1982). *Corporate Cultures.* Reading, MA: Addison-Wesley.

Dess, G.G. and Robinson, R.B., Jr (1984). Measuring organizational performance in the absence of objective measures: the case of the privately-held firm and conglomerate business unit. *Strategic Management Journal, 5, 3,* 265–273.

Eccles, R.G. (1991). The performance measurement manifesto. *Harvard Business Review, 69, 1,* 131–137.

Eccles, R.G. (1998). The performance measurement manifesto, reprint 91103. In the *Harvard Business Review on Measuring Corporate Performance, 25–45.* Boston, MA: Harvard Business School Press.

Ernest, R.C. (1985). Corporate cultures and effective planning. *Personnel Administrator, 30, 3,* 49–60.

Furnham, A. and Gunter, B. (1993). *Corporate Assessment: Auditing a Company's Personality.* London, UK: Routledge.

Harrison, R. (1972). Understanding your organization's character. *Harvard Business Review, 50, 23*, 119–128.

Kaplan, R.S and Norton, D.P. (1996). Using the balanced scorecard as a strategic management system. *Harvard Business Review, 74, 1*, 75–85.

Marcoulides, G.A. and Heck, R.H. (1993). Organizational culture and performance: proposing and testing a model. *Organization Science, 4, 2*, 209–225.

Nicholson, N. and Johns, G. (1985). The absence culture and the psychological contract: who's in control of absence? *Academy of Management Review, 10, 3*, 397–407.

Peters, T. and Waterman, R. (1982). *In Search of Excellence*. New York: Harper, Row.

Schein, E.H. (1985). *Organizational Culture and Leadership: a Dynamic View*. San Francisco, CA: Jossey-Bass.

Venkatraman, N. and Ramanujam, V. (1987). Measurement of business economic performance: an examination of method convergence. *Journal of Management, 13, 1*, 109–122.

Zamanou, S. and Glaser, S.R. (1994). Moving towards participation and involvement: managing and measuring organizational culture. *Group and Organization Management, 19, 4*, 475–502.

9 Data Analysis

9.1 Introduction

Data analysis frightens a lot of students (and practitioners) in the social sciences. Particularly when words such as 'multivariate analysis', 'multiple regression' or even 'statistics' are mentioned. In our experience, data analysis presents one of the most significant stumbling blocks to successful completion of any research project whether of an academic or commercial nature. A researcher can have shown exemplary planning skills, a thorough grasp of the theoretical underpinnings of their research area, excellent interpersonal skills to formulate a research plan with both supervisor and client contact, and have obtained rich, usable data from a representative sample of the target organizational population. These issues are all vitally important to good research. But if the researcher is then unable to analyse his/her data effectively, all the best practice principles employed to that point run the risk of going to waste.

Without understanding how to analyse data, a researcher will not be able to interpret that data, nor draw any conclusions or recommendations from it. S/he will not be able to assess the effectiveness of his/her research design, and will be prevented from presenting anything meaningful to his/her client or supervisor. It is for these reasons that data analysis forms a lynchpin of the research process. And it is critical to understand that statistics are not confined to the world of academia. In the 'real world' of consultancy, it is often an organizational researcher's grasp of data analysis and statistics that differentiates him or her from other consultants, or at least from less competent ones.

Within the specific boundaries of a research project, data analysis is critical to success. Indeed, at the outset of the project, a good researcher should consider possible types of analysis as a necessary stage in the planning process, particularly if this will require some background reading on a particular technique, or will necessitate obtaining a particular software package, for example. However, as with the selection of a design approach to address a research question, the researcher should *not adapt the research question to fit an analytical technique* with which s/he is confident or s/he prefers. Instead, consideration of possible analytic techniques is necessary since it may influence the measurement approach adopted for the research. A large number of analytical approaches are available to the researcher, some qualitative in nature, others quantitative. Almost all of these are straightforward to use (with some background reading where necessary) but all require an appreciation and understanding of when and why they should be used; that is, when are they appropriate and why should they be selected over other methods?

It is beyond the scope of this text to present a comprehensive introduction to statistical analysis, its mathematical basis or theoretical explanations of the formulaic underpinnings of the discipline. Indeed, we must assume for brevity's sake that the reader has a fairly comprehensive knowledge of statistics and of SPSS for Windows, and feels competent in both areas. For those who need a refresher in statistical theory, please refer to Clegg (1983), Howell (1998) or Robson (1994). It is also beyond our scope here to treat in great depth the various procedures and tests which will be introduced below. Instead, this section will present the researcher with:

- A suggested structure for deciding on test/analysis types;
- A guide to selection and interpretation of bivariate- and multivariate-derived data, with suggestions for further reading;
- More detailed information on some specific approaches to data analysis from both quantitative and qualitative perspectives, including multi-dimensional scalogram analysis, content analysis, meta-analysis and structural equation modelling.

9.2 Statistical data analysis: finding a test

The following plan outlines the process required to identify the most efficient statistical test or tests for any research-derived *quantitative* data. Some special cases of qualitative data analysis are dealt with separately in Sections 9.4 and 9.5, below. The first five points should be addressed prior to data collection – they are important since they may serve to frame the measurement approach you adopt to collect the data. They will also feed into later selection of an analytic strategy. The latter three points apply following data collection and lead directly into selection of an analytical technique.

1. Identify what type of research you are undertaking, e.g. hypothesis testing, inferring statistical robustness of a psychometric tool, exploring data, evaluating an intervention of some sort;

2. Identify the type of data you have obtained – are these data categorical, ordinal or interval in nature? (see glossary for a definition of 'levels of measurement');

3. If hypothesis testing, decide whether one- or two-tailed tests are most appropriate to answer the research question;

4. Identify dependent and independent variables (DVs and IVs);

5. Conduct a power analysis (see Chapter 7 for more on this), prior to collecting your data – this will provide you with a good idea of the sample sizes necessary to ensure accuracy of statistical tests;

6. Screen the data for missing values, outliers and types of distribution (normal, skewed, kurtotic, etc.) and clean data where necessary via transformation and/or exclusion;

7. Identify sample sizes contained within your data (total sample size, group sizes, etc.);

8. Decide on the test you wish to use.

Deciding on the most appropriate test (stage 8) rests very much on the responses to the other seven points, as well as the quality of the data collected by the study.

Finding an appropriate test

Fundamental questions which will narrow the search for a suitable test include:

*   Whether your data are categorical, ordinal or interval level. Only interval - level data can draw on parametric tests; other data types are restricted to non-parametric tests;

*   Whether you are interested in only one variable (requiring univariate tests), two variables (requiring bivariate tests) or more than two variables (requiring multivariate tests).

Having answered these questions, you should be able to identify the test or tests most appropriate to your aims and data. You can do this by answering the following questions:

1. Are you interested in *differences* between groups, e.g. pre- and post-intervention, or between work teams? If so, possible tests will include:

Differences between two groups only by level of data:
*   ***t*-tests** – if data are *interval* (unrelated samples *t*-tests are used where the samples are unmatched; related, where samples are matched or include the same participants);
*   **Mann–Whitney *U* or Wilcoxon** – if data are *ordinal* (Mann–Whitney *U* for independent groups, Wilcoxon for related groups);
*   **McNemar change test or Chi-square test of independence** – if data are *nominal* (McNemar change test for related groups, Chi-square test of independence for independent groups).

*Differences between **more than two groups** by level of data:*
- **ANOVA (analysis of variance) or MANOVA** – if data are *interval* [whether ANOVA (repeated measures for related groups, one-way ANOVA for independent groups) or MANOVA is selected will depend on the number of independent and dependent variables of interest – if two or more of each, MANOVA will be required];
- **Kruskal–Wallis or Friedman** – if data are *ordinal* (Kuskal–Wallis if independent groups, Friedman if related groups);
- **Complex chi-square** – if data are nominal.

2. **Are you interested in** *relationships* **between factors/variables**, e.g. between job satisfaction and performance at work? If so, possible tests include:
- **Pearson's product moment correlation co-efficient** – if data are *interval*;
- **Spearman rank correlation co-efficient** – if data are *ordinal*;
- **Phi co-efficient** – if data are *nominal*.

3. **Are you exploring patterns in the data set,** e.g. in a questionnaire measure which purports to tap into various different 'constructs'? If so possible tests include:
- **Exploratory principal components factor analysis** – looks for groups of variables that share common variance, from the assumption that these groupings are 'caused' by the same unobservable (latent) factors. Has some tight restrictions in terms of type, level of data and sample size;
- **Cluster analysis** – groups variables together on the basis of similarity of the patterns of scores on them. Less restrictive than factor analysis in terms of property requirements of the data;
- **Multi-dimensional scaling** – looks for variables that share similar patterns of scores across respondents, and draws a plot of variables so that those responding most similarly are located proximally on the plot. Again, less restrictive than factor analysis. A variation of this technique with even less restrictions on data type is multi-dimensional scalogram analysis (MSA) – see Section 9.5 for an in-depth discussion of this technique.

4. **Are you interested in categorizing participants according to certain characteristics**, e.g. whether two groups of workers are best distinguished by variations in commitment, or by job and organizational tenure?
- **Discriminant function analysis** – requires two or more continuous predictor variables and attempts to categorize cases according to these predictor variables into a categorical dependent variable.

5. **Do you wish to predict one or more outcome factors using the data you have collected**, e.g. predicting individual performance by examining workers' affective reactions to the workplace?

- **Simple regression** – if you have one interval-level predictor variable and one interval-level outcome variable;
- **Multiple regression** – if you have one interval-level outcome variable and more than one interval-, ordinal or categorical-level predictor variable and wish to determine which predictor variable(s) best predict(s) the outcome variable;
- **Logistic regression** – if you have one categorical outcome variable and two or more categorical or interval-level predictor variables and need to determine the best predictor variable(s);
- **Discriminant function analysis** – if you have more than two interval-level predictor variables and a categorical outcome variable.

6. **Do you wish to infer the statistical robustness of a questionnaire scale**, e.g. an existing scale such as the OPQ or 16-PF, or a new scale developed to measure, say, workplace integrity?
- **Alpha, split-half, Guttman reliability analysis** – produces a reliability co-efficient by examining correlations between scale items or between half-scale means;
- **Confirmatory factor analysis** – if the factor structure is established, e.g. with the 16-PF's sixteen personality factors, the number of expected factors can be specified;
- **Exploratory factor analysis** – if the factor structure is unknown, or alternative factor solutions are suspected, can be used to identify patterns of scale items.

9.3 Statistical data analysis: the tests

Tables 9.1 and 9.2 provide the researcher with an *aide-mémoire* as to the use of different forms of bivariate (data pertaining to two variables) and multivariate (data pertaining to more than two variables) statistical analysis, the requirements of each test and some guidance in interpreting test output. For background reading, see the following texts:

Basic statistics
Clegg, F. (1983). *Simple Statistics*. Cambridge, UK: Cambridge University Press.
Howell, D.C. (1998). *Fundamental Statistics for Behavioural Sciences*. - Cincinnati, OH: South Western College Publishing.
Robson, C. 1994). *Experiment, Design and Statistics in Psychology*. London, UK: Penguin.

Bivariate data analysis

Blalock, H.M., Jr. (1988). *Social Statistics* (Second Edition). Singapore: McGraw-Hill.

Fife-Schaw, C. (1995). Bivariate statistical analysis. In G.M. Breakwell, S. Hammond and C. Fife-Schaw (Eds.), *Research Methods in Psychology*. London, UK: Sage Publications.

Minium, E.W., King, B.M. and Bear, G. (1993). *Statistical Reasoning in Psychology and Education*. New York: John Wiley and Sons.

Multivariate data analysis

Hair, J.F., Anderson, R.E., Tatham, R.L. and Black, W.C. (1992). *Multivariate Data Analysis*. New York: Macmillan.

Hammond, S. (1995). Introduction to multivariate data analysis. In G.M. Breakwell, S. Hammond and C. Fife-Schaw (Eds.), *Research Methods in Psychology*. London, UK: Sage Publications.

Nesselroade, J.R. and Cattell, R.B. (Eds.) (1988). *Handbook of Multivariate Experimental Psychology* (Second Edition). London, UK: Plenum Press.

Tabachnick, B.G. and Fidell, L.S. (1996). *Using Multivariate Statistics* (Third Edition). New York: Harper Collins College Publishers.

Table 9.1   Bivariate data analysis: applications, restrictions and interpretation

Test	Used to ...	Requirements/restrictions
t-test	Examine differences between two groups of participants, e.g. before and immediately after an organizational intervention	DV interval- or ratio-level Sensitive to outliers Dependent variable normally distributed
Mann–Whitney *U* test	Examine differences between two independent groups of participants	DV ordinal level
Wilcoxon test	Examine differences between two related groups of participants	DV ordinal level
McNemar change test	Examine differences between two related groups of participants	DV nominal level
Chi-square test of independence	Examine differences between two independent groups of participants	DV nominal level
ANOVA	Examine variable differences between more than two groups of participants, e.g. before, immediately after and 4 months after an organizational intervention; the likelihood of staff in each of three departments to leave the company	DV interval- or ratio-level Sensitive to outliers DV normally distributed Each group randomly sampled from the population Linear relationships between all dependent variables

Test	Used to …	Requirements/restrictions
Phi co-efficient	Examine relationships between two variables	Nominal level variables
Spearman rank correlation co-efficient	Examine relationships between two variables	Ordinal level variables
Correlational analysis	Examine relationships between two variables, e.g. tenure and job satisfaction; perception of organizational communication and production performance; underpins multiple regression and factor analysis	Interval-level variables Linear relationship between variables

Table 9.2   Multivariate data analysis: applications, restrictions and interpretation

Test	Used to…	Requirements/restrictions
Multiple regression	Predict outcomes, using one or more predictor variables, e.g. predicting staff turnover from age, organizational commitment, rating of supervisor	Interval-level DV Linear relationship between variables Homoscedasticity (residuals and variables should be normally distributed) Large sample (see Chapter 7 for more on sampling issues)
Exploratory factor analysis (principal components)	Explore patterns in a data set by examining correlations between variables and describing these patterns as parsimoniously as possible, e.g. to explore the factor structure of a new measure of corporate identity	Interval-level data Normally distributed data Number of items in analysis should allow for at least 3 items per hypothesized factor Sample should have 3 times the number of members as items Items must adequately cover all areas of the research domain (i.e. be content valid)
Confirmatory factor analysis (principal components or maximum likelihood)	Test the adequacy of a theoretical prediction by examining variable correlations, e.g. to test the factor structure of the 'Big 5' personality dimensions	As above

Test	Used to...	Requirements/restrictions
Hierarchical cluster analysis	Identify homogeneous groups of cases based on selected attributes, e.g. attempting to predict whether or not someone is married according to their age, sociability rating, and total number of friends	Predictor variables must be interval-level and may need to be standardized so that they fall on the same scale
K-means cluster analysis	As for hierarchical cluster analysis, but you must know beforehand how many clusters you expect	Knowledge of expected number of clusters
Discriminant function analysis	Identify the distinguishing characteristics of one or more groups based on several potentially discriminating measures, e.g. identify whether two work teams are best differentiated in terms of cohesiveness or structure	Interval-level data Normal distributions Sensitive to outliers Each group contains >20 people if there are less than 5 predictors No individual can appear in both groups The spread of scores on predictors should be roughly equal
Reliability analysis	Examine the internal consistency of a proposed or existing scale containing a number of given items, e.g. with a new measure of organizational climate, or an existing measure of job satisfaction	Interval-level data Normally-distributed data Construct validity of proposed scale items
Multi-dimensional scaling (not MSA)	Determine the pattern or structure contained in a matrix of observations and present this in a psychologically meaningful way, e.g. by exploring people's representations of their psychological contract at work	Predictor variables must be interval-level Multi-dimensional scalogram analysis (MSA) is a variant of this approach and does not require interval-level data (see Section 9.5 for more information)
MANOVA	Examine differences between more than two groups of participants on more than one variable, i.e. on a combination of variables, thereby addressing variable combinations or interactions by group	DV interval- or ratio-level Sensitive to outliers Dependent variable normally distributed Each group randomly sampled from the population Linear relationships between all dependent variables

9.4 Content analysis

Content analysis is used to analyse transcription data and any other types of data that can be reduced to textual form (e.g. discourses and historical materials). Content analysis can even be used to analyse non-textual data such as works of art and architecture. However, most applied social science applications are concerned with analysing material that can be presented to content analysts in text form. The technique comprises both mechanical and interpretative components (Krippendorf, 1980). The mechanical aspect involves physically organizing and subdividing the data into categories whilst the interpretative component involves determining what categories are meaningful in terms of the questions being asked. The mechanical and interpretative elements are inextricably linked in a reciprocal process involving the researcher switching back and forth between the transcripts and the more conceptual process of developing meaningful coding schemes.

There are three main forms of content analysis: qualitative, quantitative and structural content analysis, each of which is described below.

9.4.1 Qualitative content analysis

This type of content analysis tends to be more subjective and less explicit about the processes by which interpretation of the target material occurs. The emphasis is on meaning rather than on quantification. Initially, the system of classification may be derived from the research question and the topic guide used by the moderator during process facilitation. Additional conceptual codes may arise from a closer examination of the data as a whole. Coded segments may include long exchanges, phrases or sentences. The transcripts are cut and then sorted. Codes can also be developed to signal useful quotations. Following this, a grid which tabulates code on one axis and focus group identifier on the other is constructed that provides a descriptive overview of the data. The aim is to locate quotations to illustrate particular themes or strands of meaning within the transcript. With this form of content analysis, the aim is not normally to assign numerical values to the data.

Computer-assisted approaches to data reduction which are designed to organize textual data can make at least the mechanics of the task much more manageable. The most well known of these is a software package called 'The Ethnograph' (Seidel et al., 1988). Coding is performed on the database and the segments coinciding with each code are then sorted so that all units of data relating to a particular theme can be readily assembled and retrieved.

9.4.2 Quantitative content analysis

This type of content analysis can be used to generate numerical values from the target material. These might be frequencies, rankings or ratings. However, the process by which these values are generated may include elements of qualitative analysis so the qualitative/quantitative distinction is far from clear-cut. Quantitative content analysis is somewhat of a misnomer as it is less a type of analysis than a way of producing data which can then be statistically analysed, i.e. the output of the content analysis is not the end of the analysis process as a whole.

The first stage of quantitative content analysis involves the selection of the material to be analysed – the 'universe' of material. In the case of transcripts of focus groups, for example, this will include all the material that has been collected while running the groups. More generally, the universe of material refers to all the material that is potentially available for analysis. Indeed, the initial definition of the universe of material is common to all forms of content analysis.

The second stage involves the selection of some unit of analysis. Units of analysis are the discrete bits of information that will be assigned to categories in the subsequent analysis. A unit of analysis (or coding unit) can be a word, a theme, a character, an item, time spent on a topic, etc. When the unit of analysis is a word, content analysis may become a relatively simple exercise of counting the occurrences of particular words or types of words (e.g. active versus passive constructions). Although this approach has some advantages, in particular that it can be easily computerized, it is limited in that the meaning of a word can change depending upon the context. A more subtle, though potentially less reliable, approach is to identify themes.

A theme is a statement or proposition about something. Sometimes, themes can be identified by the presence or absence of specific words (e.g. self-referential statements may be identified by the presence of 'I' and 'me'). However, the identification of themes will often require some interpretative action on the part of the coder/s.

In order to conduct a thematic content analysis, the researcher needs to generate a coding frame. The coding frame is a set of categories into which instances will be allocated. The categories should be exhaustive (i.e. all instances can be assigned to a category) and exclusive (i.e. all instances should be assigned to only one category). The coding frame can be developed either on the basis of the substantive content of the target material (e.g. categories could be different types of environmental issue) or on the basis of theoretically determined categories (e.g. internal and external attributions). To some extent, a theoretically derived coding frame is more analytic, whilst a content-derived coding frame is more descriptive. Of course, different coding frames can be applied to the same material.

Thematic content analysis requires an assessment of the reliability of the coding. This is typically done by using more than one coder to code the same material. Inter-rater reliability is then assessed by computing an agreement index such as Cohen's kappa (see Hammond, 1995, for more on this).

Quantification of the material is then required. The output of a content analysis is often the frequency of occurrence of the different coding categories, e.g. how many times does a particular coding category appear in a transcript (or text, etc.). Comparisons between different source materials may then be assessed. However, it is possible to evaluate the content along an ordinal dimension or dimensions. This increases the scope for statistical analysis of the data. Ranking may be used when a number of instances are being analysed, e.g. a researcher could rank focus groups on the degree to which group members used personalized examples to illustrate points in their arguments. Rating scales may also be used in some cases.

9.4.3 Structural content analysis

This type of content analysis involves the development of a representation of the relationships between elements in the target material. In order to do this, both qualitative and quantitative aspects of the data have to be considered.

Structural content analysis is appropriate for the analysis of complex systems of which naturally occurring focus groups are an excellent example. Variants of this approach, such as cognitive mapping (Axelrod, 1976), have often been applied to aspects of decision-making. As well as being relevant to decision-making, this approach is useful for investigating belief systems and social representations. Structural content analysis involves some of the same processes and techniques as are used in quantitative (and qualitative) content analysis. However, the rules governing the relationships between response categories also need to be defined. This allows both qualitative and quantitative aspects of the target material to be represented.

These relational rules will vary depending upon the research aims. Research into political decision-making, for example, might examine belief systems about crime and what should be done about it. As well as being able to examine the effects of group contexts on expressed beliefs, one can compare the belief systems of members of different parties (or other groups), and explore change in the belief systems over time. Relational rules would relate to co-variation and potential causality, e.g. does the political make-up of the group influence the way crime is discussed? Do views on particular policies tend to come from people who believe in certain causes of, or punishments for, crime? etc.

9.4.4 Advantages and disadvantages

Content analysis is not without its problems. It is heavily reliant on the multiple judgements of a single analyst. As the analyst may be (unknowingly or otherwise) keen to find support for a particular view of the data, it is advisable to involve two or more people independently in the coding of the transcripts so that the reliability of the analysis can be systematically assessed.

Other problems include concentrating only on what is mentioned. Sometimes what is not mentioned or strategically side-stepped by a sample of respondents may be as important. If it doesn't appear in a transcript/other written material, it cannot be content analysed. Also, talking about themes in the data in isolation may ignore the complex context in which 'themes' are embedded. In a focus group, for example, content is generated by communication and interaction in the collective sense. Structural content analysis may go some way to dealing with this problem, though the techniques of structural analysis are relatively underdeveloped and, where they are developed, tend to be tailor-made to deal with very specific problems.

9.4.5 References and further reading

Axelrod, R. (1976). *Structure of Decision: the Cognitive Maps of Political Elites*. Princeton, NJ: Princeton University Press.
Cassell, C. and Symon, G. (Eds.) (1994). *Qualitative Methods in Organizational Research: a Practical Guide*. London, UK: Sage Publications.
Hammond, S. (1995). Using psychometric tests. In G.M. Breakwell, S. Hammond and C. Fife-Schaw (Eds.), *Research Methods in Psychology*. London, UK: Sage Publications.
Krippendorf, K. (1980). *Content Analysis: an Introduction to its Methodology*. London, UK: Sage Publications.
Seidel, J., Kjolseth, R. and Seymour, E. (1988). *The Ethnograph: a Program for the Computer-assisted Analysis of Text Based Data*. Littleton, CO: Qualis Research Associates.

9.4.6 Other forms of content analysis

Researchers working within the framework of **discourse analysis** have established specific procedures for handling textual data, which are beyond the scope of this section. The reader is referred to the following sources for pursuit of this particular approach to data analysis:

Potter, J., and Wetherall, M. (1987). *Discourse and Social Psychology: Beyond Attitudes and Behaviour*. London, UK: Sage Publications.
Marshall, H. (1994). Discourse analysis in an occupational context. In C. Cassell and G. Symon (Eds.), *Qualitative Methods in Organizational Research: a Practical Guide*. London, UK: Sage Publications.
Coyle, A. (1995). Discourse analysis. In G.M. Breakwell, S. Hammond and C. Fife-Schaw (Eds.), *Research Methods in Psychology*. London, UK: Sage Publications.

Fantasy theme analysis is a form of discourse analysis based on an entirely different set of epistemological assumptions (Bormann, 1972). It is concerned with how communication affords dramatization (e.g. story telling) which in turn creates social realities for people. Dramatization is of interest only in the collective sense as providing insights into the cultural, emotional and motivational style of a particular community or population of people. The focus group method provides the ideal forum for the investigation of 'dramatized communication'. A detailed consideration of how to conduct fantasy theme analysis can be found in Bormann (1972).

Bormann, H. (1972). Fantasy and rhetorical vision: the rhetorical criticism of social reality. *Quarterly Journal of Speech, 58*, 396–407.

9.5 Multi-dimensional scalogram analysis

9.5.1 Introduction

MSA is a specific type of multi-dimensional scaling developed to allow a flexible exploration of conceptual systems either at the individual or group level (Canter et al., 1985). The focus of the method is to understand the subjective or personal meaning invested in a given subject and is based on the assumption that individuals have a unique way of construing their world. The MSA method is argued to be useful when the research question focuses on the general conceptual processes underlying the explanations people give for behaviour, or on the understanding of categories people use to make sense of their world (Canter et al., 1985).

Canter et al. (1985) argue that the desire for quantitative, computer analysable results places a number of restrictions on data, since data must be collected in a way that is congruent with the procedure used to analyse it, which may or may not be appropriate to the issue being studied. Using open-ended, less-restrictive procedures, they argue, allows participants to express their own views; if these data could also be structured enough to allow systematic analysis, an ideal compromise would be achieved. MSA provides such an approach via a multiple sorting process that can be computer analysed. Participants are asked to sort a number of elements into categories they themselves choose. They are then asked to name those categories, allowing participants the freedom to impose their own views on the data.

MSA techniques are structural modelling techniques but differ in their assumptions about the nature of input data and constraints on solutions from factor analytic models. Metric properties of data are not assumed and linear association coefficients are not required. The main tenet of MSA procedures is to represent psychological distances or similarities in terms of 'physical' distances in geometric 'space', whilst making very few assumptions about the data. MSA procedures 'plot' each item as a point in geometric space and attempt to find a configuration of points so that a plot can be divided into clear regions which distinguish the items on the basis of each variable. The more similar the items are, the more proximally they will be grouped or clustered in the plot. Two types of plot may be generated and examined: one plot shows the configuration of all points across all participants; the second describes data points for each participant at an individual level.

9.5.2 Method

MSA can be used to explore patterns in any qualitative data set, whether containing categorical, ordinal or interval-level data, allowing relationships between variables or categories and original items contributing to those categories, to be represented in a visual space. For the sake of brevity, we will describe here the stages involved in the MSA method for exploring the 'meaning' in individuals' patterns of responses using a card sort data collection approach.

1. Develop item/card set according to theoretical rationale for area of interest, e.g. people's understanding of what it means to be a soldier, perceptions of the concept of work integrity, etc.

2. Content validate items with subject matter experts; pilot items for ambiguity of wording, meaning, etc., adapting/deleting items where necessary. Number each card prior to exercise.

3. Run 'card sort' exercise with target group(s), asking each participant individually to sort the cards according to your rationale (into mutually exclusive groups, or non-mutually exclusive groups depending on the MSA package available for analysis). Note the groups according to item number and ask each participant to 'name' each group using their own label.

4. Input the data according to the requirements of the analysis package. Output will include numerical representation of each item's location on the graphical plot, as well as graphical output. Graphical output will include an aggregated plot as well as plots for each individual participant. Item numbers will appear on each plot and will need to be linked back to the original items. A 'coefficient of contiguity' value above 0.9 must be obtained for MSA to be regarded as stable, i.e. for there to be interpretable patterns within the data rather than totally random responses from participants.

5. On obtaining output, first examine the aggregated plot for any 'clusters' of items, linking item numbers back to original card sort items. This provides the first impression of patterns in the data (see Figures 9.1 and 9.2 for examples). Tentatively group items according to their location on the plot, getting a 'feel' for each cluster's meaning by looking back at component items.

6. Now examine each individual plot – the location of items on each individual plot will be the same as for the aggregated plot, but each individual may *not* have grouped their items in the same way. Individual plots will be numbered according to the groups of items that each participant identified originally, not according to the item numbers themselves. The researcher must look for clusters of same-number groups which *map onto* the aggregated plot groups in order to interpret the meaning of each group according to each individual. In doing this, the group names originally put forward by each participant can be used to describe the clusters appearing on the aggregated plot.

7. Once group names have been identified for each cluster on the aggregated plot (and 'confused' items have been interpreted as best they can, e.g. by including some items in more than one group, etc.), the researcher can name each cluster by looking for underlying meaning in all group names obtained from participants.

8. If appropriate, clusters can then be separated by partitioning the plot space (see Wilson, 1995), or otherwise representing differences between groupings.

Note that other researchers have applied the technique in very different ways, e.g. to explore: the meaning of 'place' within environmental psychology (Canter, 1983); group decision-making (Wilson and Canter, 1993); and conceptual development in education (Wilson and Canter, 1990), and the reader is referred to these sources and others mentioned at the foot of this section for further information. Wilson (1995) explains in simple terms how the results from a content analytic process may feed directly into an MSA analysis.

9.5.3 An applied example

To illustrate the process outlined above, an applied example of card sort-based MSA is presented in Case Study 9, below. The researcher in this example was successfully able to examine similarities and differences between two professional groups in terms of the psychological meaning of the *implicit* contracts each participant held with their employing organization. In this way, it was possible to shape and interpret qualitatively derived data using a multivariate quantitative method of analysis and present in an immediate, graphical way, participants' psychological representations of the 'meaning' of their relationships with their respective organizations. This graphical output is presented in Figures 9.1 and 9.2.

Case Study 9: Exploring the psychological contract using MSA

O'Hara (1998) used MSA to explore the psychological contract construct with groups of police officers and advertising agents, in order to draw out differences in the way each group represented their relationship with their employing organization and to explore, in a general sense, the utility of using MSA for this kind of exploratory work by examining the overall patterns of responses reported by participants. Participants were engaged individually in a card sorting task – forming the basis of the MSA analysis – each of 27 cards containing a behavioural or attitudinal statement pertaining to the psychological contract as depicted in work published to date, including, for example:

- Helping out colleagues when necessary
- Perception that the organization recognizes effort at work
- Working extra hours whether paid or not
- Working to the letter of employment contract
- Willingness to accept geographical transfer within company

O'Hara had placed a tentative structure on the cards in terms of the areas which she believed they were tapping into based on the reports of previous researchers. However, due to the exploratory nature of the work, participants were asked to group the cards together in any way they saw fit, to represent 'meaning' to them (groups of cards were necessarily mutually exclusive due to the requirements of the software package used). Some participants managed to divide all the cards into groups, others only used a few cards but each grouping from each participant was named by that participant, recorded, and input into a simple software package. The output of the MSA analysis reported the 'psychological space' depicted by both police and advertising groups when describing their psychological contracts at work, with clusters of card sort items displayed within this space in an aggregated sense (that is, the overall representation of both groups) and at individual level. By tracing items back to their original meaning, and to the group names provided by each participant, and examining and interpreting clusters of items as one would factor analysis-derived 'factors', O'Hara was able to determine similarities and differences in the meaning of psychological contracts for police and advertising groups. Figures 9.1 and 9.2 illustrate the obtained plots for both professional samples: each item is represented by a small dot, with surrounding circles representing the researcher's interpretation of item groupings, based on the aggregated plot, then traced back to individual MSA plots for original group labels.

The reader should note that the orientation or position of items/groups on the plot is not meaningful, merely the 'distance' between items/groups and the clustering of items into groups. Clustering of items suggests that they together *mean* something to the sample (although this must be verified by checking back to individual plots), while distance between groups suggests the psychological proximity or distance that groups perceive between the meaning of item clusters.

The professional groups, in fact, show some similarities in their groupings of items: 'organizational citizenship' and 'decorum', for example, were grouped in a similar way by both samples, as was the central grouping in each plot – 'commitment'. However, differences are also apparent. Whilst advertisers group 'careerism' and 'distrust' independently and place some psychological distance between the groups, police officers combine these groups, suggesting perhaps that for the police sample (and not for the advertisers), perceptions of self-oriented professional development and careerist tendencies are seen in the same way as negative workplace reactions such as cynicism and suspicion of the organization. In addition, 'job security' is a police-derived grouping which is notably absent from the advertisers' plot, again suggesting a difference in each sample's experience of work.

Figure 9.1   MSA plot for advertising agents

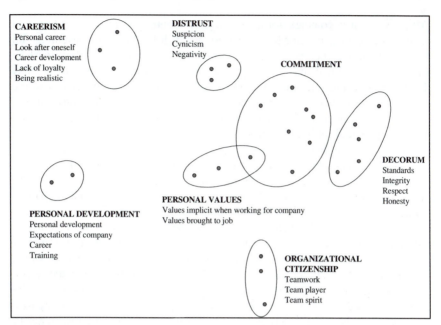

Figure 9.2   MSA plot for police officers

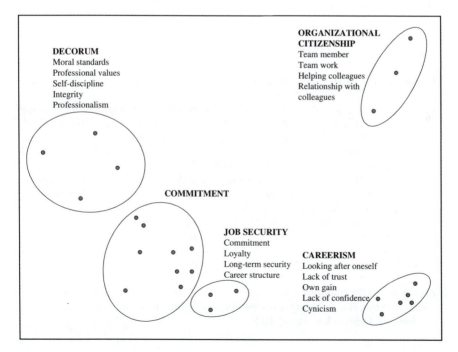

9.5.4 Advantages and disadvantages

MSA is a fairly complex form of analysis, requiring careful collection and categorization of data prior to the analysis itself. It is also time-consuming and exhaustive during the analysis phase, where each participant's output must be closely inspected and linked to aggregated output before any conclusions may be drawn from the data. Interpretations, too, are necessarily subjective and the researcher must maintain a very objective stance to avoid conveniently 'fitting' the data to match any initial theory driving the research. *Post hoc* rationalization is also a potential pitfall, as with much exploratory research, and is difficult to avoid. Even by returning to the original sample and discussing the accuracy of results, participants are also likely to rationalize what they see retrospectively.

However, MSA's advantages are numerous. The technique represents one of the only analytic approaches which retains the rich, individual and subjective nature of qualitative data, while simultaneously applying the structure of a quantitative analysis. As such, it is a powerful tool and can provide deep insight into data which may otherwise prove too complex to interpret. The graphical representation of output provides a neat, thumbnail picture of the way in which individuals cognitively represent an area of interest and while item distances on an MSA plot are in no way absolute, they do provide an indication of the psychological distance or proximity in peoples' perceptions of item groupings. Overall, MSA is a useful, powerful technique which requires the researcher to understand fully the underpinning method prior to its use, but which may provide a revealing further analysis of qualitative data deriving from content analytic or other methods.

9.5.5 References and further reading

Canter, D. (1983). The purposive evaluation of places: a facet approach. *Environment and Behaviour, 15, 6,* 659–698.

Canter, D., Brown, J. and Groat, L. (1985). A multiple sorting procedure for studying conceptual systems. In M. Brenner, J. Brown, and D. Canter (Eds.), *The Research Interview: Uses and Approaches.* London, UK: Academic Press.

O'Hara, C. (1998). The psychological contract: a multi-method approach. Unpublished MSc thesis, University of Surrey, Guildford, UK.

Wilson, M.A. (1995). Structuring qualitative data: multidimensional scalogram analysis. In G.M. Breakwell, S. Hammond and C. Fife-Schaw (Eds.), *Research Methods in Psychology.* London, UK: Sage Publications.

Wilson, M.A. and Canter, D. (1990). The development of professional concepts. *Applied Psychology: an International Review, 39, 4,* 431–455.

Wilson, M.A. and Canter, D. (1993). Shared concepts in group decision making: a model for decisions based on qualitative data. *British Journal of Social Psychology, 32,* 159–172.

Zvulun, E. (1978). Multidimensional scalogram analysis: the method and its application. In S. Shye (Ed.), *Theory Construction and Data Analysis in the Behavioural Sciences.* London, UK: Jossey-Bass.

9.6 Meta-analysis

9.6.1 Introduction

Consider an applied research question which involves quantifiable variables. Perhaps, 'how effective are transformational leadership approaches in improving team satisfaction?' or 'how are job satisfaction and employee productivity related?' Such questions have attracted a fair degree of research interest over the years, with the result that many dozens (and sometimes hundreds) of studies have been undertaken to explore them. Faced with an expansive literature and the task of synthesizing it prior to embarking on a fresh research venture, many prospective researchers will undertake to obtain the key papers within their chosen area of interest, and summarize findings using a discursive, qualitative approach.

As Wood (1995) points out, qualitative narrative approaches to reviewing existing literature have limited utility if the researcher is interested in *aggregating* and *quantifying* research findings in any given domain. Guzzo et al. (1987) put forward the notion of a 'continuum of quantification' when considering literature reviews. At one end of this continuum fall narrative literature reviews. Towards the centre of the continuum fall semi-systematized approaches which involve summations of the significant and non-significant findings reported in the literature as an indication of the degree to which the research community as a whole refutes or endorses any given hypothesis. At the extreme quantitative end of the continuum fall a group of statistical techniques known as 'meta-analysis' which are designed to aggregate experimental and correlational results across a range of individual studies.

Unlike traditional reviewing methods, meta-analysis uses the summary statistics from individual studies as the data points. A key assumption of this form of analysis is that each study provides a differing estimate of the underlying relationship within the population. By aggregating results across studies, the researcher can gain a more accurate representation of the relationship present within the population than is provided by the individual study estimate when taken in isolation. This set of techniques has grown up in response in order to provide 'some means of making sense of the vast amounts of data that have accumulated' in many areas of applied social science research (Hunter et al., 1982: 27). Taking the example given at the beginning of this section, 'how are job satisfaction and employee productivity related?', several meta-analytic studies have been undertaken to provide an overall assessment of the relationship between these variables. Vroom (1964) considered 20 studies in his meta-analysis and reported a non-significant correlation of 0.14; more than 20 years later, Iaffaldano and Muchinsky (1985) undertook a meta-analysis of over 200 studies and reported a very similar non-significant correlation of 0.15.

Glass (1976) coined the term 'meta-analysis', and introduced most of the currently used procedures to the social sciences.

> Meta-analysis refers to the analysis of analyses . . . the statistical analysis of a large collection of analysis results from individual studies for the purpose of integrating the findings. It connotes a rigorous alternative to the casual, narrative discussions of research studies which typify our attempts to make sense of the rapidly expanding research literature. (Glass, 1976: 3).

9.6.2 The meta-analytic process

Glass et al. (1981) and Hunter et al (1982) outlined the meta-analytic methods typically applied in social science research today. These approaches are underpinned by a similar process: collection of relevant studies followed by treatment of each study's findings in such a way that they may be expressed as a common statistic. This common statistic is most often referred to as a measure of 'effect-size', i.e. an index of the strength and power of the relationship between study variables, which also takes into account various sources of error likely to bias the individual estimates of effect size identified across studies.

Glass et al.'s (1981) procedure for undertaking meta-analysis is summarized by Wood (1995) as follows:

1. Select the independent and dependent variables of interest.
2. Identify, locate and obtain all relevant and usable studies containing information of interest.
3. Code each study for characteristics which might be a predictor of study outcomes, i.e. might relate to size of effects obtained, e.g. age, sex, length of intervention, etc.
4. Calculate estimates of effect size for the IV–DV pairs of interest (this requires application of statistical formulae, discussed below).
5. Calculate the mean and standard deviation of effect size across studies.
6. Examine those study characteristics identified in (3) which correlate with study effects.

Hunter et al.'s (1982) process extends that proposed by Glass et al. (1981) by including steps to correct for study artefacts. Hunter et al.'s (1982) procedure duplicates Glass et al.'s (1981) first four stages and goes on to include:

5. Calculate the mean effect size across studies. Effect size for each study is then weighted by sample size.
6. Calculate the variance of effect size.
7. Determine the extent to which differences in variances of effect size are due to sampling error, errors of measurement and range restriction.

8. If a large percentage of the variance across studies can be attributed to measurement artefacts alone, it is concluded that the average effect size is an accurate estimate of the relationship between the variables.

9. If, however, a large proportion of the variance is unaccounted for, then study characteristics are examined to determine their correlation with effect size (stage 6 of Glass et al.'s procedure).

Crucial to the meta-analytic process is the notion of 'effect size', which is a function of significance level of sample size, according to the following formula:

$$\text{Effect size} \quad = \quad \frac{\text{Significance level}}{\text{'Sample size'}}$$

In order to combine findings across a number of studies, it is important to use a comparable statistic. Glass et al. (1981) report the use of *d* (standardized differences between mean scores), as follows:

$$d \quad = \quad \frac{\text{(Mean of experimental group – Mean of control group)}}{\text{Standard deviation of control group}}$$

Hunter et al. (1982) consistently use *r* – Pearson's product moment correlation co-efficient, while Mullen (1993) uses Fisher's *Z* as a measure of effect size. It is worth referring to the original sources listed at the end of this section for more detailed accounts of the statistical procedures for calculating effect size. This is also true of the procedures required to assess degree of sampling error, measurement error and range restriction, as identified by Hunter et al. (1982) and Hunter and Hirsh (1987).

9.6.3 Problems with meta-analysis

Despite its potential for synthesizing large numbers of research findings and reporting them in a fairly digestible and accessible format, meta-analysis has a number of potential drawbacks:

- **File-drawer effect** – this is an issue which besets all social science research. It refers to the fact that not all studies are published and, therefore, that many findings which had the potential to be included in a meta-analytic study reside in the 'file drawer' of the researchers who undertook the original work. Although some academics have suggested that editorial review boards for journals act principally as arbiters of quality, and therefore that unpublished work would probably not justify inclusion in meta-analytic studies anyway (Hunter et al., 1982), it is also true that such boards generally favour 'significant' findings when selecting research for publication. Less directly (but perhaps more seriously), it also seems likely that researchers themselves will act as censors of their own work if they do not obtain the 'desired' result, and will not therefore put this research forward to be considered for publication. Some workers have attempted to address these problems by developing formulae to assess how many non-significant studies would need to exist before a null relationship between variables of interest is reported (Rosenthal, 1979).

- **Defining the domain of interest** – it may sometimes be problematic to decide on which studies to include in, or exclude from, a meta-analysis due to indistinct boundaries around the domain of interest. In such cases, the analyst must include a specific explanation as to the rationale for inclusion of some studies and exclusion of others.

- **Qualitative findings** – due to meta-analysis' reliance on quantitative statistical procedures, qualitative research findings are necessarily excluded from any meta-analysis. Where a particular domain of organizational study draws heavily on qualitative approaches, this may lead a meta-analyst to include an unrepresentative sub-sample of findings in his/her analysis as only a limited number contain quantitative data.

- **Availability of descriptive statistics** – many academic journals now require all papers submitted for review to include basic descriptive statistics for the principal variables included in the study (e.g. means, standard deviations, sample sizes, inter-correlations, etc.). Without these basic data, regardless of the potential relevance of a given study finding, that study cannot be included in a meta-analysis. This omission of descriptive data is particularly prevalent in older reported studies and in less prestigious academic journals where publication is not necessarily contingent on the provision of such information.

- **Covariates for inclusion** – as noted in the above meta-analytic procedures (Section 9.6.2), potential mediating or moderating factors (e.g. age, sex, grade, etc.) should also be included in order that results are not over-simplified. However, it remains open to the judgement of the researcher as to which additional factors to include/exclude in a meta-analytic study, again leaving the procedure open to error.

9.6.4 References and further reading

Glass, G. (1976). Primary, secondary and meta-analysis of research. *Educational Researcher, 5*, 3–8.
Glass, G., McGraw, B. and Smith, M.L. (1981). *Meta-analysis in Social Research.* Beverly Hills, CA: Sage Publications.
Guzzo, R.A., Jackson, S.E. and Katzell, R.A. (1987). Meta-analysis analysis. *Research in Organizational Behavior, 9*, 407–442.

Hunter, J. and Hirsh, H.R. (1987). Applications of meta-analysis. In C.L. Cooper and I.T. Robertson (Eds.), *International Review of Industrial and Organizational Psychology*. Chichester, UK: Wiley.

Hunter, J., Schmidt, F, and Jackson, G. (1982). *Meta-analysis: Cumulating Research Findings across Studies*. Beverly Hills, CA: Sage Publications.

Iaffaldano, M.T. and Muchinsky, P.M. (1985). Job satisfaction and job performance: a meta-analysis. *Psychological Bulletin, 97, 2*, 251–273.

Mullen, B. (1993). Meta-analysis. *Thornfield Journal, 16*, 36–41.

Rosenthal, R. (1979). The 'file drawer problem' and tolerance for null results. *Psychological Bulletin, 86*, 638–641.

Vroom, V.H. (1964). *Work and Motivation*. New York: Wiley.

Wood, P. (1995). Meta-analysis. In G.M. Breakwell, S. Hammond and C. Fife-Schaw (Eds.), *Research Methods in Psychology*. London, UK: Sage Publications.

9.7 Structural equation modelling

9.7.1 Introduction

Structural equation modelling (SEM) has been described as a 'collection of statistical techniques that allows examination of a set of relationships between one or more IVs, either continuous or discrete, and one or more DVs, either continuous or discrete' (Tabachnick and Fidell, 1996: 709). In very broad terms, the field involves the amalgamation of multiple regression and confirmatory factor analytic techniques to assist in the assessment of *developed* models. It is not intended for empirical generation of models as with techniques such as exploratory factor analysis (Cuttance and Ecob, 1987). The technique has enjoyed wider use in recent years with the advent of increased computing power, allowing previously untestable hypotheses and models to be more closely scrutinized.

Within SEM, researchers are most often concerned with measurement of, and relationships between, 'latent constructs'; that is, constructs which are themselves implicit and unmeasurable, but which are believed to underpin the explicit variables used to measure them. For example, Eysenck and Eysenck (1975) argued that one of their three principal bipolar personality factors, 'extraversion' (a 'latent construct'), may be estimated by explicitly measuring the sub-factors which underpin it, namely activity, sociability, risk-taking, impulsiveness, expressiveness, reflectiveness and responsibility. Thurstone's (1938) study of 'primary mental abilities' assumed that three sub-factors (visual intelligence, verbal intelligence and processing speed, themselves comprising measurable sub-components), when combined, accounted for the latent construct 'g' or general intelligence. Within SEM, measurement in itself is regarded as error-prone, and the technique of SEM accounts for measurement error when calculating relationships between latent and observed variables. By explicitly modelling measurement error, SEM users may derive unbiased estimates of the relationships between latent constructs.

At its heart, SEM is based on a comparison of covariance structures between a previously constructed theoretical model and an empirically derived data-based model. If the two models (or at least, their covariance matrices) are consistent with one another, the originally conceived structural model may be considered to be a plausible explanation for observed relationships between measured and latent variables. Effectively, SEM represents a more complex form of regression/factor analytic-based modelling which can quantify several sets of relationships simultaneously, and can also control for error covariances resulting from, for example, the research sample misunderstanding two survey questions which contained the same word, etc.

9.7.2 Measurement and structural models

SEM requires construction of both *measurement* and *structural* models. Measurement models describe the relationships between measured variables and latent constructs or underlying factors. Structural models describe the relationships between the latent constructs themselves. To illustrate this, we may consider an example of a sample of construction workers whose intentions to stay with, or leave, their company are of interest to the researcher. Initial exploratory interviews and further background research by the researcher has shown that several underlying constructs (which the researcher may be able to measure using newly constructed questionnaire items) may predict workers' intentions to leave or stay: their job satisfaction, commitment to the company and their perceptions of the current job market. To tap into each of these three predictors, questionnaire scales are developed, each containing three items (which we code as 'j1–3' for job satisfaction, 'c1–3' for commitment and 'm1–3' for job market perceptions). Intention to leave is measured using two pre-existing scales, coded as 'i1' and 'i2'. Armed with this information, it is possible to construct measurement and structural models. As stated above, measurement models are used to address the relationship between observed variables (the questionnaire items) and latent variables (job satisfaction, etc.); structural models address the relationship between latent variables (our three predictor constructs and the intention to leave construct). Thus, Figure 9.3 depicts both measurement and structural models. 'Endogenous' variables are used to describe the section of the model we want to predict; 'exogenous' variables describe the section of the model involved in prediction.

9.7.3 Identification, achieving normality and constructing the model

In order to use SEM, any model should be 'identified' and include normally distributed variables. Identification involves ensuring that the number of independent covariance equations, $q(q+1)/2$, must be greater than the individual number of parameters to be estimated, where 'q' represents the number of parameters to be estimated (i.e. the number of arrows shown on the diagram). For our model, $q(q+1)/2 = 14(15)/2 = 105$ and the total number of parameters to be identified is 14, so the model should be identified.

Figure 9.3   Proposed measurement/structural model for predicting construction workers' intention to leave

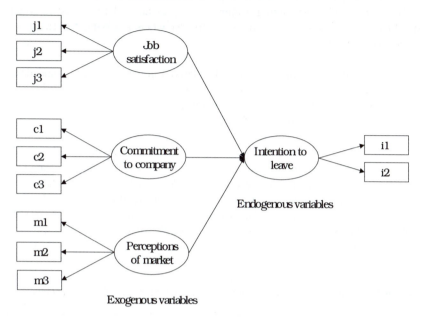

Observed variables should be normally distributed to use the majority of common SEM algorithms (e.g. weighted least squares, generalized least squares and maximum likelihood) and may require transformation if they are not. Assessments of skewness and kurtosis should be obtained for evidence of normality and loglinear transformations used if necessary. In addition, since we should assume that ordinal-level data only are obtained by the measures, polychoric correlations must be calculated for the correlation matrix.

Constructing the model itself will depend on the package selected – the authors are most conversant with LISREL for Windows, but even this package is continuously re-iterated and updated, so the process for construction (and the programming involved) will not be dealt with here. For the purposes of explaining the process of model construction, we will assume that the model has been specified successfully and that the software package has accepted the data in order to build the model.

9.7.4 Estimation of parameters and assessing goodness of fit

The software package used for the analysis, e.g. LISREL, will output a path diagram similar to that shown in Figure 9.3, but will also show parameter estimates for each path between each variable and each construct. At this stage, the researcher should look out for parameter estimates which fall outside the –1 to +1 range which denote problems with the original data set.

The package will also output a number of 'goodness of fit' statistics which should be considered along with other criteria when assessing the fit of the model. These include:

1.   Overall fit between theoretically derived covariance matrix and data-derived covariance/correlation matrix;
2.   Adequacy of individual parameter estimates;
3.   Theoretical implications for the model.

Overall fit may be assessed using chi-square and other statistics which provide a general indication of the general fit of the model. However, note that the chi-square statistic is sensitive to large sample sizes and to non-normal data and should be treated with caution. Other fit indices not requiring normal data are shown in Table 9.3, which also shows the minimum/maximum acceptable probability values for each to infer a reasonable fit of the model with the obtained data:

Table 9.3   Alternative goodness of fit statistics and their acceptable value range

Goodness of fit measure	Value required
Goodness of fit index (GFI)	>0.95
Adjusted goodness of fit index (AGFI)	>0.90
Root mean square error of approximation (RMSEA)	<0.05
Root mean square residual (RMR)	<0.05

Adequacy of individual parameter estimates may be assessed by examining the direction and size of the relationship between each variable and each construct. If negatively keyed items are used in any of the scales, these should be negatively related to the latent construct in question. Size of relationship is denoted by parameter value: if any parameter is small, reasons underlying this should be investigated – the variable may have little power in predicting the construct and could be removed from the model if this is theoretically justifiable.

Adaptations of the model, due to low parameter estimates or for other reasons such as error in the data, must be *theoretically* justifiable – it may be, for example, that removal of one of the market perceptions variables significantly improves the overall fit of the model. In order to remove this variable, the researcher must understand the theoretical implications for the model, and should not rely purely on empirical evidence specific to his or her single sample. It may be that this variable will be shown to be an efficient predictor of the market perceptions construct with another sample of construction workers.

9.7.5 Modifying the model

The latter comments made in the section immediately above pertain to possible modifications or amendments to the model to improve overall goodness of fit. Most SEM packages will provide the researcher with a series of 'modification indices'; that is, suggested amendments to the model, with the associated improvements in overall fit that can be expected. As mentioned above, any such modifications *must be theoretically justifiable*. An example of a justified modification may be to add an error covariance to the model if two or more items contain error not related to the model itself. For example, two items causing respondent confusion by using a specific word, e.g. 'disgruntled' or 'dynamic', may be identified by the SEM package, which may suggest the addition of a new parameter to lessen the impact of this error source. If there is a good reason for this modification, it may be justified. It is not, however, justifiable blindly to follow all of a package's suggested changes for improving model fit, without considering the implications for the model's *meaning* and theoretical underpinnings. It should also be noted that any modifications to the model will require the researcher to re-estimate the model from scratch.

9.7.6 Advantages and disadvantages

SEM is a complex technique which requires a comprehensive understanding of its statistical underpinnings before it should be attempted. It places significant restrictions on the type of data used, e.g. normally distributed, interval-level (although this can be ameliorated by using polychoric correlations) data, and a reasonable sample size. It is also based on a fundamental assumption of causality, which may not sit well with those models whose constructs are more reciprocally related (as is the case in much 'real world' organizational research). Finally, the technique requires a certain level of competence with computer-based software packages (e.g. LISREL) which is likely to require some training prior to use.

However, SEM is a powerful analytical tool, very useful for developing complex attitudinal/behavioural models where numerous relationships can be assessed simultaneously, and represents a significant step forward in hypothesis testing and in statistical model building. It is becoming increasingly widely used in the social sciences, evident in the large number of journal papers published in the past 15 years that draw upon it (see, for example, Hansen, 1989; Heck et al., 1989; Marcoulides, 1989; Marcoulides and Heck, 1993), thanks to improved software packages and a wider recognition of its strengths, and it seems likely that this trend will continue.

9.7.7 References and further reading

Cuttance, P. and Ecob, R. (1987). *Structural Equation Modelling by Example: Applications in Educational, Sociological and Behavioural Research*. Cambridge, UK: Cambridge University Press.

Eysenck, H.J. and Eysenck, S.G.B. (1975). *The Eysenck Personality Questionnaire*. Sevenoaks, UK: Hodder and Stoughton.

Hansen, C.P. (1989). A causal model of the relationship among accidents, biodata, personality and cognitive factors. *Journal of Applied Psychology, 74, 1*, 81–90.

Heck, R.H., Marcoulides, G.A. and Glasman, N.S. (1989). The application of causal modelling techniques to administrative decision making: The Case of Teacher Allocation. *Educational Administration Quarterly, 25, 3*, 15–31.

Marcoulides, G.A. (1989). Structural equation modelling techniques for scientific research. *Journal of Business and Society, 2, 2*, 130–138.

Marcoulides, G.S. and Heck, R.H. (1993). Organizational culture and performance: proposing and testing a model. *Organization Science, 4, 2*, 109–225.

Tabachnick, B.G. and Fidell, L.S. (1996). *Using Multivariate Statistics* (Third Edition). New York: Harper Collins College Publishers.

Thurstone, L.L. (1938). *Primary Mental Abilities*. Chicago, IL: University of Chicago Press.

10 Reporting Research Findings

10.1 Introduction

This chapter provides an overview of the reporting process, including written reporting to academic (institutional and journal) and organizational audiences. It then goes on to discuss in some detail the presentation of research findings to organizational and academic groups. Throughout this section, we present tips and suggestions based on our own personal experiences as organizational researchers (whether our roles have been as student, supervisor or practitioner).

10.2 Reporting to an academic audience

Each educational institution will have established its own protocol for submitting research dissertations and reports which you will need to study in detail. The best way to approach this is to examine previous dissertations submitted for the degree for which you are a candidate, in particular those which obtained higher than average marks. This will give you a feel for the length, scope and quality of what is expected at each particular academic level. You may have got the impression from glancing through previous dissertations that they are assessed by their weight! This is not the case. It is the *quality* that matters and quantity is not necessarily an indicator of this. The tighter, the more succinct and focused the report, the higher its quality is likely to be. When it comes to academic research reports, it is often the case that 'less is more'.

Some educational institutions use publication standards as their protocol for dissertation reports. The best way to get a feel for this kind of writing is to study high-quality journal articles which publish material in your field. This will provide you with ideas about how to structure your report, its style and tone as well as content. Section 10.3 also provides some tips and hints on structuring an academic research report for journal publication.

> There is no better way of learning how to write up research than: (a) to 'analyse' the way journal articles are written and (b) to write and obtain feedback from your supervisor who is already likely to be experienced in writing for academic publication purposes.

Generally speaking, most reports will be required to adhere to a similar format to that presented below:

Abstract (100–150 words)
List of contents
List of figures/tables
Introduction
Questions/hypotheses
Method
  Design
  Sample, including organizational details as appropriate
  Measures/materials
  Procedure
Results
Discussion
  Description of results
  Interpretation/explanation
  Limitations of study
  Implications of study
  Further research
Conclusion
References
Appendices

Each of these sections will now be introduced in a little more depth.

Abstract
This provides a succinct overview (100–150 words) of what you focused on, the key issues/questions/hypotheses addressed, the design, method/measures used, the key findings and any arguments made in the paper which provide it with an overall 'story line' or particular thrust. Details are omitted from the abstract. Its purpose is to present the big picture.

Introduction
This will begin with an objective or key focus, and will move on to provide some background material including the reasons why you deem the topic to be important. It will describe the theoretical (and/or epistemological) basis of the research with rationale (i.e. why this as opposed to other approaches). The introduction should lead to the derivation of specific hypotheses or questions or issues to be addressed and will then briefly outline the way in which you decided to tackle them as a preface to the method section. It will link the theoretical rationale with the design and methodological/measurement rationale, thereby indicating that the study has internal logic and coherence.

The purpose of the introduction is to:

- Indicate why it is that you selected to do what you did and its importance/relevance to your particular branch of the social sciences;

- Demonstrate your knowledge and insight into the domain of interest (in both academic and practical terms);
- Demonstrate your ability to bring a research-based (scientist–practitioner) approach to bear on real-life practical considerations and concerns;
- Provide an interpretative framework and focus for the report, facilitating the construction of a coherent argument which runs throughout the report;
- Outline the questions/issues/hypotheses you have arrived at and how these were derived.

Method
Design: Describes the design used with a brief rationale.
Sample: Describes the sample, how it was derived, from what population and why, including estimates of how representative it is of the population. If appropriate, details of the organization from which respondents were drawn will need to be provided here.
Measures/materials: Describes (with rationale) the measures used, from which source, their psychometric properties (if appropriate) and in what form they were presented. All materials/apparatus used will need to be described in sufficiently replicable detail.
Procedure: Describes how you went about collecting data in replicable detail, including any problems and how they were overcome, all decisions made along the way, etc.

Results
Where appropriate, data analysis should be presented for each hypothesis or question or issue in turn. If this is not appropriate, a logical or meaningful structure can be developed which builds up from simple to complex elements. Rationales for each choice of data analysis technique must be provided. The level of statistical detail you report will depend on the protocol within your academic department. Otherwise, as a minimum, report choice of test(s) (including a rationale for test selection), variables used within the test and in what form (categorical, ordinal, interval), the result obtained, and the probability of this occurring by chance (plus relevant degrees of freedom, and distribution descriptives where appropriate, e.g. mean, standard deviation, etc.).

If the conventional format is inappropriate for the particular approach you have taken (e.g. your data are qualitative) you will need to consult your supervisor for advice. In most cases, qualitative research can be written up along the same lines, although it will perhaps form more of a continuous 'narrative' than a quantitatively oriented report. A source worth consulting on this issue is Wolcott (1993).

Discussion
The discussion should present a description of the results obtained relative to

the questions asked/hypotheses addressed, moving on to discuss the practical and theoretical significance of the results. Within the overarching framework of a coherently constructed argument, the discussion will move from description to interpretation/explanation and then to speculation (i.e. looking to the future). This section must be critical, qualified by the limitations of the study and with reference to the findings reviewed in the introduction. The organizational implications of the findings should also be discussed. A discussion will often end with some ideas for future research, suggesting how subsequent researchers could build and improve on your research approach and findings.

Conclusion
Summing up the main argument(s) or key finding(s) and the conditions/qualifiers under which these apply.

References
Use the protocol laid down by your educational institution for recording references. Ensure that you report your references using a consistent protocol.

Appendices
Be careful these do not end up as the dumping ground for everything and anything (e.g. a print-out of your entire dataset, or output direct from a statistical package with no explanation of its meaning). Insert only what is really necessary and relevant (i.e. documents which *add value* to your research report).

As has already been discussed, the writing-up phase is not something to be tagged on to the end of a project and completed in a hurry (see Chapter 3 for more on this). The writing process is continuous, which means that by the time you reach the report-writing stage, most of it is already done. Plan your time so that your supervisor (and friends/relatives/partners) have time to look through what you have written and perhaps, more importantly, to provide you with constructive feedback. It is no good giving your supervisor something to read the night before you're supposed to submit the final report! Chances are that he or she won't have time to read it there and then, let alone provide you with any constructive input on how to shape or polish it. Plan your time and get a draft to your supervisor well in advance of the deadline.

> Plan your writing time, draft the report, seek feedback, redraft, seek feedback, final draft and submission.

10.3 Writing up for academic publication

Once you have submitted your research findings to fulfil course requirements, you may wish to continue the process and adapt your findings for publication in an academic journal. There can be a number of advantages to this, most notably gaining credibility in both academic and professional circles as a published author on a particular topic. Becoming an established 'expert' in your chosen field of research through publication can improve opportunities for advancement in an academic career, further courses of study, or (if used to 'market' your services to prospective employers or clients) in a professional setting. In this section, we outline the similarities and differences in writing up research findings for an acknowledged academic journal, as opposed to writing up a college dissertation or project report.

As noted in the previous section, some academic institutions require research findings to be written up in 'journal' style, and most institutions will require a similar structure to be followed as that outlined above (i.e. Abstract, Introduction, Method, Results, Discussion). Most academic journals follow this general framework, although there are certain points of structure and format which are specific to each journal. The guidelines for academic publication can be obtained directly from the journals themselves by contacting the editor or a member of the editorial team.

In addition to these idiosyncratic differences in journals' 'house styles', more fundamental differences exist between journals in what they will and will not accept for publication, as well as between requirements for writing up a college 'thesis' and those to secure academic publication of a paper. These differences (and some helpful tips on the publication process) are introduced below:

- In general, research written up for academic publication will need to be **briefer and more 'punchy'** than that submitted as part of a college course. Because they have finite space within which to publish research, academic journals are less tolerant of 'loose', flowery language, lengthy introductions, literature reviews and discussions. Your paper should have a tight, coherent 'story' and should keep to that story throughout. Issues of tangential interest should be omitted or relegated to a line or two in the discussion.

- The people reviewing your paper will be acknowledged experts in their field. As a result, your introduction and associated **literature review needs to include all the relevant previous research** published in that area. Omitting (selectively or otherwise) particular research findings from your review *will* be noticed by the review team and is likely to lead to rejection of your paper.

- Academic journals are becoming less and **less likely to publish 'cross-sectional' research**. Much research conducted as part of an academic course is tightly constrained by time and resources with the result that, often, the study design will be cross-sectional, i.e. the research will focus on a particular organizational issue on a 'moment in time' or 'snapshot' basis, rather than following that issue over time, or across organizational settings. While some journals will still consider such papers, it is important to outline the limitations of findings obtained via such a design, in terms of their level of generalizability to the wider population and over time.

- Most research students will write up their **research findings for academic publication in collaboration with their project supervisor**. Your supervisor is likely to have some experience of preparing papers for publication and this experience will be invaluable.

- It is also worth considering **distributing a draft paper for review by other academics within your department** prior to sending the paper to your target journal. This will provide helpful and constructive criticism and may pre-empt some of the comments likely to be made by journal review teams. Such feedback can then be used to further tweak and improve your draft paper.

- Many academic journals have **specific minimum requirements for reporting results** of findings. These generally include reporting descriptive information (e.g. means, standard deviations) and (where appropriate) inter-correlations between study variables, for all variables included in the research. This is partly due to the growing use of meta-analysis within the social sciences and the requirements of this technique in terms of descriptive background data. If you are aiming for publication in a specific journal, take the time to find a recent published paper similar in structure or design to your research and follow the protocol implicit in that paper. The paper selected as a model needs to be recent since changes in protocol can occur fairly rapidly in some journals.

- There will be **differences in the quality and scientific rigour** required of research published by different academic journals. This generally reflects the perceived quality of those journals within the relevant research community. Within most social science disciplines, an informal hierarchy of journal quality/prestige will operate – ask your supervisor about this within your particular discipline.

- **Your paper may be more suited to one or two journals than to others**, due to the particular interests of the editorial teams of those journals. Again, your supervisor should have a good idea of the most appropriate destination for your paper.

- It is also important to note that **you cannot attempt to get published in more than one journal at the same time**. As a result, it is worth taking some time to consider which academic publication would be the most appropriate for your paper.

- Bear in mind that **your paper is unlikely to be accepted for publication immediately**. The publication process can be a long one since the process of review can take 6 months or more and it can be even longer before you receive feedback on your paper. When you do receive feedback, it may be that your paper has been accepted without revision (although this is rare), but more likely that some minor or even major changes will be required before the paper can be published. These changes could relate to any element of the paper, including introduction, review of the field, sample structure, analyses used, discussion points, generalizability of findings, etc. and will require further tweaks and amendments before the paper is accepted. It may be that the paper will be rejected out of hand if the review team feel that any element is 'fatally flawed', perhaps due to problems with the design, underlying logic of the 'story', or any aspect of the paper which cannot be modified with relative ease. In this case, it is likely that you will need to undertake further research before approaching an alternative publication.

- As suggested immediately above, **feedback from a review team, while often constructive and useful, can be harsh and negative**. For this reason, you need to be fairly resilient when receiving feedback from a review team. Even if this feedback seems unnecessarily harsh and damaging, it will be possible to use the information to positive effect in making changes to the draft. When re-submitting a revised draft to the same journal, it is clearly important to outline exactly how you have addressed every criticism (minor and major) made by the review team.

10.4 The client report

Feedback to participating organizations is an essential part of the research process, too often forgotten in the excitement of having finished the project and (hopefully) passed the course! Feedback forms a critical part of the 'psychological contract' secured at the outset with an organization which if violated, can mean that your future relationship with that company is severely jeopardized as are future research prospects for other students and the educational institutions of which they are part. The researcher has a professional responsibility to provide feedback of some kind to participating organizations. Some organizations will be satisfied with a report, others will also want you to present your findings at a board meeting or similar forum, particularly if the findings have valuable practical implications.

Unless explicitly requested, it is not enough, or indeed appropriate, to send the company a copy of your dissertation. This document will be written in a largely inaccessible form and thus will not be very organization-friendly. This does not mean that you should oversimplify what you have found (and thus patronize the reader), merely that the information can be presented in a more digestible form than that typical of the conventional research report. The 'client report' for example will need to be prefaced by an 'executive summary'. This is similar in purpose to, yet also fundamentally very different (in terms of content) from, the research abstract. In many instances, the executive summary is all that will end up being read since it is often the practical significance of these findings which is of most interest to a client organization. Other readers will dip into the report at a more detailed level but will not wish to get bogged down with too much detail. An example of an executive summary is provided in Case Study 10.

The executive summary should (in plain English):

- Spell out what was done;
- How it was done;
- When it was done;
- Who and how many were involved;
- What was found;
- What the implications are of what was found;
- What is recommended.

Case Study 10: An example of an executive summary presented to a call-centre company

Introduction
During Spring–Summer 1999, a research project was undertaken jointly between CALLME's inbound department and an independent consultant, which focused on the attitudes and perceptions of CALLME's staff in various departments within the call-centre. More specifically, the project examined current staff perceptions of CALLME's organizational 'climate', levels of commitment, satisfaction and feelings of belonging and the impact of these attitudes/perceptions on staff performance.

Sample size
The project secured a reasonable sample size (150 staff), making conclusions drawn from the study robust and accurate.

Method
Using a mixture of established and newly developed psychometric tools, Jack Spratt of the University of Southern England was able to analyse the perceived climate of a number of CALLME's departments. Perceptions of climate were set against individual performance data, including absenteeism, lateness, intention to leave and percentage scheduled hours worked, in order to examine the impact of employee perceptions of their workplace on individual performance.

Findings and implications
From the study, it was found that daily key performance indicators (KPIs), including absenteeism, lateness and percentage of scheduled hours worked, were best predicted by staffs' perceptions of certain aspects of their workplace. Elements of CALLME's culture which appeared to have the greatest impact on KPIs were:

- Perceived 'morale', i.e. the general atmosphere of the workplace;
- Perceived 'information flow', i.e. accessibility of information to employees;
- Perceived 'involvement', i.e. inclusion in work-related decisions.

Those employees who reported more positive perceptions of each of these areas of CALLME's culture displayed lower absenteeism and lateness figures and worked a greater percentage of their scheduled hours. In contrast, employees' reported intentions to stay with, or leave, CALLME were best predicted by their level of organizational commitment and by the type of 'psychological contract' which they held with the organization (ranging from 'transactional' – financially-oriented – to 'relational' – relationship-oriented). Highly committed and 'relational' employees were found to be the most likely to stay with the organization long-term.

Recommendations
On the basis of the study's findings, it is recommended that, as a priority, CALLME organizes cross-grade and cross-departmental focus groups to discuss these issues in more depth. It is suggested that these focus groups address issues of staff involvement with decisions at work, current levels of information accessibility and the general climate of the call-centre, in order to identify areas where staff feel improvements could be made. A further exploration of the important components of staffs' relationships with CALLME (their psychological contracts) should also form part of focus group discussions.

The executive summary might also serve as an important form of feedback to those involved in the research (e.g. those who actually completed questionnaires or who participated in interviews). Alternatively, the executive summary may provide the *basis* for feedback throughout the organization though not in the exact same form (e.g. in a 'cut-down' version as part of a newsletter or memo).

A full client report will need to be structured as a narrative or 'story' as follows:

Executive summary (1 page)
See above.

Background to the research (1 page)
A brief account of why the topic is of interest and on what basis particular questions are being asked; relevance to the organization.

Method and procedure (1 page)
Summary of design, methods and procedures used.

Results (5 pages maximum)
Where possible, presented graphically and coupled with brief descriptions/explanations to clarify.

Interpretation/practical significance (1 page)
What it all means and implies from a practical point of view, limitations and conditions under which the interpretations apply, and links with previous related research in similar contexts.

Recommendations (1 page)
These will need to be tentatively phrased with the particular conditions under which they hold true explained as qualifiers.

The report will need to be as brief as possible, with the guidelines above appropriate to the kind of research project pursued at masters level. Length will also vary depending on the type of data obtained. Qualitative data can take up a lot of space, but one should avoid providing endless verbatim quotations within the report even if they are highly pertinent to what it being reported or argued. Of most interest to the participating organization will be a summarized version of the narratives obtained from employees (e.g. from interviews, focus groups).

Make sure you have not included anything potentially libellous or insensitively written, and that particular participants are not identifiable within the report. Ask your supervisor to read the report and to provide constructive suggestions and comments well before you submit it to the organization. Ensure that the report is presented well in terms of written English as well as its overall accessibility/digestibility and attractiveness. This may mean getting the report bound professionally. If possible, involve the client organization (particularly your organizational 'champion' – see Chapter 4 for more on the role of the 'champion') in the report-writing process, including additional/revised information as necessary to ensure that the report is as client-friendly as possible. Once the final draft is complete (and has been agreed by representatives from the organization), send several copies for distribution and attach a covering letter thanking the organization for their contribution to the research, and providing a contact number for queries and follow-ups (e.g. you may be invited to present your findings at a business conference, to a board of directors or within a similar forum).

It should be noted that feedback to a company can raise a dilemma for the researcher. Some of the information arising out of the research may not be what the client wants to hear and may even be personally compromising. One has to consider that what employees have reported may be: (1) not what they would wish to pass on, and (2) not pleasant for the client to hear. The decision as to how much if any information and analysis is discussed with the client has to be an individual one. Clearly no attributable information should be given; the confidentiality agreed with participants must be absolute. However, if the research forms part of a potentially long-term relationship between you, the researcher and the company, then the relationship with the client (as well as study participants) is also an important one. Thus, while diplomacy in the analysis phase may be appropriate, there is little point in hiding non-attributable information which will form part of a longer-term study. Honesty is (as in consultancy) the best policy, even if this means lost corporate access.

10.5 References and further reading

Barrass, R. (1991). *Scientists Must Write*. London, UK: Chapman and Hall.

Becker, H.S. (1986). *Writing for Social Scientists: How to Start and Finish your Thesis, Book or Article*. Chicago, IL: University of Chicago Press.
Preece, R. (1994). *Starting Research: an Introduction to Academic Research and Dissertation Writing*. London, UK: Pinter.
Wolcott, H.F. (1993). *Writing up Qualitative Research*. London, UK: Sage Publications.

10.6 Presenting research findings

Presentation can be daunting for anyone, no matter how experienced. A good presentation is one which is well prepared and delivered with confidence. This section will take you through a number of steps which will help you to prepare a presentation of your material whether to an academic or organizational audience.

10.6.1 Step 1: Audience analysis

Analyse your audience using the following pointers as a guide. They will help you to frame and contextualize your presentation by considering the background to it, the make-up and motivations of your audience, what to focus on, what to avoid and how to 'pitch' the presentation effectively:

1 **Why are you presenting to this audience?**

2 **Audience analysis**
   - Knowledge of subject
   - Opinions about the subject
   - Opinions about you/the organization you represent
   - Their reasons for attending the presentation
   - Advantages to them resulting from the presentation
   - Disadvantages to them resulting from the presentation
   - Age group
   - Sex distribution
   - Vocabulary understanding level
   - Open-mindedness
   - Possible prejudices/objections

3 **What techniques are likely to elicit a negative reaction?**

10.6.2 Step 2: Determine how you will manage the attention of your audience

People are limited in the amount and complexity of information that they can take in and remember. If the presentation is delivered as an unbroken sequence of facts or disorganized monologue, people will become lost. To engage and maintain attention, build in variety and take active steps to manage understanding:

Build in variety
Concentration span when listening to someone speak varies across individuals but on average can only be maintained for about 10 minutes unless active steps are taken to introduce variety into the delivery. This can be done by varying the type of 'stimulation' you create during the presentation by engaging all the senses (or as many as you can realistically engage).

- *The spoken word* – vary volume, tone, emphasis, pace in rhythm with what you are arguing and the points you are making; invite questions (to hear other 'voices') and introduce spoken excerpts from other voices.

- *Visual support* – use overheads, flip-charts, examples/demonstrations, pictures, video material, slides, handout material, appropriate use of colour.

Maximize the use of all the senses, though take note of the fact that overuse of one particular sense can tire the receiver. Introduce constant pattern and systematic (versus chaotic) change.

Manage understanding
Categorize your material into meaningful chunks: package the information into manageable units of meaning (the size of which will depend on the audience):

- Present the material in a logical/coherent order that makes intuitive sense to the audience and that aids assimilation of information;

- Pitch the presentation at the appropriate level: what do they know already? What level of understanding can you assume?

- Introduce new information gradually;

- Provide examples: meaning can be obtained by attaching new information to existing information. Build associations using metaphors, analogies and case examples;

- Provide intermittent summaries at regular intervals throughout the presentation;

- Provide verbal 'signposts' to indicate what is coming next: e.g. 'There are two important things to consider here'; 'I have just … so now I am going to …';

- Substantiate and justify your statements, with illustrations and examples that people can relate to;

- Use anecdotes to illustrate your points, ensuring their relevance. Be brief rather than long-winded in your explanation;

- Provide opportunities for the audience to ask questions for clarification/elaboration.

10.6.3 Step 3: Clarifying presentation objectives

Clarifying the objective is critical to an incisive presentation. A clearly stated objective should provide a very firm guide as to what to include/not to include in the presentation.

The stated objective should comprise a simple, precise statement of the 'outcome' (behaviour, reaction) you wish to elicit from the audience as a result of your presentation. What do you want them to be doing (thinking, feeling) or doing differently by the end of the presentation? In writing your objective, use **action** words like 'describe', 'identify', 'delineate'. For example, 'By the end of my presentation, the audience will be able to describe and critically evaluate three perspectives on ... x', 'to identify the advantages and disadvantages of y' ... etc. Even if the intention is to get people to understand or appreciate or to think or feel differently, use action words to articulate these aims. That is, ask yourself what exactly might constitute evidence of 'thinking differently', 'feeling in a particular way' or of 'understanding', 'appreciation' or 'awareness'?

In writing the objective, begin with the phrase: 'By the end of the presentation, the audience will be able to ...'

Always keep the objective in mind when preparing the content and structure of the presentation. The objective should frame content and structure, and also delivery.

10.6.4 Step 4: Structuring the presentation

Structure: Tell them what you are going to tell them (introduction), tell them ('meat'), tell them what you told them (conclusion/consolidation). People have difficulty listening to and assimilating material that is presented in an incoherent and disorganized lump. To aid assimilation, structure the presentation into:

Introduction
↓
Development
↓
Consolidation

The presentation must be logically framed and made explicit at the outset. This will aid the formation of an argument and also provide a 'guide' for the audience in following the argument. The proposed structure can be outlined on an overhead, flip-chart or handout to which you can intermittently refer throughout the presentation

Introducing your presentation
Introducing the presentation is important as a means of:

- Providing an overview of what is to come;
- Managing expectations about what you will and will not deliver/guiding the audience on what they can get out of the presentation;
- Inspiring interest and engaging attention;
- Outlining the structure or agenda of the presentation to provide the audience with a presentation 'map';
- Indicating what type of back-up material you will be providing.

The introduction should last no longer than 10% of the total delivery time.

Development
This comprises the main argument or thrust of the presentation.

Consolidation/conclusion
This is essential as a means of reinforcing what has been said. Recall the 'recency effect' – i.e. people will often only remember the last thing they have heard. This can take the form of a question and answer session, coupled with a comprehensive summary of the main points covered by the presentation.

> The longer the presentation and/or the more complex the argument, the greater the need for intermittent summaries and 'milestone' points along the way.

10.6.5 Step 5: Producing Content

Planning is essential if you want to achieve your objectives successfully. Clarifying the objective is the first stage of planning since it is this that will provide the basis for selecting and structuring the presentation material. The objective should specify what exactly it is that you want people to know and/or feel as a result of the presentation

To produce the content, ask:

- What will they need to **know**?
- What will they need to **do**?
- What do I need to demonstrate?

Brainstorm your answers to these questions. This brainstorm will produce the 'content' of the presentation. Categorize the material and then arrange it into a logical/coherent sequence.

10.6.6 Step 6: Construct visual aids

The visual aids most commonly used for presentations are: overhead projectors, flip-charts, slide projectors and computer-generated displays linked to overhead projector systems. Choice of visual aid is tied to:

- Size of audience;
- Formality of meeting;
- The purpose for which the visual aid is to be used, e.g. flip-charts are most suited to informal meetings involving small numbers of people.

The purpose of using visual aids is:

- To provide structure;
- To present an outline of the presentation;
- To provide 'signposts';
- To simplify explanations/clarify interrelationships;
- To illustrate a point;
- To spell out unfamiliar/complex ideas;
- To change pace;
- To provide a lasting impression.

How to use visual aids appropriately:

```
Ensure visual aids are:

CLEAR

MEMORABLE

LEGIBLE

TO THE POINT
```

- Do not have more than (about) seven lines on your slide, otherwise it will be difficult to read and ideas will become 'clouded';

- Images of letters (on the screen) should never be less than 5mm high for each metre of viewing distance (e.g. 50mm at 10m);

- Produce acetates using presentation/graphics software, where possible;

- Ensure that on using the visual aid, you can still see the audience, the audience can see you and, most importantly, they can see the visual display.

> Do not use visual aids over-enthusiastically and/or to take the attention away from yourself and what you are saying: this will clutter the presentation and detract from the argument. Never use visual aids as an excuse not to interact with the audience.

10.6.7 Step 7: Build in the use of questions

Questions can stimulate interest and engage people. Assuming that it is possible for you to involve the audience through the use of questions, draw on the following points:

- Use specific and focused rather than general/vague questions to tailor and contain the audience response;

- Use questions to get the audience to really *think* about the material you are presenting;

- Ask questions that test out understanding;

- Use questions to break up the presentation (e.g. as a means of consolidation mid-way through the presentation);

- It is more effective to simply pose a question rather than to pounce on someone to answer it;

- Help the audience to relate the material of your presentation to their own experience;

- Avoid leading questions (where the answer you expect is obvious from the way you have put the question), multiple questions (where you combine two or more questions in one) and closed questions (which invite yes/no answers).

10.6.8 Step 8: Overall preparation

Planning:

Purpose   Why am I doing the presentation? Is it the most effective way to communicate the information I want to convey? What is my objective?

Subject	Am I clear on the material? Is it relevant to my audience?
Audience	Who will be there? Can I influence who attends? What do they already know?
Time	When is it? How long have I got to prepare? How long have I got to make the presentation?
Venue	Where? Size? Suitably equipped?

Preparation:

Material	Have I collected all I need? Have I differentiated the 'must-knows', 'should-knows', and 'nice-to-knows'? Have I rejected the 'already-knows' and 'do-not-need-to-knows'?
Notes	What method can I use? Is it formal enough to need a script? Will keywords be more appropriate?
Structure	Have I clearly identified three stages in my presentation: introduction, development, consolidation. Is my introduction short and sharp? Will I be getting the 'must-knows' across early on? Have I sufficient material/variety to maintain interest? Is my summary accurate?
Visual aids	Do I need any? What type? Will they have the required impact? How long have I got to prepare them? Should I produce them professionally?
Rehearsal	Can I arrange for someone to watch me and provide feedback? Does the amount of material fit in with the time allowed? Are my notes manageable? Can I read them easily? Are my visuals clear? Do they support what I say? How does the presentation 'feel' overall?

On the day:

Arrival	Have I allowed time for travel emergencies? Do I have early access to the venue? Is the equipment appropriate? Does it work? Is it positioned correctly?
Nerves	Have I time to relax before I start? Have I been to the loo?!? Should I get some fresh air first? Am I going to stand or sit?
Delivery	Introducing yourself, who you are and where you come from/who you represent.
Self-assessment	Self-reflection and determination to improve.

10.6.9 Step 9: practice and seek feedback

Use the categories of presentation analysis illustrated in Table 10.1 to examine your own performance and/or for purposes of feedback from others.

Table 10.1   Analysing your presentation performance

Category of analysis	Definition	Example
Structuring		
Stating structure/ summarizing	Giving a condensed overview of material which is about to be/has been presented	'During this session I will …' 'To recap, the following issues …'
Indicating transition	Signalling when the presentation is moving to a new topic or level of detail	'Moving on …' 'Just to clarify …'
Integration		
Linking to other points	Forging a connection or link between two or more points within the presentation or between the presentation and other material	'This ties in with what I said earlier.' 'As I noted earlier …'
Linking to experience	Connecting the presentation with the experience of the audience	'I appreciate that most of you will feel rather sceptical about…'
Elaboration		
Giving examples and illustrations	Providing verbal, visual or other examples to illustrate/clarify/elaborate	'For example …' 'Just to illustrate …'
Providing substantiation/ support	Substantiating with reference to sources of 'proof'	'Research by XXX has shown that …'
Using repetition deliberately	Repeating points or phrases deliberately for impact	'To repeat …' 'You can save time … you can save effort … you can save trouble …'
Using pauses or variation	Varying pitch, pace or intensity of voice, pausing	

Introduction: How was the presentation introduced? Was the introduction treated in sufficient depth and detail? What was the impact of the introduction on the group?

Development: How much new information was conveyed? Too much/too little/about right? Did the development unfold logically and in a connected fashion?

Was each point treated and explained in as much detail as possible? What use was made of examples and other material familiar to the audience?

Was any use made of questions? What type? What was the degree of participation and involvement? How was this achieved?

Was the pace of the session too fast/too slow/about right?

Was audience interest maintained throughout the presentation? What level of eye-contact was achieved?

What use was made of visual aids? What was their impact? How acceptable was the speaker's tone, volume and speed?

What supporting material was used and how effective was it? How would you assess the speaker's confidence? Level of credibility? What contributed to/detracted from this?

Consolidation: What scope did the presenter give for receiving feedback? How much reinforcement was given? Was it effective? How balanced was the entire presentation?

10.6.10 Step 10: Polish up your presentation and speaking skills

There follow some tips and hints for improving overall presentation and public speaking skills.

> Preparation is three-quarters of the presentation completed.

- Talk from note headings rather than read from a fully prepared script – if you lose your place it is very difficult for you to find it again and can also be very dull for the audience. *Know* your subject and your visual aids.
- Involve the audience – draw ideas from them, make the talk 'live', talk *to* the audience and engage in eye-contact.

> Demonstrate understanding of the audience point of view.
> Be modest.

- Be tactful and diplomatic;
- Clearly project your voice;
- Vary tempo, speed and pace.

> Be yourself – the importance of personal style.
> Relax and enjoy!

- Emphasize certain words to highlight important aspects of the material;
- Use gestures to punch home ideas;
- Use *spontaneous* humour;
- Use the active tense as much as possible;
- Be cheerful, positive and project with authority/confidence, but take care not to be too certain that you are right and the audience is wrong!
- Demonstrate 'energy'; carry the audience along.

> The importance of mental and physical rehearsal.
> The importance of positive self-dialogue.

> ### DO NOT:
> - Bluff your way through.
>
> - Allow nervous habits to get in the way, like jingling keys, twiddling with pencils or blue-tack, making paper-clip necklaces!
>   - Be monotonous.
>   - Be patronizing.
>   - Use jargon.
>   - Use too many visual aids.
>   - Pad out the presentation with 'waffle'.
>   - Use abstractions.
>   - Deliver poor, planned jokes.
>   - Use metaphors excessively.
> - Use 'defence rousers': judging, coercion, manipulation, disinterest, being superior, or too certain.

11 Concluding words

In this book, we have attempted to provide an overview of the process of research investigation from start to finish. We have provided advice on how to deal with the various steps along the way and information on which to base the many hundreds of decisions (big and small) that need to made in the pursuit of sound research.

As will be clear from the approach we have adopted throughout, we feel that this text should provide a starting point for understanding the intricacies of organizational research. We have attempted to cover a broad range of issues, techniques and approaches pertinent to the applied social researcher. Where additional information would be beneficial, we have also provided some key references and suggestions for further reading. We hope that by providing a 'road map' for undertaking research in applied settings, we have dispelled some of the fears and concerns experienced by many prospective researchers.

As researchers ourselves, we are always keen to receive feedback on our work (whether positive or negative!), in order that we may develop and improve within our profession. As such, we would be pleased to receive comments and (constructive!) criticism on any aspect of this book. Please forward any such correspondence to Michael Carmichael at Sage Publications, or e-mail us at feedback@organisational-solutions.co.uk. We look forward to hearing from you.

Glossary

Action research – a term used to describe interactive research, with the researcher taking an active role, applying his/her skills in order to iteratively diagnose, action change and continue evaluative research in a cyclical process. This style of research is consistent with the view of the social science researcher as a scientist–practitioner, remaining true to the principles of objective, scientific research but acknowledging the importance of practical implications of that research in applied (organizational) settings.

A posteriori – an outcome of experience or observation, e.g. a conclusion deriving directly from experimentation or research.

A priori – occurring prior to, and independent of, experience or observation, e.g. a hypothesis that is developed before evidence is collected to support or refute it.

Bivariate analysis – a form of statistical analysis involving two variables, sub-dividing into tests that look for differences between groups (e.g. *t*-test, ANOVA) and tests that attempt to detect an association or relationship between two variables (e.g. **correlational analysis**).

Common method variance – the artificial inflation of relationships between variables when all data derives from the same source, particularly prevalent in quantitative questionnaire-based research. Part of the problem is due to respondents' propensity to use certain response styles (e.g. preferring to use the central portion of a response scale, or using extreme options only), as well as due to respondents' striving to simplify conceptualization of various ideas and constructs collected via the same method (e.g. collecting data relating to job satisfaction, organizational commitment and perceptions of team climate, using a single questionnaire-based survey method).

Correlational analysis – a form of statistical analysis which identifies the strength and direction of relationship between (typically two) variables. For example, the relationship between age and job satisfaction, or between team coherence and leadership style. Correlations can be calculated for categorical (phi co-efficient) as well as ordinal (Spearman's rank correlation co-efficient) and interval/ratio (Pearson's product moment correlation co-efficient) variables.

The statistical test selected must recognize the *lower* level of measurement of the variables being analysed. For example, a correlational analysis undertaken between team coherence (measured at the ordinal level via a rating scale) and leadership style (measured at the categorical level in terms of whether the leader is 'autocractic' or 'democratic') would need to be carried out at the *categorical* level (using the phi co-efficient) since this is the lower level of measurement of the two variables.

Critical incident technique – a research method requiring the researcher to elicit from a participant (usually via interview techniques) specific examples of a particular type of event or behaviour. The technique's name derives from its use in safety-critical environments as a means to identify the behaviours surrounding 'near miss' or 'critical' incidents.

Deductive – deducing specific instances with reference to general laws or principles (i.e. theories). Research hypotheses generated in this way derive from established theoretical and conceptual frameworks clearly established and accepted by the research community. See **inductive** for a contrasting definition/approach.

Dependent variable – a variable under investigation whose variation under different conditions the researcher is attempting to describe, explain or understand.

Empirical – based on observation and experience rather than theory or logic.

Epistemology – the theory of knowledge and investigation of what distinguishes defensible belief from opinion, by investigating the validity/scope of, and methods used to derive, a particular view.

Error – discrepancies exist between what is measured and the true value of the measurement target. Measurement error can be illustrated in the following simple formula:

$$observation = reality - error$$

Error in organizational research can derive from all manner of sources depending on the method and design used to obtain data, e.g. **halo** error, leniency/severity error from performance rating scales; differences in coding method used to content analyse qualitative interview data; differences in the ability of participants to introspect when completing a self-report measure of personality, etc. The goal of the researcher should be to minimize error as far as is practicable by applying rigorous design and methodological constraints.

Ethnographic research – the study of individuals and groups within their natural setting, with data collected to reflect the 'cultural reality' of participants' (often referred to as **informants** within ethnographic research) beliefs, values and customs. Within an organizational setting, ethnography can be used to gain a comprehensive understanding of an individual's or group's perspective on a particular issue, e.g. an individual's perceptions of their department's culture; a team's behaviour while undertaking a work-related task. Ethnographic research attempts to minimize preconceptions or hypotheses about an individual or group and allows participants to generate data themselves, via the researcher's careful observation or facilitation within a naturalistic setting.

Factor analysis – consists of a number of statistical techniques, the underlying aim of which is to simplify complex sets of data. At its heart, factor analysis provides a means of simplifying correlational relationships between numerous variables, in order to uncover any underlying 'structure' which may exist in the data. Applications are various and include establishing the structure of 'traits' underlying personality, understanding the relationship between various performance criteria, exploring the relationship between established work-related constructs (e.g. organizational commitment, job satisfaction and job involvement). *Exploratory* factor analysis allows the researcher to generate hypotheses about relationships between variables by *exploring* the underlying relationships between variables. *Confirmatory* factor analysis is concerned with confirming or refuting existing hypotheses about relationships between variables.

Gantt chart – used primarily in project management, a chart in which a series of horizontal lines shows the amount of work done (or projected) in certain periods of time for certain tasks.

Generalizability – the degree to which a specific finding can be applied to a broader group or **population**, i.e. the degree to which the finding is *generalizable* to the wider population.

Halo effect – typically found in rating scale-based judgements of performance across various tasks or competencies. This effect refers to the overarching perception of the judge or assessor of an individual's capability/performance, which then leads to their rating of an individual at a similar level across tasks regardless of actual performance on those tasks. Other rating scale-based effects or errors include: primacy (only taking into account early evidence in the ongoing judgement of an individual's performance/behaviour); recency (only taking into account later evidence in ongoing behavioural judgements); 'similar to me' (an assessor judging an individual's level of performance on the degree to which they are similar to, or different from, him/herself); leniency/severity/central tendency (the tendency to use only certain portions of a rating scale while judging the performance of a series of individuals, leading to unrepresentative restrictions in range of performance reported).

Hypothesis – a tentative proposition made as a basis for further exploration, often based on limited evidence. A *null* hypothesis (i.e. the assumption that the hypothesis is unfounded) may only be rejected in light of sufficient evidence that the hypothesis is supported.

Independent variable – a variable whose value the researcher is typically able to manipulate or change in investigating differences in a **dependent variable** or variables. Changes in the independent variable are often hypothetically related to changes in the dependent variable.

Inductive – inductive research designs involve general inferences being drawn from specific instances. These may not be based on established theoretical frameworks but may, through thorough investigation and analysis of empirically derived data, lead to the development of new or revised theories. These new theories may then be tested under a hypthetico-**deductive** approach.

Informant – typically found within ethnographic research (and deriving from anthropological study) an individual from whom a researcher is able to obtain information relating to the customs, values, attitudes and behaviours of the individual or wider group.

Levels of measurement – a four-way classification is most typically used when considering the various levels of measurement present in social science research. The level of measurement adopted will have implications for the way in which data are analysed and the degree of precision with which conclusions from the data may be drawn. *Nominal* or *categorical* measurements are those which reflect qualitative, rather than quantitative differences between levels. Data are categorized into nominal (named) groups, e.g. pass/fail, yes/no, male/female, sales/administration/finance division. Categorical measurement systems require that each observation or data point falls into only one category (mutual exclusivity) and that each data point can be categorized into a category (exhaustiveness).

These criteria of mutual exclusivity and exhaustiveness apply to all levels of measurement, whose definitions follow. *Ordinal*-level measurement systems allow data to be rank ordered with reference to an external criterion (e.g. size, value, rating), and may be assigned a quantitative value. Whilst these values indicate the order in which a series of data points may fall (e.g. a supervisory rating of 'excellent' or '5' will be higher than a rating of 'poor' or '1'), we can conclude nothing about the magnitude of difference between the points (i.e. we only know about the *order* of values, not the *size* of difference between scale points). *Interval* scale measures, however, assume that the difference between each scale point is equivalent. For example, the difference between Z scores of 2.0 and 2.5 (i.e. 0.5) is equivalent to that between -0.7 and -1.2 (0.5). *Ratio* measurement systems take this one stage further and introduce an *absolute zero* value, as well as equal interval scale points. Examples of ratio measurement scales are time and distance (both of which possess an absolute zero point).

Meta-analysis – a means (typically quantitative and using statistical procedures) for determining the cumulative relationship/difference between target variables within a social science research paradigm, drawing on more than one existing study. By making statistical adjustments to published research findings, it is possible to construct comparable measurements of a given phenomenon (e.g. the relationship between organizational commitment and job satisfaction). By applying a fairly straightforward statistical formula to existing findings (and this may include several dozen, or many hundred research findings), it is possible to calculate the overall *effect size* for that relationship or difference.

Methodology – a system of methods used in the study of a particular phenomenon.

Multi-dimensional scalogram analysis – a method used to understand the subjective or personal meaning invested by an individual or group of individuals in a given topic. The method is most useful when a research question focuses on the general conceptual processes underlying the explanations people give for behaviour, or on the understanding of categories people use to make sense of their world.

Multivariate analysis – a form of statistical analysis that deals with more than two variables at the same time (e.g. multiple regression, factor analysis, cluster analysis, etc.).

Non-parametric – statistical tests which do not make rigid assumptions about the nature of data under analysis, unlike **parametric** tests. Non-parametric tests are best suited to the analysis of data collected using ordinal or categorical systems of measurement.

Non-probability sampling – techniques used where **probability sampling** approaches are not possible due to issues of practicality, time, resources, etc. Specific techniques include: purposive, quota, convenience and snowball.
 Purposive sampling involves selecting individuals from a population according to an underlying interest in particular groups (e.g. union members in a factory organization).
 Quota sampling involves identifying individuals with particular characteristics, on the assumption that these different characteristics are distributed systematically throughout a population, and so, selecting the correct *quotas* of people displaying variations of the characteristic will ultimately result in a representative sample.
 Convenience sampling involves the researcher obtaining data from anyone 'convenient' (friends, family, work colleagues, etc.).
 Snowball sampling involves including members of the target population by drawing on existing contacts and on their contacts.

Each of these forms of sampling carries with it certain caveats which will almost certainly impact on the accuracy and generalizability of conclusions which can be drawn from research findings based on samples obtained via any of these methods.

Paradigm – a 'world view' underlying the theories and methodology of a particular scientific subject, leading to a particular way of looking at a given phenomenon.

Parametric – statistical tests which make specific assumptions about the nature of the data being analysed. Typically, parametric tests assume that the data are normally distributed, that samples have been drawn randomly from the population and that the variances of population scores in each group are equivalent. Tests that do not make these assumptions about the nature of data are termed **non-parametric**.

Participant – the term now most commonly used to describe a person participating in a research project. This term has largely superseded the word *'subject'* to describe those involved in research. Other terms, such as **'informant'**, may be used in certain contexts, e.g. when adopting an **ethnographic** data collection approach.

Path modelling – a technique used to determine which of a number of 'pathways' connects one variable with another. It is based on the assumption of causality, i.e. that variations in one or more variables cause variations in the target variable, and is generally applied in the social sciences under the guise of **structural equation modelling**.

Performance – performance at work is not the consequence or result of job behaviour, it is *the act itself*. This distinguishes individual, team and organizational performance from 'effectiveness', i.e. an evaluation of the results or outcomes of performance and 'productivity', i.e. the ratio of effectiveness to the cost of achieving that level of effectiveness. Selecting an appropriate *criterion* to assess performance or the outcome of performance (effectiveness) can be problematic. Ideally, the researcher should be confident that a criterion selected is: *objective* (its measurement will be the same, regardless of the measur*er*); *reliable* and *valid* (it accurately assesses performance across situations and over time); able to *discriminate* fairly between different levels of effectiveness; and is *accessible* (i.e. the data can be obtained with relative ease).

Population – the collection of all units of analysis (within organizational research, these units could be individual employees, teams or even organizations) defined by the research question (i.e. of interest to your study).

Positivism – a system of thinking which assumes that any proposed theory or law can be scientifically verified or is capable of mathematical or logical proof.

Positivist approaches emphasize the use of rigorous scientific methods in the exploration of a particular paradigm or phenomenon.

Power – statistical power refers to the capacity of a given test to *correctly reject the null hypothesis*. The power of a test is dependent on four factors: *test used* (**parametric** tests are generally more powerful than **non-parametric** tests); *effect size* (the observed difference or relationship between study variables – the larger the effect size, the greater the power); *significance level* (the lower the significance level the lower the power of the test); and *sample size* (the larger the sample size, the more powerful the test).

Probability sampling – a probability or random sample describes a sample selected in such a way that all members in the population have a known chance of selection. They are preferable to **non-probability sampling** techniques because they are more likely to produce representative samples and also enable estimates of the sample's accuracy to be made. Probability sampling techniques include: simple random, systematic and stratified sampling.

Simple random sampling (SRS) involves completely random selection of individuals from the total population and assumes the availability of a complete list of population members.

Systematic sampling is a very similar technique to SRS, differing only in that it does not rely on the generation of random sample members but instead involves the researcher selecting a suitable 'sampling fraction' (e.g. 5% of the total population) and from the population list, selecting every n^{th} sample member (e.g. every twentieth sample member).

Stratified sampling involves the selection of appropriate strata on which to base a sampling frame (e.g. age, sex, divisional membership, etc.) and then applying SRS or systematic sampling techniques to each stratum to ensure that the sample is as representative of each stratum as possible.

Process consultation – an approach to interaction with an organization (typically in organization development research and practice) which sees the consultant acting as a 'helper' and facilitator, providing an outside view of an organizational problem, but acting principally as a sounding board to allow the client to take and retain ownership of the problem and to generate his/her own means of addressing that problem. The process consultant's primary area of expertise is in communicating the skills of diagnosis and intervention to the client in order that s/he can use these skills directly, rather than relying on the consultant over time.

Psychometric – literally defined as 'measurement of the mind', psychometric instruments are constructed according to a specific rationale, which assumes that they possess **reliability** and **validity**. Any instrument investigating psychological functioning (whether used for the collection of data regarding aptitudes, competencies, personality characteristics, attitudes, motives, mood states, etc.) which conforms to the strict requirements for reliability and validity, and which also displays objectivity, is standardised and is able to discriminate fairly between individuals, may be described as 'psychometric' in nature.

Q-sort – a data collection method which can be used to assess, in a highly structured and systematic way, people's understanding of an issue, from their own unique standpoint, and has the potential to integrate qualitative and quantitative information. The technique itself requires participants to sort a set of cards (each card describing a different element of the target phenomenon) into a normal distribution in terms of their construction of that phenomenon, i.e. the relative importance they assign to each element.

Qualitative research – typically adopting research methods whose underlying aim is not to quantify data obtained, qualitative research approaches are becoming increasingly popular in the applied social sciences. Such approaches often aim to *explore* a specific issue from an **inductive** perspective, perhaps in an effort to generate new theory. However, qualitative research methods can employ quantitative modes of analysis (e.g. multi-dimensional scalogram analysis, content analysis of interview/focus group data) and can be very effectively used to supplement and enrich **quantitative, deductive** research.

Quantitative research – contrasting with **qualitative** research approaches, this type of research is concerned with the measurement and *quantification* of data, often deriving from an underlying hypothetico-**deductive** approach to a research question, i.e. attempting to test out an established theoretical viewpoint.

Reliability – a cornerstone of **psychometric** theory, reliability is concerned with the degree of data consistency across a defined dimension. Reliability may be assessed in terms of consistency across time (test–retest reliability) and internal consistency (e.g. split-half reliability, alternate forms reliability). Accepted wisdom dictates that a reliability co-efficient should exceed $r = 0.7$ in order for the temporal or internal consistency of a given measure to be of adequate reliability.

Repertory grid technique – this data collection method involves three stages: the elicitation of 'elements' (i.e. people, objects, events or in fact anything with reference to which an individual constructs meaning); the elicitation of 'constructs' (in relation to the elements); and the construction of a grid matrix of elements and constructs. Qualitative data obtained using the first two stages may be placed in a quantitative framework within the third stage in order to assess the consistency of construct elements across individuals.

Sample – a set of individuals selected from a population and intended to represent the population under study. Samples are drawn on the basis that it would be impractical to investigate all members of a target population. It is possible to collect samples using **probability** and **non-probability** sampling techniques.

Sampling error – the amount by which a sample's characteristics deviate from the **population's** characteristics, expressed in terms of the standard error statistic.

Sampling frame – the list of members from a given **population** from which the **sample** may be drawn.

Skew – refers to the degree to which a given variable's distribution exhibits normality, i.e. the mean, median and mode are proximal. In positively skewed distributions, the mean typically exceeds the median, which in turn exceeds the mode. In negatively skewed distributions, the opposite pattern prevails.

Structural equation modelling (SEM) – researchers using SEM are most often concerned with measurement of, and relationships between, 'latent constructs'; that is, constructs which are themselves implicit and unmeasurable, but which are believed to underpin the explicit variables used to measure them. The method involves the amalgamation of multiple regression and confirmatory factor analytic techniques to assist in the assessment of *developed* models.

Theory – a system of ideas intended to explain a phenomenon, especially a system based on general principles and therefore independent of the target phenomenon. Within organizational research, a theory may relate to a supposition about how two or more variables are interrelated, which may or may not have been empirically tested.

Triangulation – the use of different research methods (e.g. qualitative and quantitative) within the same study to collect data from alternative sources. These data can be used to assess the validity of findings from alternative sources, and can enrich and inform findings collected using a single research approach.

Validity – when pertaining to **psychometric** research, validity comprises: content, construct and criterion-related validity. *Content* validity concerns the degree to which scales which purport to tap into each dimension of interest cover each dimension comprehensively, using items which are agreed to be relevant and consistent by subject matter experts. *Construct* validity concerns the extent to which each of an instrument's dimensions reports statistical independence from each other dimension, and is conceptually and theoretically watertight. It may be that relationships between a given instrument and other established instruments provide evidence for construct validity, where the two scales are intended to measure similar (or distinct) constructs. *Criterion* validity concerns the degree to which there exists a relationship between key dimensions of the instrument and 'real-world' criteria of interest, e.g. individual- and group-level performance outcomes.

Index

absenteeism, 139
abstract, 172
access, organizational, 44–51
action research, 13
alpha change, 132

balanced scorecard, 139
beta change, 132
bottom-line performance, 134, 139
buy-in, organizational, 47

case studies, 54–6
client report, 177–80
common method variance, 108
communicograms, 111
content analysis, 151–5
    qualitative, 151
    quantitative, 151–3
    structural, 153
criterion, 123

data analysis, 143–70
    content, 151
    meta-, 161
    multidimensional scalogram, 155
    statistical, 144
    structural equation modelling, 165
data collection, 67–113
    diary methods, 109
    focus groups, 80
    interviews, 69
    observation, 96
    psychometric, 87
    surveys, 99
deductive, 11
diary methods, 109–13
discussion, 174–5

ethics, 61–5

factor analysis, 58, 149
focus groups, 80–7

gamma change, 132

inductive, 11
internet, 31–6
    citing sources, 36
    evaluating sources, 34
    search engines, 33
interviews, 69–74
    guidelines, 71
    semi-structured, 70
    structured, 69
    unstructured, 70
introduction, 172

literature review, 36–40

meta–analysis, 161-5
method, 173
multidimensional scalogram analysis,
155–60

observation, 96–9
operationalization, 40
organizational culture, 93, 135

path modelling, 58, 165
performance, 122–142
    group, 129
    individual, 125
    organizational, 135
positivism, 11
presentations, 181–90

psychometric research, 87–96
publication, academic, 174–7

Q-sort, 78–80
qualitative, 12
quantitative, 12

reliability, 89
repertory grid, 75–8
reporting research, 171–90
    academic, 171
    non-academic, 177
research
    project plan, 22
    proposal, 27, 46
    starting, 16
research design, 52–66
    case study, 53
    correlational, 57
    experimental, 58
    selecting, 60
research question, 40
results, 173

sampling, 114–21
    convenience, 118

limitations, 118
power analysis, 118
purposive, 117
quota, 117
simple random, 116
snowball, 118
stratified, 116
systematic, 116
scientist-practitioner, 7, 10
single case, 54, 55
statistical tests, 144–50
    bivariate, 148
    descriptions, 147–50
    multivariate, 149
    selection of, 99
structural equation modelling, 165–70
surveys, 99–108
    attitudinal data, 102
    behavioural data, 101
    demographic data, 99
    layout, 106
    wording, 104

turnover, employee, 138

validity, 90–93